IMAGES
of America
SMYRNA

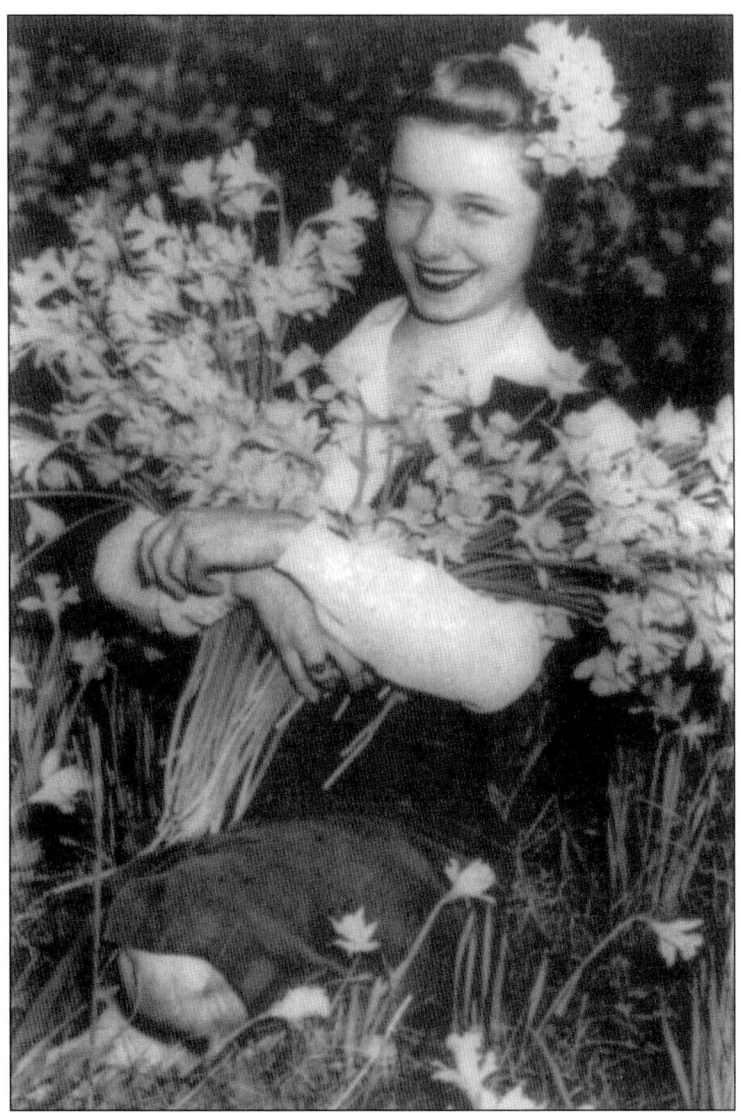

Harriette Rice Brawner, seen here in the early 1940s, holds an armful of jonquil blossoms from the yard of her grandmother, Mrs. P.M. Rice (née Blanch Ruff Rice). Rice's residence was on the southwest corner of Church and King Streets, the present location of Carmichael's Funeral Home. Rice was Smyrna's largest jonquil gardener. From late February to the end of April, she would allow local schoolboys to sell the jonquils to tourists along the former route of US Highway 41, known as the Dixie Highway. The boys sold the flowers for 10¢ or 15¢ a dozen, but they had to give Rice half of the money they collected. Smyrna, at the time a small community of around 1,500 residents, was known for being the "Jonquil City of the South." (Courtesy Parker Lowry.)

ON THE COVER: In 1953, a large number of the almost 4,000 Smyrna residents turned out for this Grand Re-Modeling Sale at the Atherton Drug Store in the heart of Smyrna. This "gigantic" sale offered door prizes, including black-and-white televisions and other small appliances. The store was located on the west side of Atlanta Street, at the approximate location of the present-day Shane's Rib Shack. A Western Auto Store was next door on the south side, and the Smyrna city hall was next door to it. (Courtesy Smyrna History Museum.)

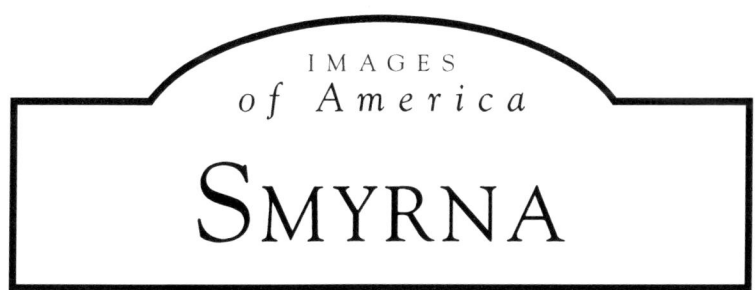
IMAGES
of America
SMYRNA

Harold Lee Smith and Kara M. Hunter-Oden

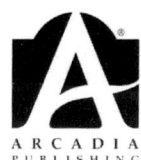

Copyright © 2014 by Harold Lee Smith and Kara M. Hunter-Oden
ISBN 978-1-4671-1089-1

Published by Arcadia Publishing
Charleston, South Carolina

Printed in the United States of America

Library of Congress Control Number: 2013937484

For all general information, please contact Arcadia Publishing:
Telephone 843-853-2070
Fax 843-853-0044
E-mail sales@arcadiapublishing.com
For customer service and orders:
Toll-Free 1-888-313-2665

Visit us on the Internet at www.arcadiapublishing.com

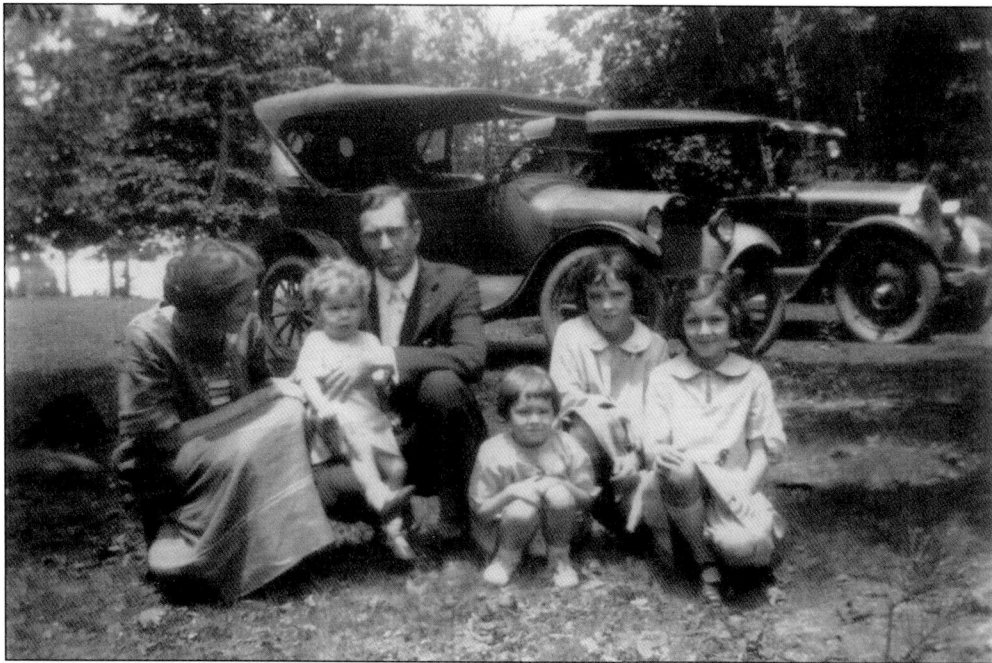

The Greens are enjoying a picnic of the Smyrna First Baptist Sunday school. Lena Mae Gann Green, the wife of Dr. Grover Cleveland Green, was active in the Smyrna Woman's Club. She is credited with suggesting the nickname "Jonquil City of the South" for Smyrna after 18 ladies got together in 1937 to organize the Jonquil Garden Club. Jonquils had been introduced to Smyrna in the late 1800s by Steven and Louisa Taylor after their son, Henry, who lived in Spokane, Washington, sent them a bag of jonquil bulbs. They planted the bulbs, which multiplied prolifically, and shared them with their neighbors, who in turn shared them with others. In the spring, almost every yard was covered with bright yellow blooms. The Taylors moved to Spokane in 1907, never realizing the legacy they had left for the town. The city officially adopted The Jonquil City as its nickname in 1949. (Courtesy the estate of Laura Alice Hamrick and the Smyrna History Museum.)

CONTENTS

Acknowledgments		6
Introduction		7
1.	Religion and Churches	9
2.	Early Pioneers	25
3.	Downtown Smyrna	37
4.	Neighborhoods	67
5.	Organizations, Clubs, and Schools	89
6.	Unincorporated Smyrna	111
About the Smyrna Historical and Genealogical Society		126
Bibliography		127

Acknowledgments

It is impossible to remember all the people and organizations that have contributed photographs and other family treasures and memorabilia over the years to the Smyrna Historical and Genealogical Society and the Smyrna History Museum. Many people provided invaluable assistance and encouragement in compiling this book and in assembling information, photographs, and other materials. We beg forgiveness for any omissions. Any photographs in this book not otherwise acknowledged are courtesy of the Smyrna History Museum.

We wish to thank the following: Betty Sharp Smith, cofounder of the Smyrna Historical Society Inc. and the Smyrna History Museum; Norma Townsend McHann; Parker Lowry; Mary Annie McDaniell Johnson; Jean and Joan Bennett; Becky Nash Paden and her brothers, John and Jim Nash; Mayor Max Bacon; former Smyrna city clerk Susan Hiott; former editor of the *Smyrna Herald* and associate editor of the *Marietta Daily Journal*, Bill Kinney; Pete Wood and his wife, Lillie Fulghum Wood; Gordon and Malinda Jolley Mortin; the estate of Lex and Leodelle Jolley; Ann and James Johnson; Pat Burns Roche; Betty Griffin McNiff; Cheryl Emmett-Bennett; Don Taylor; Erica Hague; and especially Kathy Moore Graham, who pitched in to assist with the late revisions in the images and text. We also thank all the other museum volunteers and members of the Smyrna Historical and Genealogical Society who have contributed to and supported its activities for the past 28 years. Thanks also to the many current and former residents of Smyrna who graciously allowed the authors to view, examine, and use their family photographs, records, and documents in the preparation of this historic overview of the City of Smyrna, Georgia.

—Harold Lee Smith and Kara Hunter-Oden
May 2013.

For every individual whose name or actions is included here, there are many thousands of equal or greater importance not included. Those chosen are simply the representatives of an era or a particular facet of life in this community, used here to tell the story of a city . . . a city of people, the people of Smyrna. Where this picture is accurate in your mind, thank all those who helped relate it to us. Where it is in error or omits what should have been included, forgive us.

—Bill E. Miles, editor, *Smyrna Herald*, 1952–1961

INTRODUCTION

In the early 1800s, the area that is today Smyrna was occupied by Indians. DeSoto encountered them when he marched into what is now North Georgia, looking for gold and other treasures for the Spanish king. The Cherokee and Creek Indians, at one time or another, claimed the territory. History says the Cherokees won the land from the Creeks in a game of "ball-play" or "stick-ball." As described by Henry Thompson Malone in *Cherokees of the Old South,* the game involved a ball made from a deer hide and sticks, about two feet long, with animal-skin netting on one end similar to what is used in lacrosse. Tradition also says that the game was played on land just north of Smyrna in an area that became Ball Ground, Georgia.

In a series of treaties, Georgia had acquired all of the lands previously owned by the Indians except the portion in the northwest section owned by the Cherokees, including where Smyrna is located. The Cherokees adopted a constitution in 1827 and established the capital of the Cherokee Nation in what is now Calhoun, Georgia. The tribe also proposed its own newspaper, the *Phoenix.* Georgia reacted quickly. The day after Christmas 1827, the Georgia General Assembly passed legislation placing the entire Cherokee Nation under Georgia law and dividing the land among several Georgia counties on December 20, 1829. In 1831, the general assembly passed additional legislation that removed the land from the previous counties and made one large county, Cherokee. They also provided that the Cherokee County land be distributed by means of a land lottery, held on October 22, 1832, at the state capital in Milledgeville. All white adult males who had lived in Georgia for the previous four years were eligible for the drawings. Also eligible were widows of soldiers, physically handicapped persons, veterans, and their descendants.

By the spring of 1832, surveyors were hard at work dividing the territory into two types of lots: 40-acre "gold" lots, so named because they were potential sources of gold, which had been discovered in Dahlonega, Georgia, a few years earlier; and "land" lots of 160 acres on which there was no expectation of finding gold.

In December 1832, the Georgia General Assembly divided the county of Cherokee into a number of counties, including Cobb, named for Thomas Welch Cobb of Lexington and Greensboro, Georgia. He was a lawyer, a US representative, and a US senator. He died on February 1, 1830, two years before the county was named for him.

W.F. Vanlandingham, a surveyor for the state of Georgia, surveyed the 17th district, third section, of Cherokee County, where Smyrna is located. The notes he made in his field books indicated the conditions of the land, the improvements made by the Indians, the approximate number of acres in cultivation and cleared, and the relative value of the land with improvements. He noted the types of vegetation and trees growing in the area. In addition, his notes established the names of the Indian occupants of the area at the time the county was organized in 1832.

Among the Indians occupying the land were a woman named Nana; Naja; Nickajack, well known even today; Chulow; Telurkirka; Old Chulow; Tatagarka, the son of Walking Stick; Wawneta; Wookana; Talatangue; Crawfish; Viskohajka; Watey; Legarita; Corn Silk; Pipi; William Vann; and Billy. These Indians owned huge tracts of land containing log cabins, corn bins, and other outbuildings.

In addition to the Indians, Vanlandingham noted the presence of Killin Moore, a white man in possession of some of the land, and a half-breed named Elizabeth Elliott, who had title to some land by legal transfer. The state of Georgia apparently rented a number of land lots to a white man

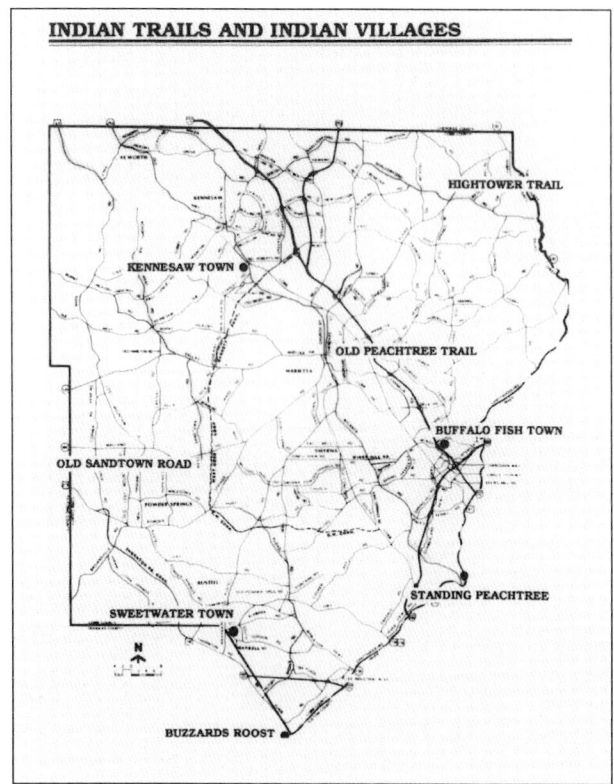

This map of Cobb County shows some of the villages and towns that existed before Cobb actually became a county in December 1832. Cherokee and Creek Indians had established most of these places prior to the arrival of English and Spanish explorers in 1732. Very little of the heritage of the Native Americans survived Georgia's acquisition of their lands through the series of treaties that eventually sent them hundreds of miles west from their homeland.

named E.E. Fishman, Esq. Another renter from the state was a man named George Robin. His land contained a blacksmith shop, three log houses, a stable, a corncrib, and six to eight acres in cultivation. The former Indian owners who had four land lots were renting to a white man named Harrell. Another owner of four land lots at the time was a white man, Colonel Rice.

According to surveyor Vanlandingham's field notes, few Indians were left in the Smyrna area, even in 1832. The Cherokees continued their struggle through the federal courts, but by 1835, some Indian leaders came to the realization that their troubles with Georgia would end only with removal and that a treaty under the best possible terms was necessary.

In December 1835, a group of about 300 Cherokees signed the Treaty of New Echota, which was ratified by the US Senate and signed by the president on May 23, 1836. One of the signers of the treaty was a man named Stand Watie. The name is similar to that of an Indian, Watie, who occupied land in the Smyrna area when the survey was conducted on June 13, 1832.

By the end of 1838, all the Indians had left voluntarily or were removed by force. All that remains of the Cherokee heritage in the Smyrna area today are a few names, like Nickajack, Odema, Noses, Chattahoochee, Etowah, and a few others.

In the meantime, a few of the "fortunate" draws in the gold and land lottery had started moving into the area. Original legislation provided that the person whose name was drawn could obtain fee simple title to the lot by paying $10 into the treasury of the state of Georgia. In December 1833, the legislature reduced the amount to $5. The landholders had five years to make the payment, but the deadline was extended several times. Finally, on December 21, 1843, the legislature set the final deadline to October 1, 1844. Lots not accepted and paid for by that time reverted back to the state.

When the first official census was completed in October 1834, there were only 1,576 people in 275 residences in all of Cobb County. A few of them had already established their homes in the Smyrna area and were looking to fulfill their dreams and needs in the near future.

One

RELIGION AND CHURCHES

Smyrna had its origins as a religious community when a few Cherokee Indians were still occupants of the area and before Cobb County was established in December 1832. Andrew Jackson was president of the United States at the time. Early settlers moved into the area that later became the location of Dickson's Shopping Center, the Crossings Shopping Center, and the present super-size Kroger.

In 1831, pioneers petitioned the Nance's Creek Primitive Baptist Church in DeKalb County to sponsor a church at that location. The petition was approved on April 1, 1832, and Concord Primitive Baptist Church was constituted on April 13, 1832, with 14 charter members. It was the first church established in Cobb County. Rev. Thornton Burke was the first pastor.

Early churches not only provided spiritual guidance; social life was centered on church-related activities like picnics, hayrides, plays, concerts, barbeques, and traditional holiday celebrations.

Around 1838, a Methodist church established an outdoor worship center. It became known as Smyrna Camp Ground, located near a spring where a brush arbor was made, log seats were provided, and a camp meeting was announced. Worshipers came from the surrounding area and stayed for several days to enjoy the fellowship.

As the population grew, more churches were organized. In addition to the congregations featured in this section, the following were also established: Fellowship Baptist (1927), Green Acres Baptist (1948), Welcome All Baptist (1955), Our Savior Lutheran (1960), Norton Park Baptist (1961), and Trinity Baptist (1973). There are currently 52 churches in Smyrna. Church leaders and members have been visible in the communities. Their contributions to civic and moral development are immeasurable.

The name *Smyrna* was chosen in recognition of one of the churches established in Asia by the Apostle Paul in the first century A.D. The biblical Smyrna was an early center of Christianity, and the name is often used in connection with a church settlement.

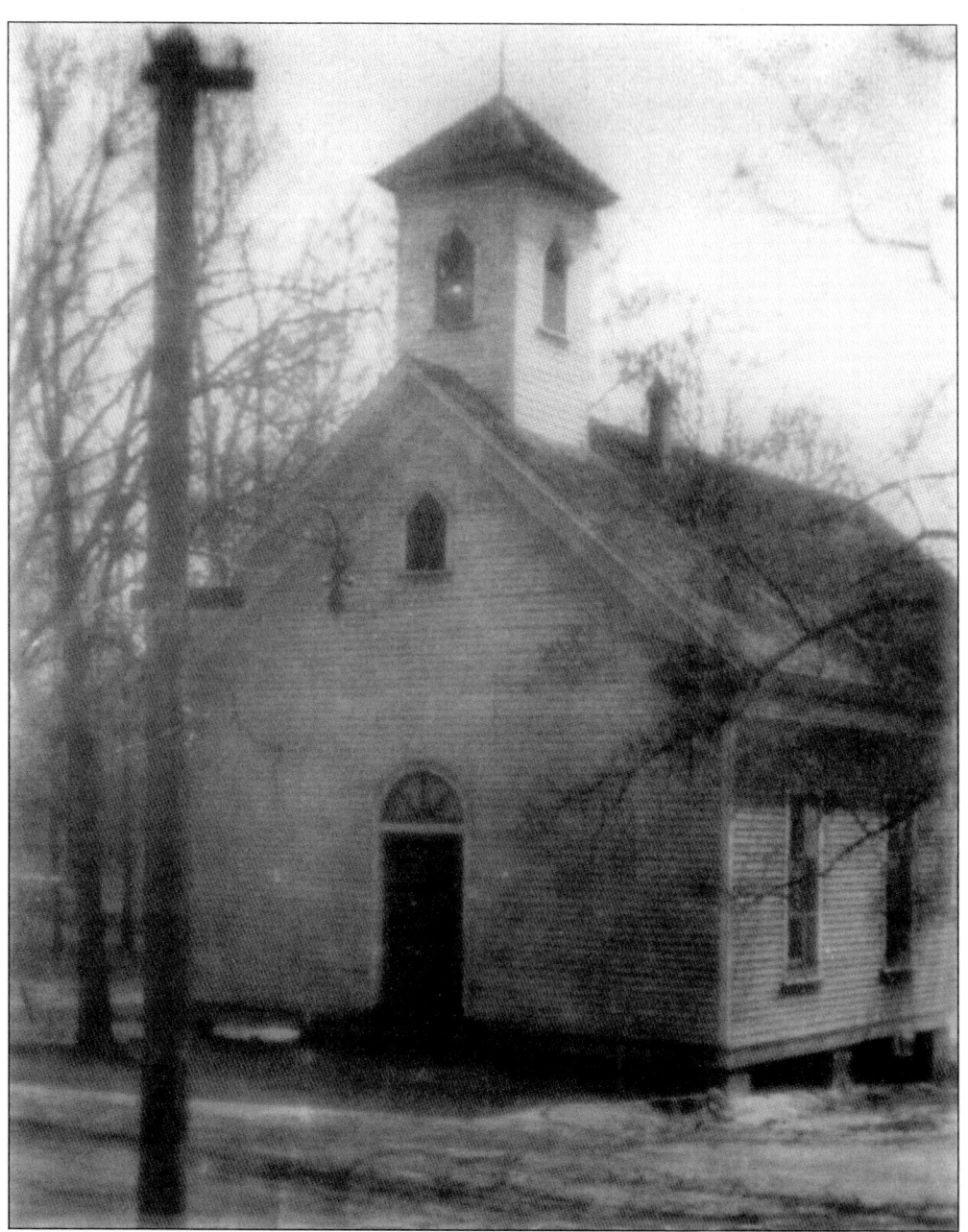

This white frame building was the first worship center constructed by the Smyrna First Baptist Church. Since its organization in August 1884, the congregation had been meeting in the Presbyterian Church facility. The new building was on Atlanta Road, approximately where the Second Baptist Church is today. This building and several others were destroyed by a fire that started in the flue of the church in March 1924. (Courtesy Mary Terry.)

Concord Baptist Church was the very first congregation of any denomination organized in Cobb County. It began holding services in a log schoolhouse in 1832. By 1889, the building shown here, Concord's fifth, was constructed near the first one. In 1909, it was moved piece by piece and completely reassembled at its present location, 4494 Floyd Road in Mableton. (Courtesy Rex Pruitt.)

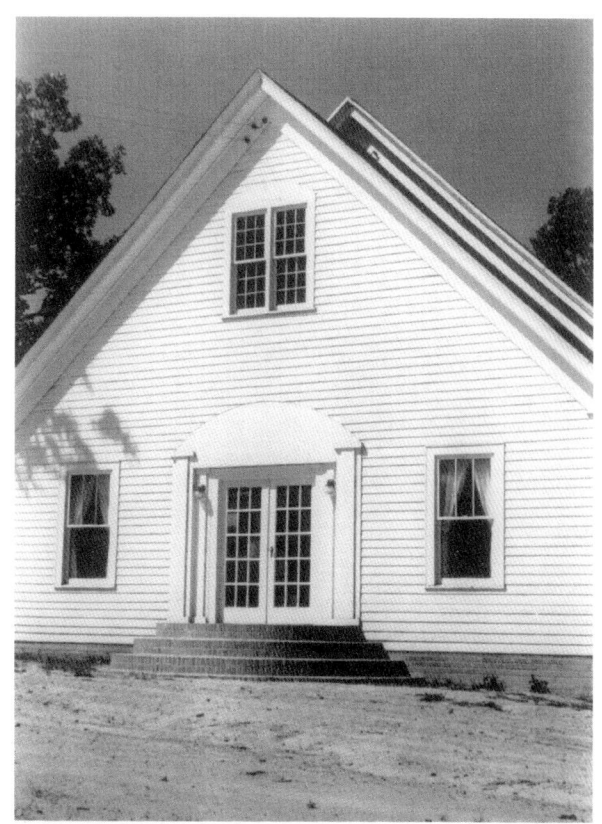

The 150th anniversary of Concord Baptist Church and a homecoming were celebrated on May 30, 1982, in the worship center constructed in 1970. Special musical programs were presented by the choir and guest performers. Invited guests were former pastors and members and public officials. Pioneer families of the church included the Barbers, Glores, Peeks, Seays, Barnses, Ganns, and Thomases, among others. (Courtesy Harold Smith.)

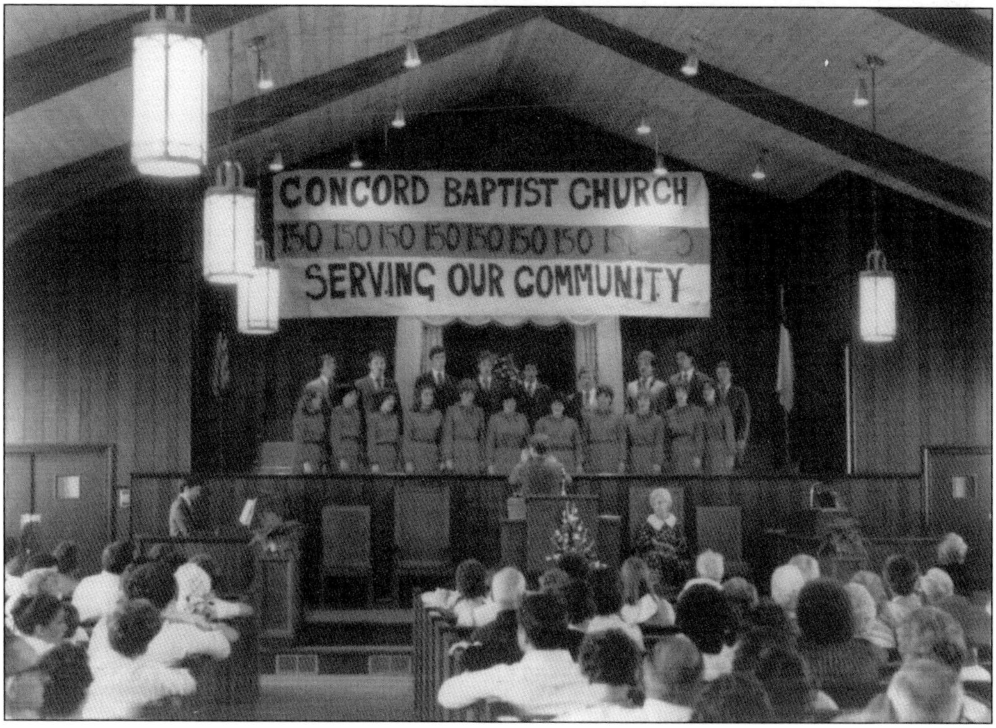

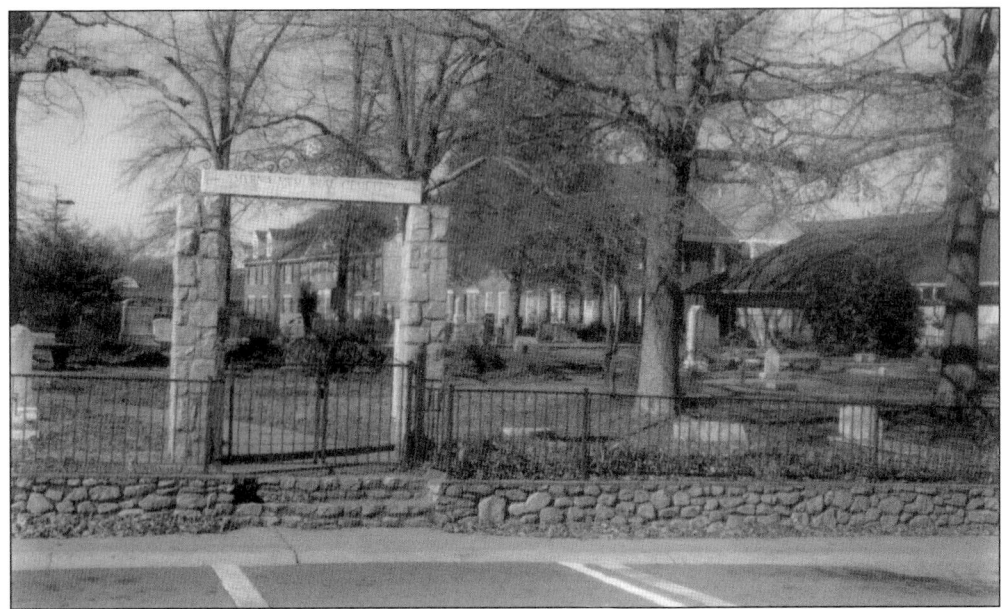

Perhaps the oldest landmark in Smyrna is Memorial Cemetery, established in 1838 by the Methodists along with their church. It is located in the heart of the city, near city hall, the Village Green, community center, library, two historic churches, and the entrance to Market Village. Money for the marble marker atop the entrance was raised by Mazie Whitfield Nelson. She died in 1977 and now rests with family members in the cemetery.

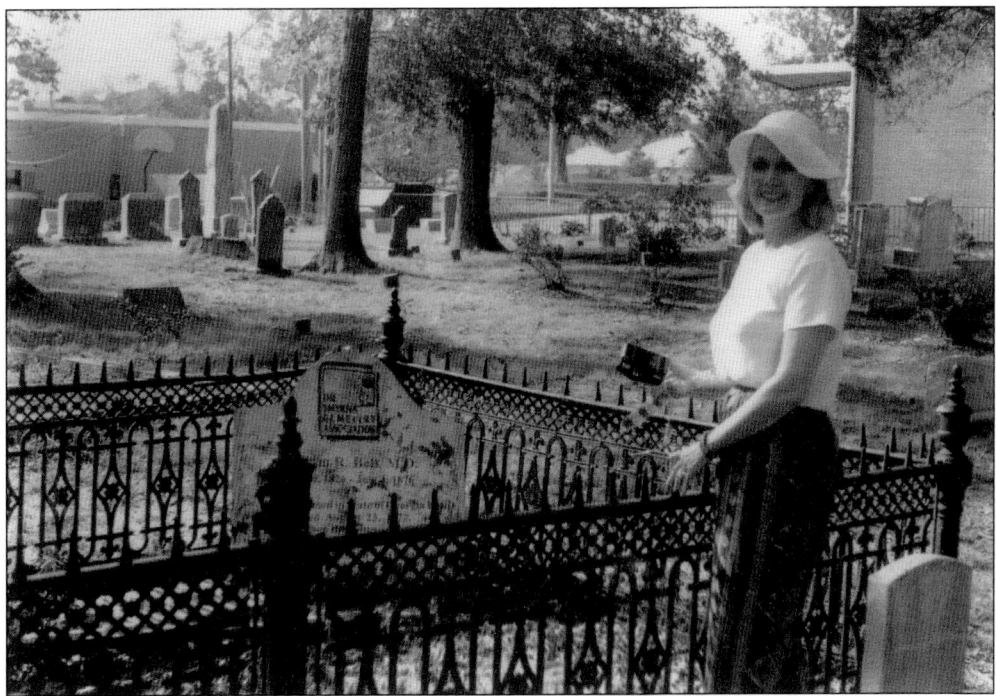

Jane Farmer is seen here photographing the graves of Smyrna's first mayor, John C. Moore, and one of the first city councilmen, W.R. Bell. These men were named in Smyrna's original charter, granted by the state of Georgia in August 1872. (Courtesy Harold Smith.)

The 1883 Methodist church was constructed of heart pinewood. A larger church was constructed in 1911. Col. B.T. Frey purchased the old church building and converted it into the 15-room Smyrna Hotel (1911–1919). The portion shown here was saved from demolition in 1954 and moved to a new location, currently next to CVS Drugs and behind the Gautschy House. It is used for office space. (Courtesy Harold Smith.)

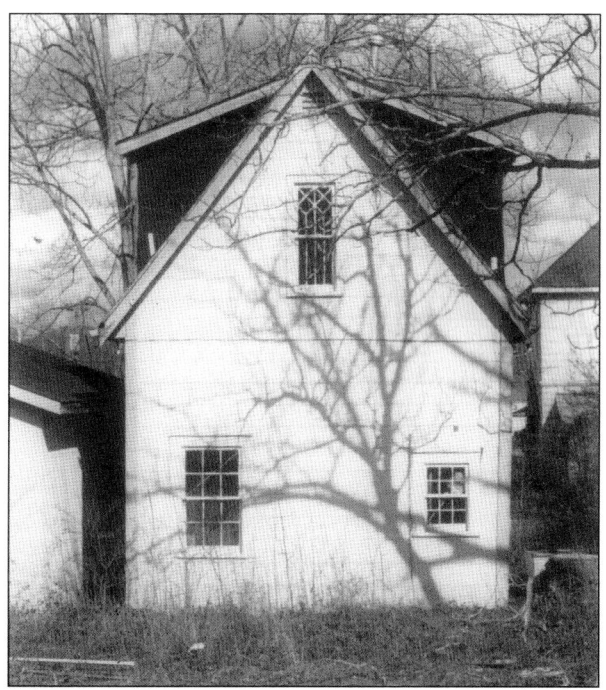

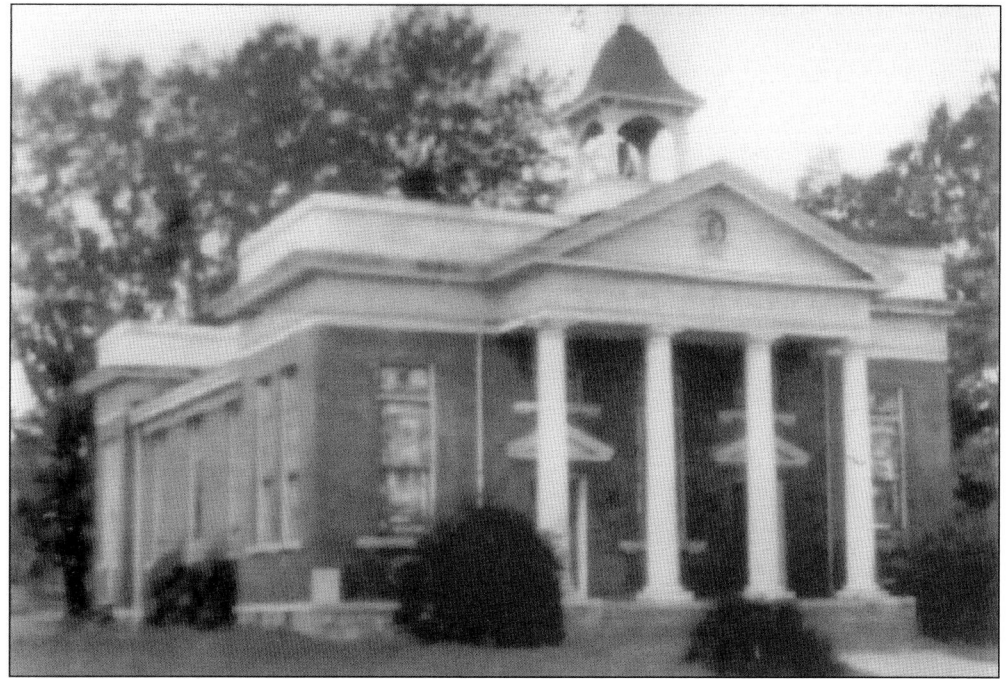

Less than 1,600 people lived in Cobb County when recently arriving pioneers established the brush arbor worship center near the present-day intersection of Church and King Streets. The center attracted worshippers from all over the area. However, about two years after construction started on the Western & Atlantic Railroad, the Methodists constructed their first building and a nearby cemetery, now Smyrna Memorial. The Methodist building (shown here), on the northwest corner of Atlanta Road and Church Street, served from 1911 to 1967. (Courtesy First Methodist Church.)

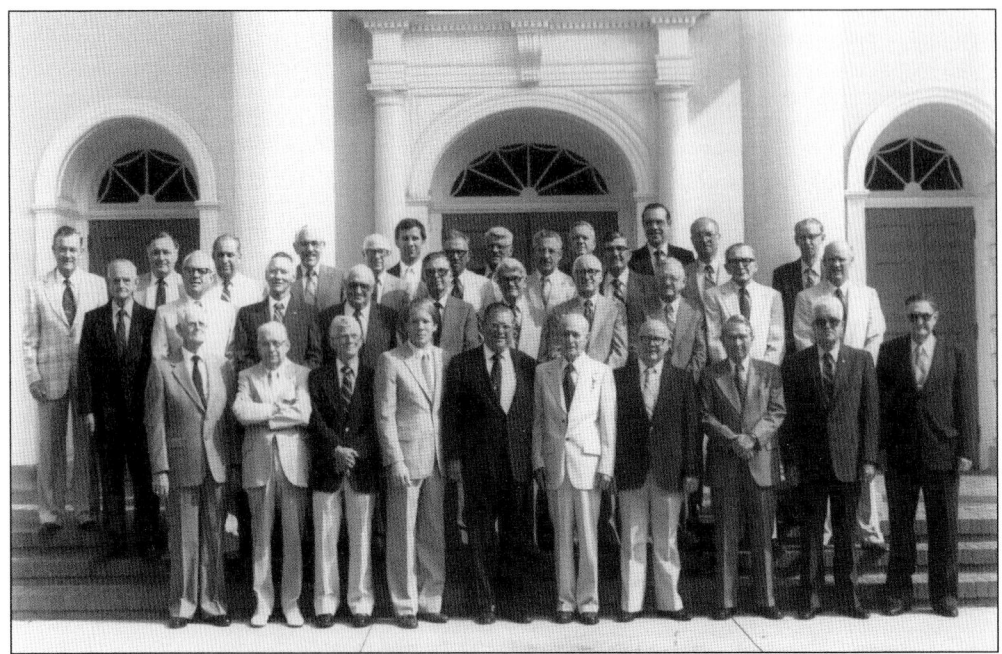

Pearce Matthews began teaching Sunday school at First Methodist Church during World War II. After his death, his son, John, taught the class for 38 years. Pictured here is the 1974 class. The present building on Concord Road was built in 1967. It contains the stained-glass windows from the previous building. The church voted to name the new building Matthews Chapel in honor of Pearce and John Matthews. (Courtesy Lois Matthews.)

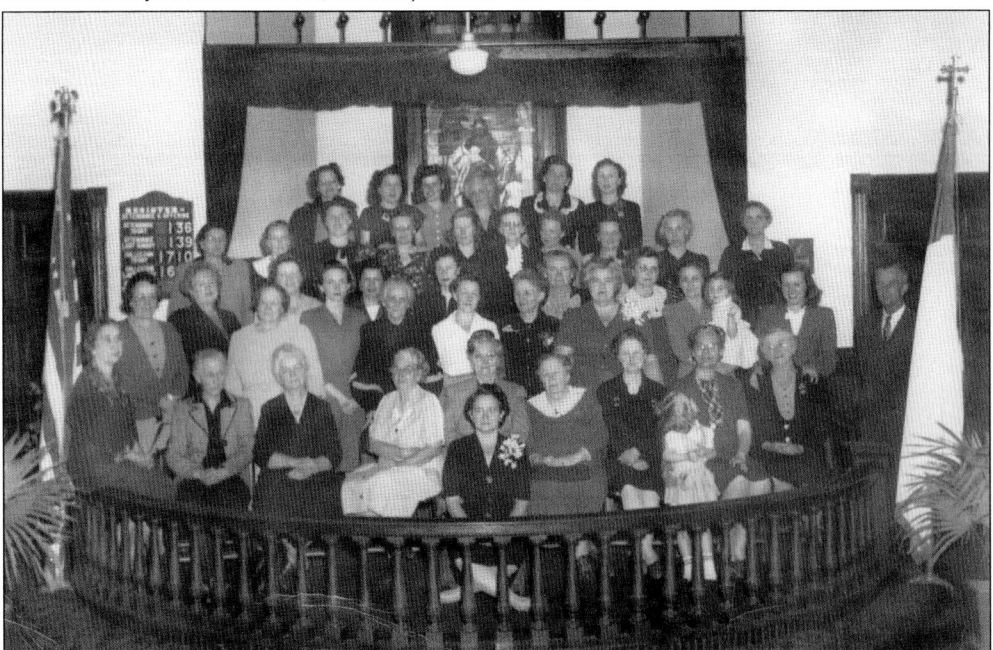

The First United Methodist Church Woman's Club (1945–1946) is pictured here with Rev. R.C. Owens (far right) in the church sanctuary. The church was located from 1911 to 1968 at the intersection of Atlanta Road and Church Street. (Courtesy Elizabeth Anderson.)

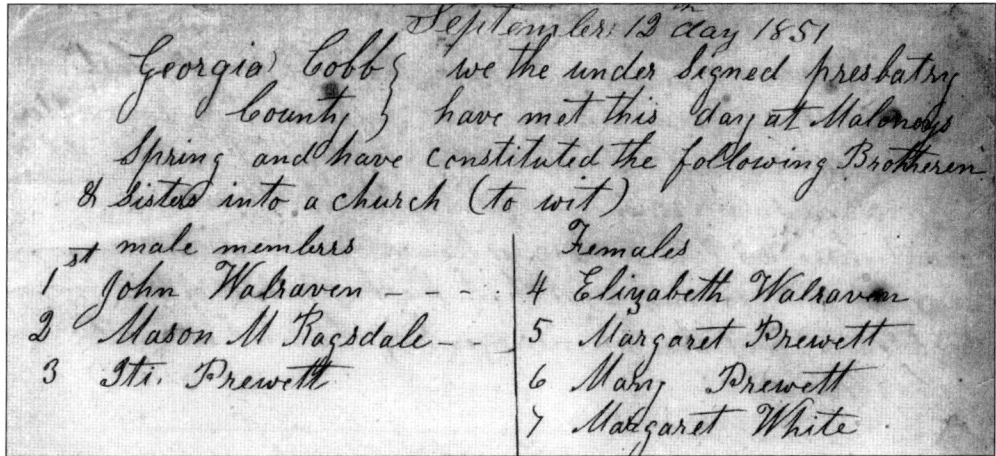

The Maloney's Spring Primitive Baptist Church was constituted on September 12, 1851. The building no longer exists, but the church cemetery is located on South Cobb Drive at Austell Road. Many past Smyrna citizens, including mayors, state legislators, county commissioners, merchants, and doctors, are buried there. The original minutes of the church (shown here) were donated to the Smyrna History Museum.

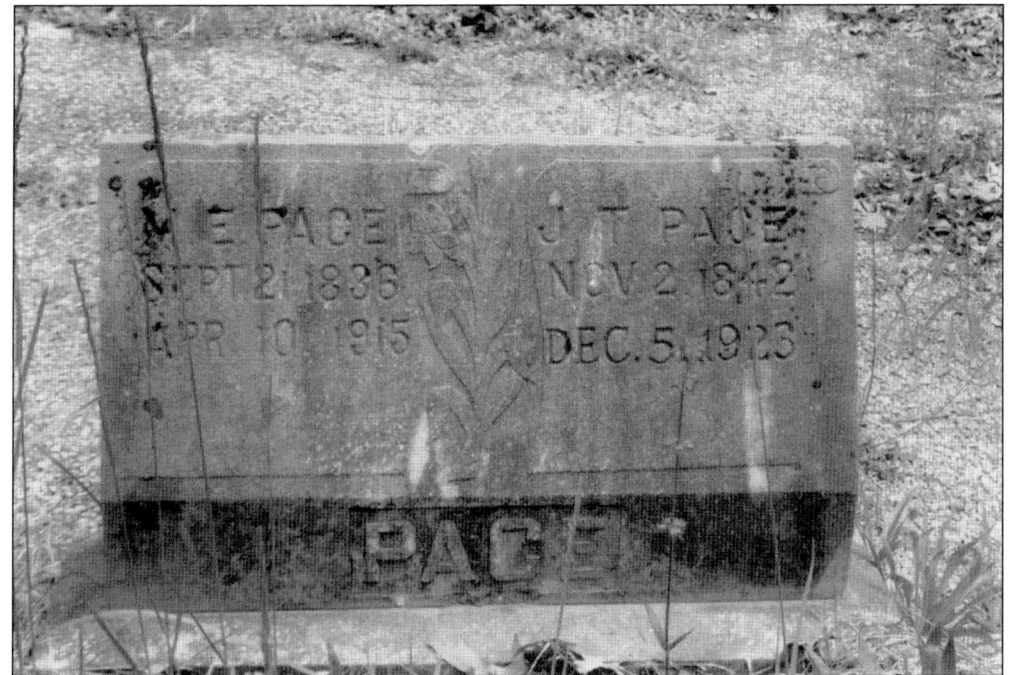

The grave of John T. Pace and his wife, Martha Elizabeth Henderson Pace, is located in the cemetery of Maloney's Spring. He served as Smyrna's mayor from 1901 to 1906 and was a Cobb County commissioner. He was the father of Dr. William Tatum Pace, a Smyrna physician, and the grandfather of Lorena Pace Pruitt, Dr. Pace's daughter and Smyrna's only female mayor (1945–1948). (Courtesy Harold Smith.)

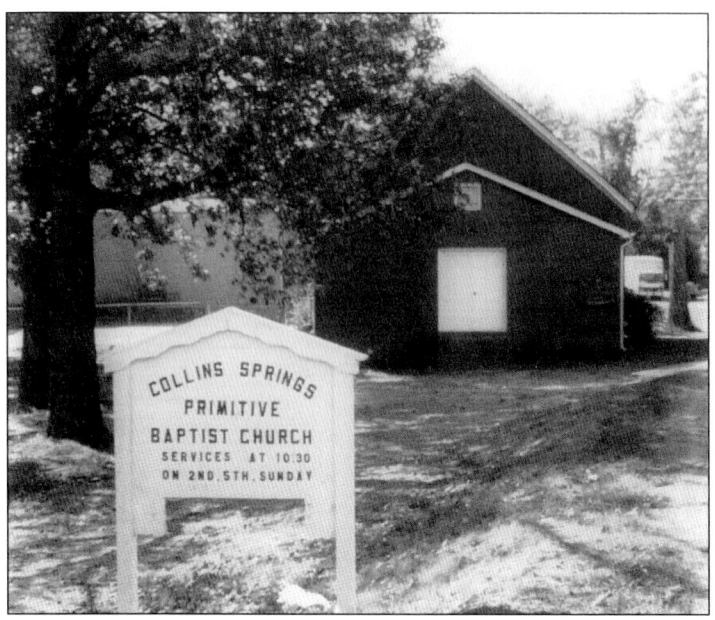

Collins Springs Primitive Baptist Church, on North Church Road, was founded in 1856. The original building was destroyed in 1864 during the Civil War. Rebuilt in 1866, the church, cemetery, and spring carry the name of James A. Collins, a pioneer and businessman. The earliest marked burial in the cemetery is Charlie M. Maner, 16-year-old son of Mr. and Mrs. W.G. Maner who died on July 21, 1857. (Courtesy Harold Smith.)

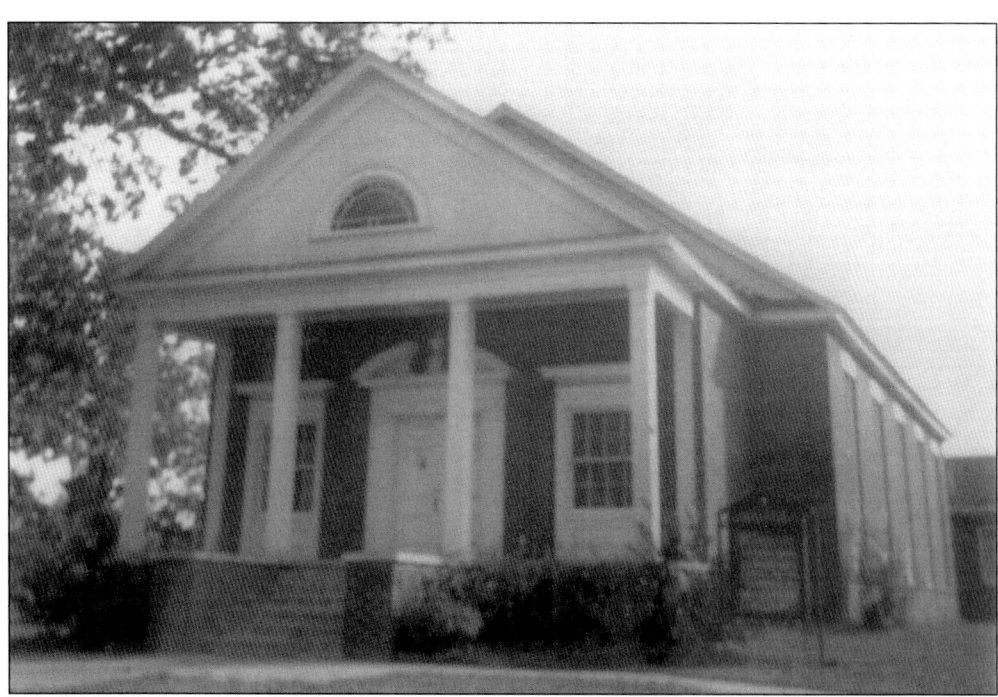

Smyrna Presbyterian Church, organized in 1874 in the building originally constructed for the Smyrna Boys Academy, was dissolved in 1905 and reestablished in 1913 in a new facility on Memorial Drive. The congregation later built on Atlanta Road. The first service in that facility (shown here) was on April 26, 1965. The old building was sold to the Smyrna Assembly of God, which in turn sold it to First Baptist Church in 1983. (Courtesy Smyrna Presbyterian Church.)

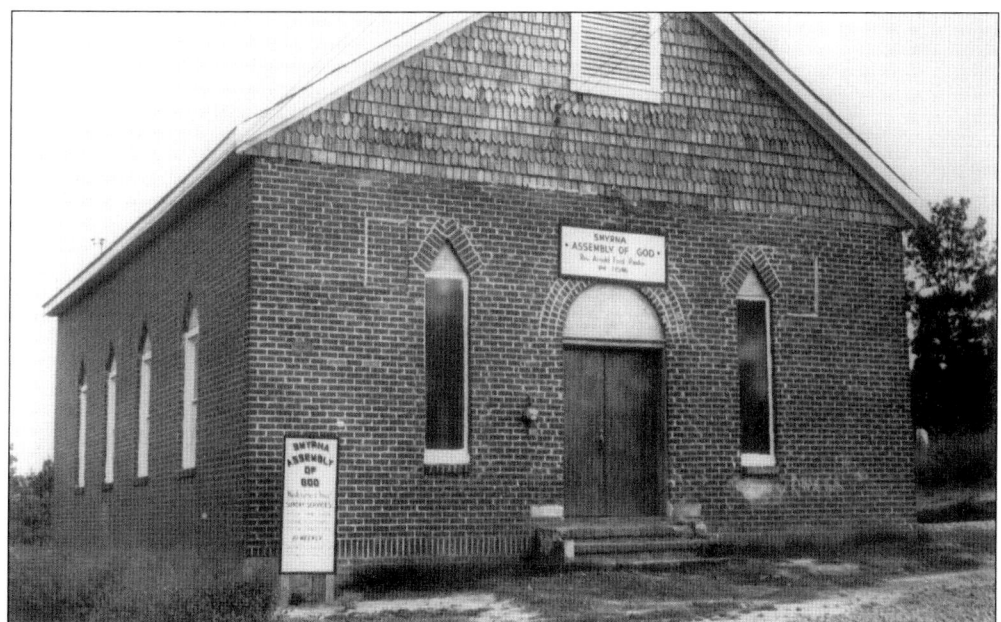

The Mount Zion Baptist Church was established as one of the earliest black congregations in all of Cobb County, in 1877. It was located at Hawthorne Street and Roswell Road, adjacent to the only African American cemetery in Smyrna. In 1949, the church moved to a new location, on Hawthorne Street (formerly Davenport Street). The building shown here was sold to the Smyrna Assembly of God in 1953.

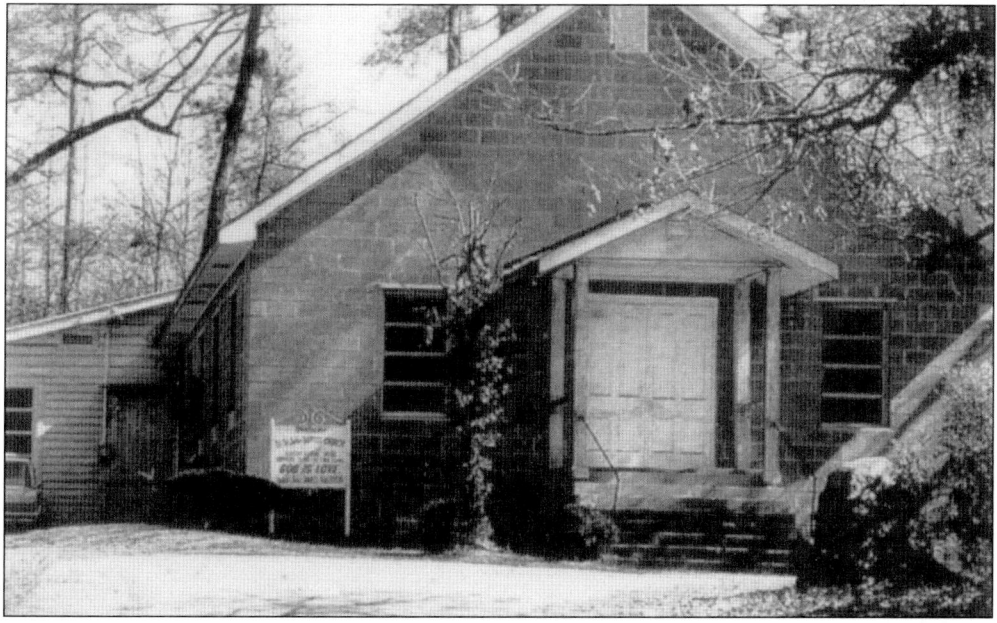

The First St. John Baptist Church was an African American church established on Settlement Road in 1871. In 1997, developers purchased 41 acres, including 22 homes and 2 churches, to construct a new subdivision. An African American cemetery and part of a Civil War *shoupade* (fort) have been preserved, located on the historic Johnson River Line, which extended almost seven miles along the Chattahoochee River to repel Union forces. (Courtesy Roberta Cook.)

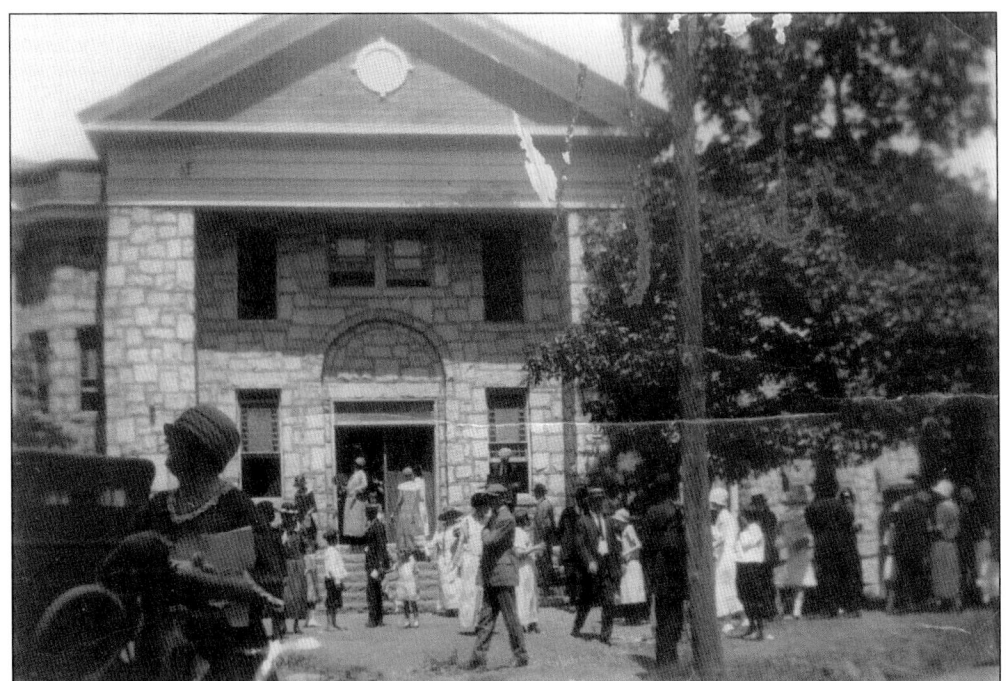

The Baptist Church of Jesus Christ was constituted with four charter members on August 30, 1884. They met in the Presbyterian church building until they constructed a white frame building in 1886. On August 10, 1924, the first service was held in this new building, constructed from Stone Mountain granite. The church changed its name to First Baptist Church of Smyrna in 1946. Alma Gilbert is seen in the left foreground. (Courtesy Evelyn Mulkey estate.)

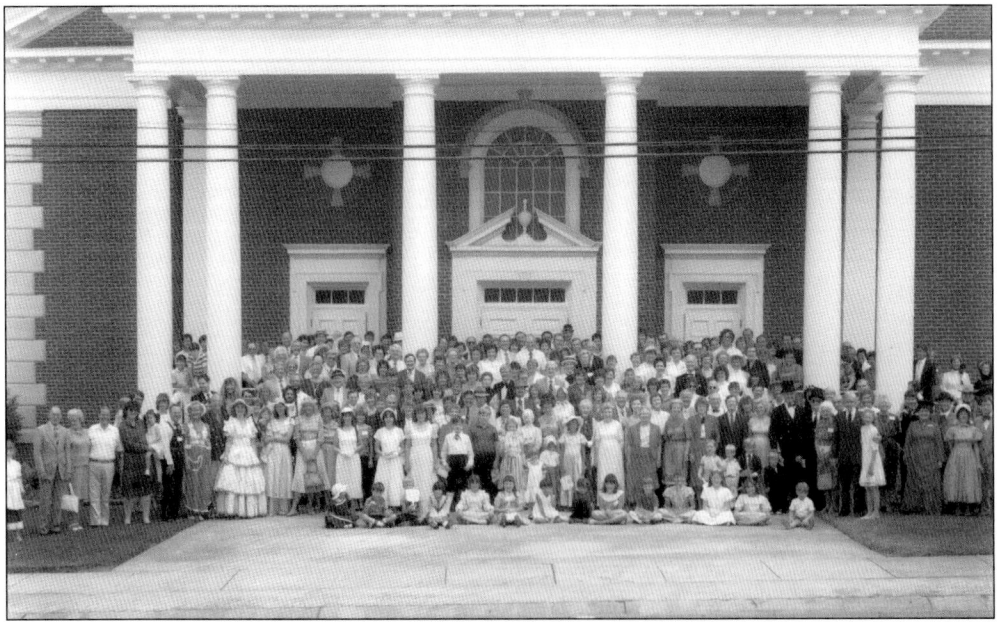

The Smyrna First Baptist Church celebrated its centennial on Sunday, August 26, 1984, with more than 1,500 members in attendance for the sermon by pastor Evan A. "Bud" Abbot. The centennial activities continued for a week. (Courtesy First Baptist Church.)

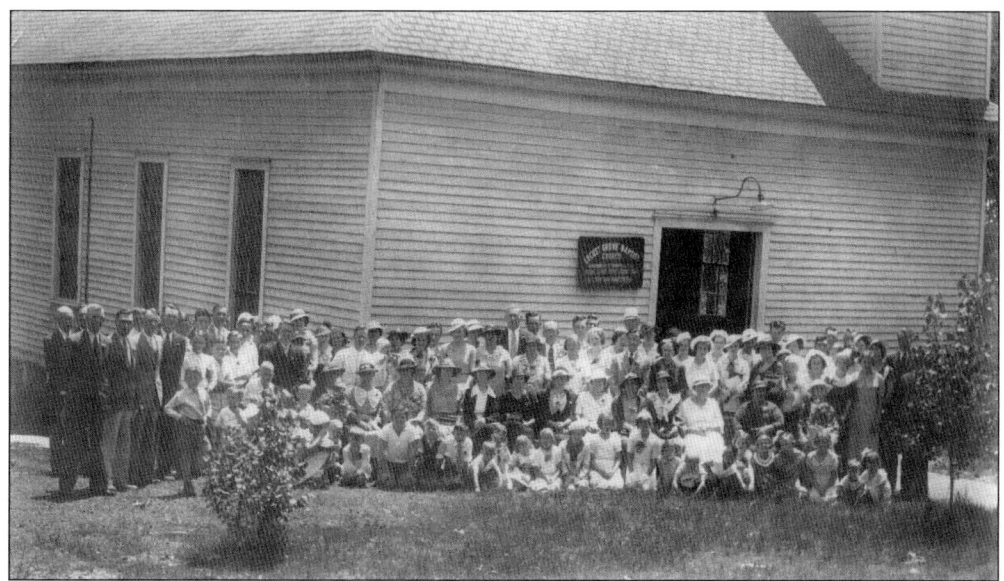

Members of Locust Grove Baptist Church pose for a 1935 homecoming in front of the original wood frame building, which served the congregation from 1920 to 1937. The church grew out of a Sunday school that was organized in October 1909. The congregants first met in a white frame schoolhouse near the intersection of Oakdale and Atlanta Roads. On July 10, 1910, a tent was erected on the site of the building. (Courtesy Locust Grove Baptist Church.)

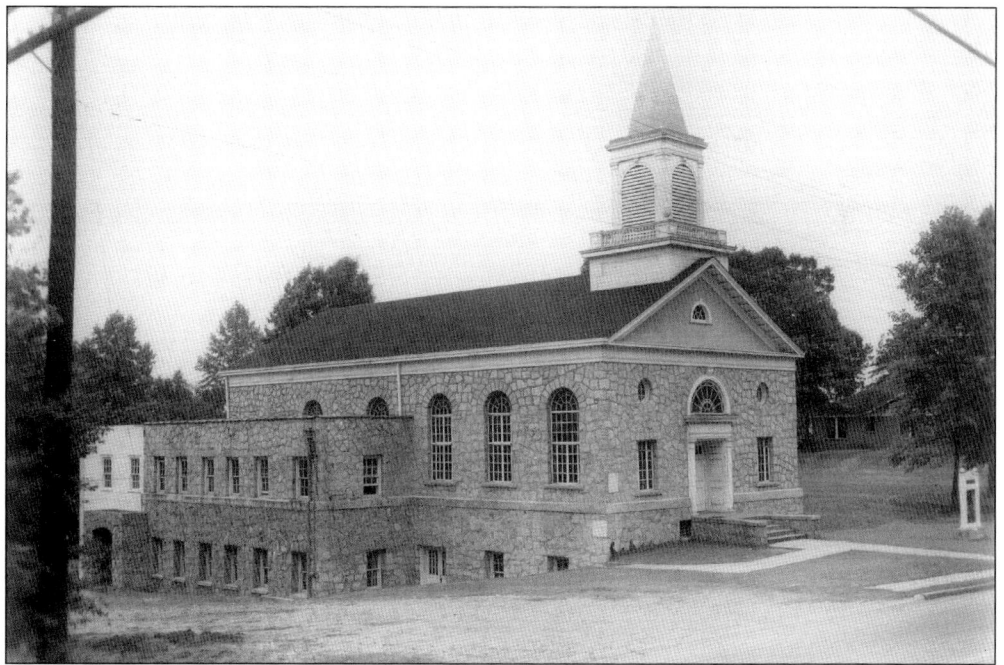

By 1938, due to growth, Locust Grove Baptist Church made plans for a new, larger building. The basement of the stone building was completed in 1937 and used as a sanctuary until the church was completed. The building was dedicated on October 20, 1940. Members played a key role in the development of the Oakdale and South Cobb area. The building currently houses St. Benedict Episcopal Church and School. (Courtesy Locust Grove Baptist Church.)

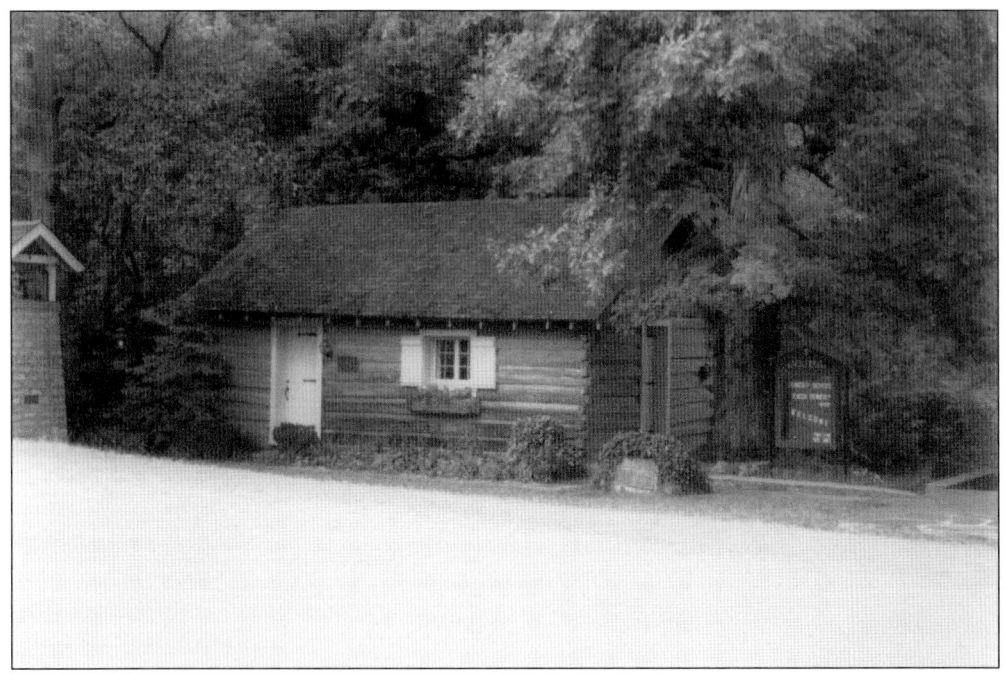

The Log Cabin Community Sunday School was organized in 1912 as an interdenominational Bible study group and met in a small log cabin. A larger cabin was erected in 1919. In the early days, it attracted people from Atlanta who had purchased large tracts of land in South Cobb County. (Courtesy Harold Smith.)

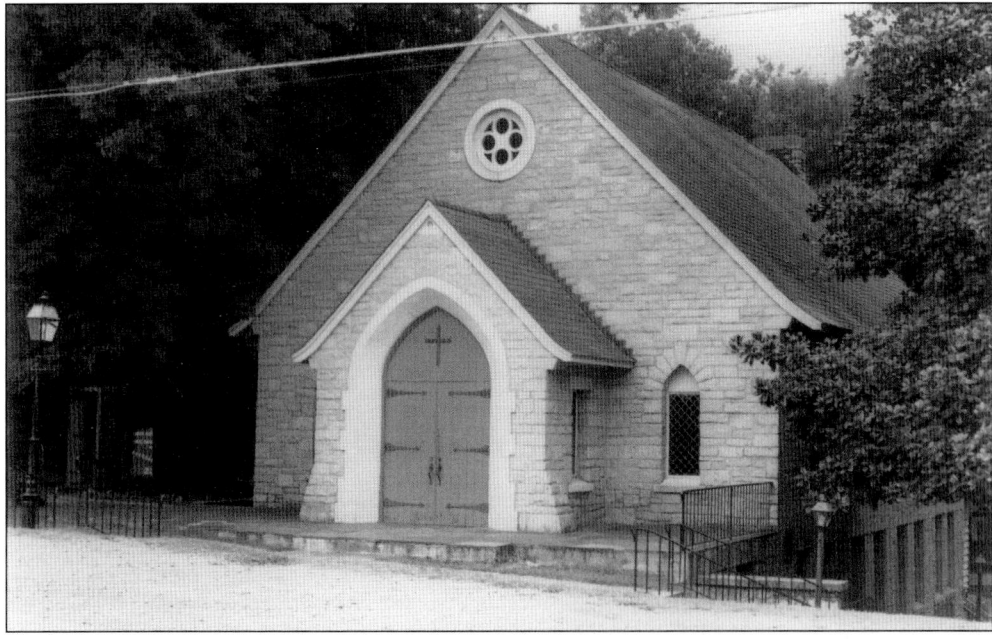

The Log Cabin Community constructed a stone building in 1949. It is a popular facility for weddings and other special occasions in addition to regular religious services. The buildings are located adjacent to each other on Log Cabin Drive, just east of Atlanta Road and south of I-285. (Courtesy Harold Smith.)

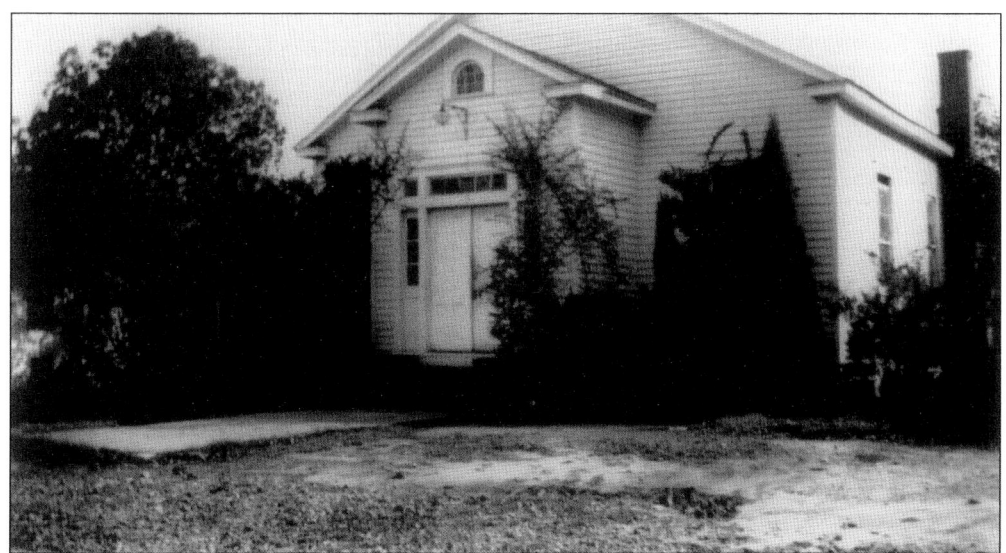

Spring Street Baptist Church was organized on October 15, 1933, with Rev. J.W. Reeves as founding pastor. Church property was donated by W.J. Osburn, who cut timber from his property on Elizabeth Street to build the church. A new brick sanctuary was constructed in front of the original wooden building, which was converted into Sunday school rooms.

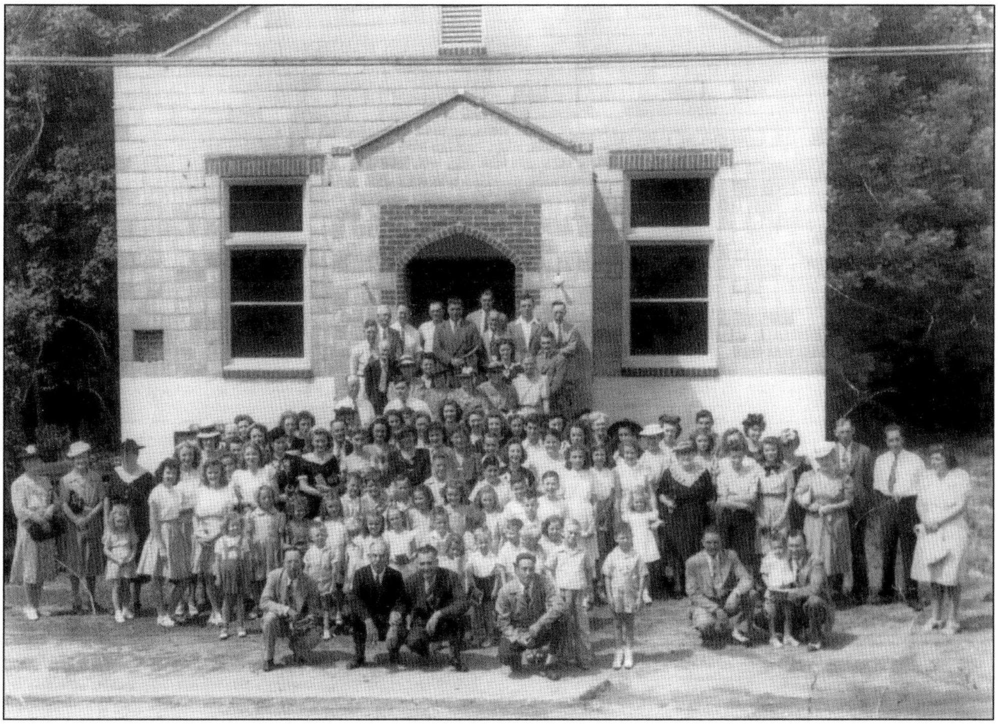

Organized with 34 charter members on September 26, 1942, Second Baptist Church began holding meetings in the old Nelms Lodge on West Spring Street. The basement of the building at the church's present location, Atlanta Road at Powder Springs Street, was completed in 1943. The sanctuary was not completed until 1946, because building materials were unattainable during World War II. (Courtesy Joann McDowell.)

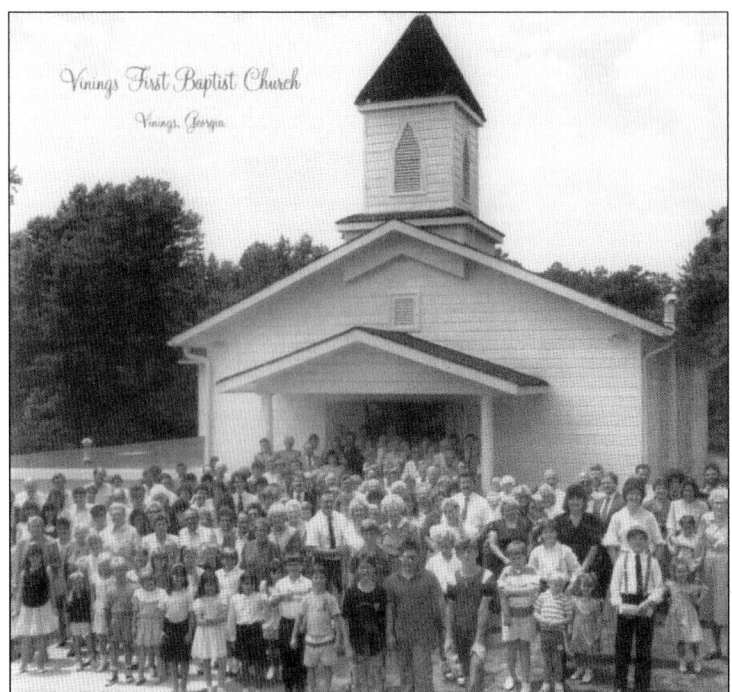

Representatives from 14 Baptist churches attended the organizational meeting of Vinings First Baptist on August 8, 1948. Services the first year were held in a clubhouse on Golf Club Drive. The congregation observed its 40th anniversary in 1988. The church relocated to 4182 South Cobb Drive in August 1992 from New Paces Ferry Road. (Courtesy Beverly McDowell.)

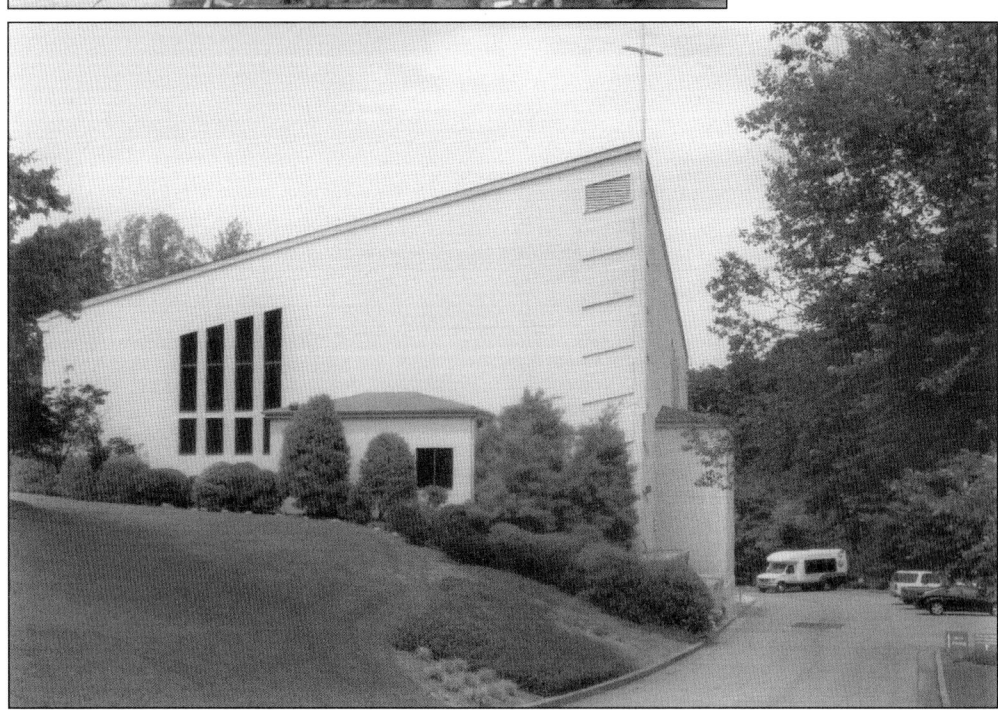

The Smyrna Assembly of God held its first meeting on January 7, 1953, at the home of W.G. Graham on North Matthews Street. Rev. Arnold Ford and a small group purchased the abandoned building of the Mount Zion Baptist Church for $550. In 1963, the congregation purchased the old Presbyterian Church on Church Street, and in 1978, it moved to its present location on King Springs Road (shown here). (Courtesy Harold Smith.)

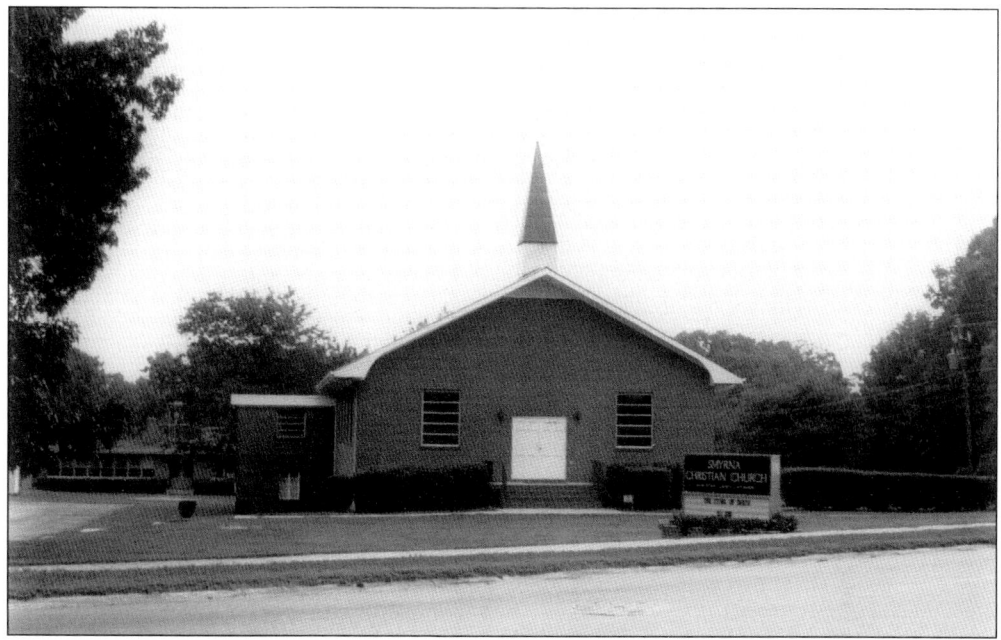

Smyrna Christian Church, on Concord Road, was organized on April 25, 1954. During the first year, the members met at the old Jonquil Theater on Atlanta Street, at the home of Mr. and Mrs. William Holden on Church Street, and at the Smyrna Woman's Club building. In 1955, the church constructed a small house on its lot and met in the home until a new sanctuary was completed in 1958. (Courtesy Harold Smith).

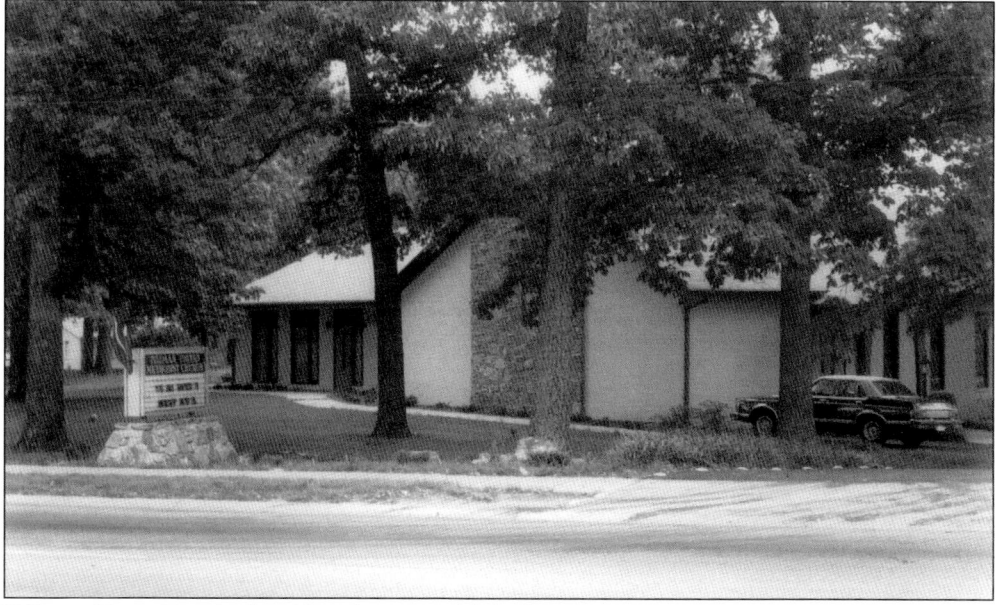

Tillman United Methodist Church was established at the home of Mr. and Mrs. R.L. Ruff Sr. on February 21, 1954. The members met at the Concord Road residence for six weeks. Then, they purchased three acres from the G.S. Brown estate, which contained a house, two buildings, and a garage. The congregation met in those remodeled facilities until a building was completed (shown here). The first service was held on July 7, 1957. (Courtesy Harold Smith).

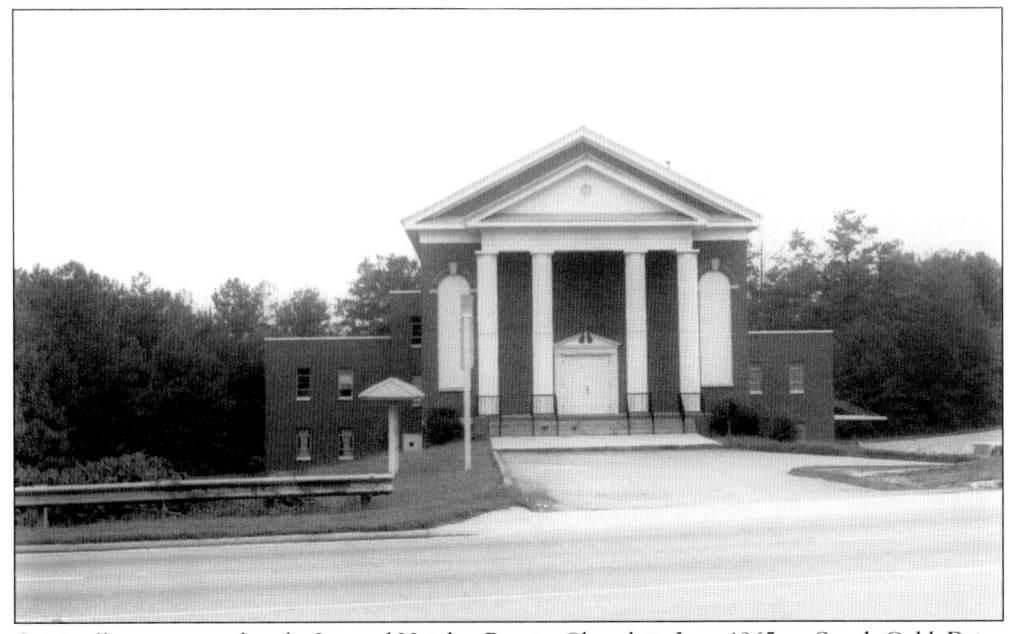

Originally constructed as the Legend Heights Baptist Church in June 1965 on South Cobb Drive by the Noonday Baptist Association, the name was changed to Community Baptist Church. It is currently owned by Vinings First Baptist Church. (Courtesy Harold Smith).

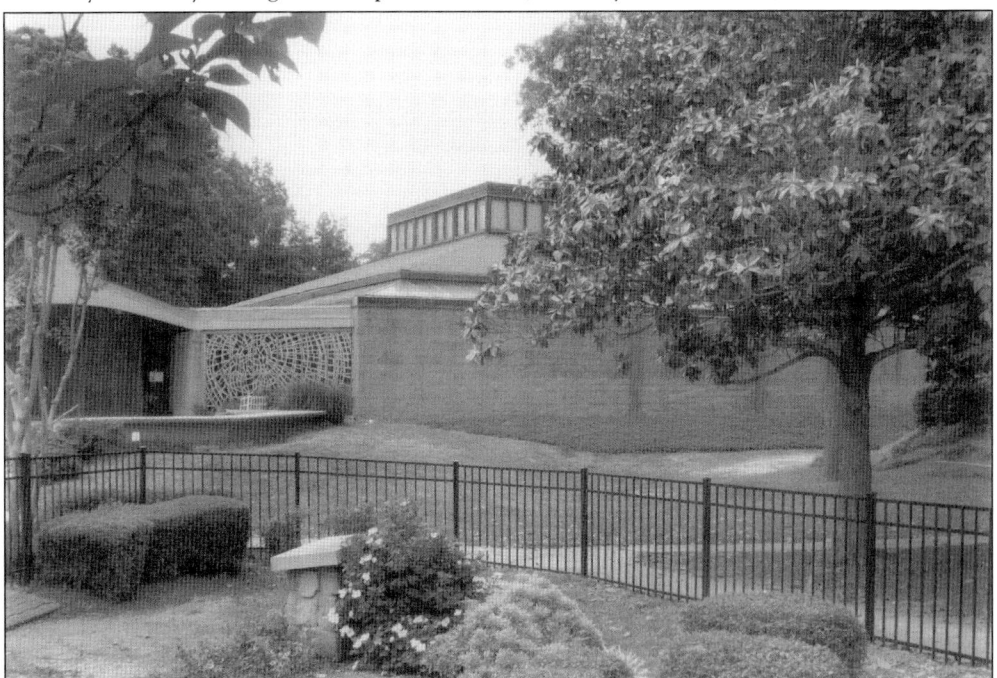

On June 1, 1966, the first Catholic church in Smyrna, St. Thomas the Apostle, was established. The first Sunday mass was held on June 5 of that year in the Wills High School cafeteria. Belmont Theater was later used. Father Richard Morrow was the first pastor. The congregation was the first in the area to have "Blue Nuns." In 1966, the church moved to the intersection of King Springs and Cooper Lake Roads. (Courtesy Harold Smith).

Two

Early Pioneers

The first official census of Cobb County was certified on March 4, 1834, by Ferdinand Jett. It was authorized by the Georgia legislature on December 21, 1833. The total population as stated by Jett was 1,576 persons. The first US census was conducted in 1840. Cobb County was enumerated by nine militia districts: 845 Roswell (originally in Cobb), 846 Powder Springs, 851 Acworth, 895 Coxes (between Smyrna and Austell), 897 Merritts, 898 Marietta (including the city of Marietta), 911 Gritters, 942 Weddingon (annexed into Paulding County), and 992 Randall's (also known as Lemon's). The county also included parts of Smyrna, Mableton, and Vinings. Some of these names are still familiar today as the names of Cobb County's 170 or so voting precincts.

When the 1840 census was completed, Cobb was found to have a total population of 7,539. There were eight Revolutionary War veterans living in Cobb at the time: John Barnwell, 88; John Colling, 80; Adonijah Edwards, 73; Israwl Eastwood, 83; Peter Glover, 79; Robert McDowell, 86; Jeremiah Nesbit, 105; and John Summers, 77. Cobb County's total population was made up of 3,269 white males, 3,185 white females, 440 male slaves, 454 female slaves, 5 free male persons of color, and 3 free female persons of color. Approximately 527 of the total population had settled in the Smyrna area militia districts. There is a difference of 183 between the breakdown figures and the county total. In addition to the people, there were 1,597 horses and mules, 9,629 cattle, 3,524 sheep, and 20,177 hogs.

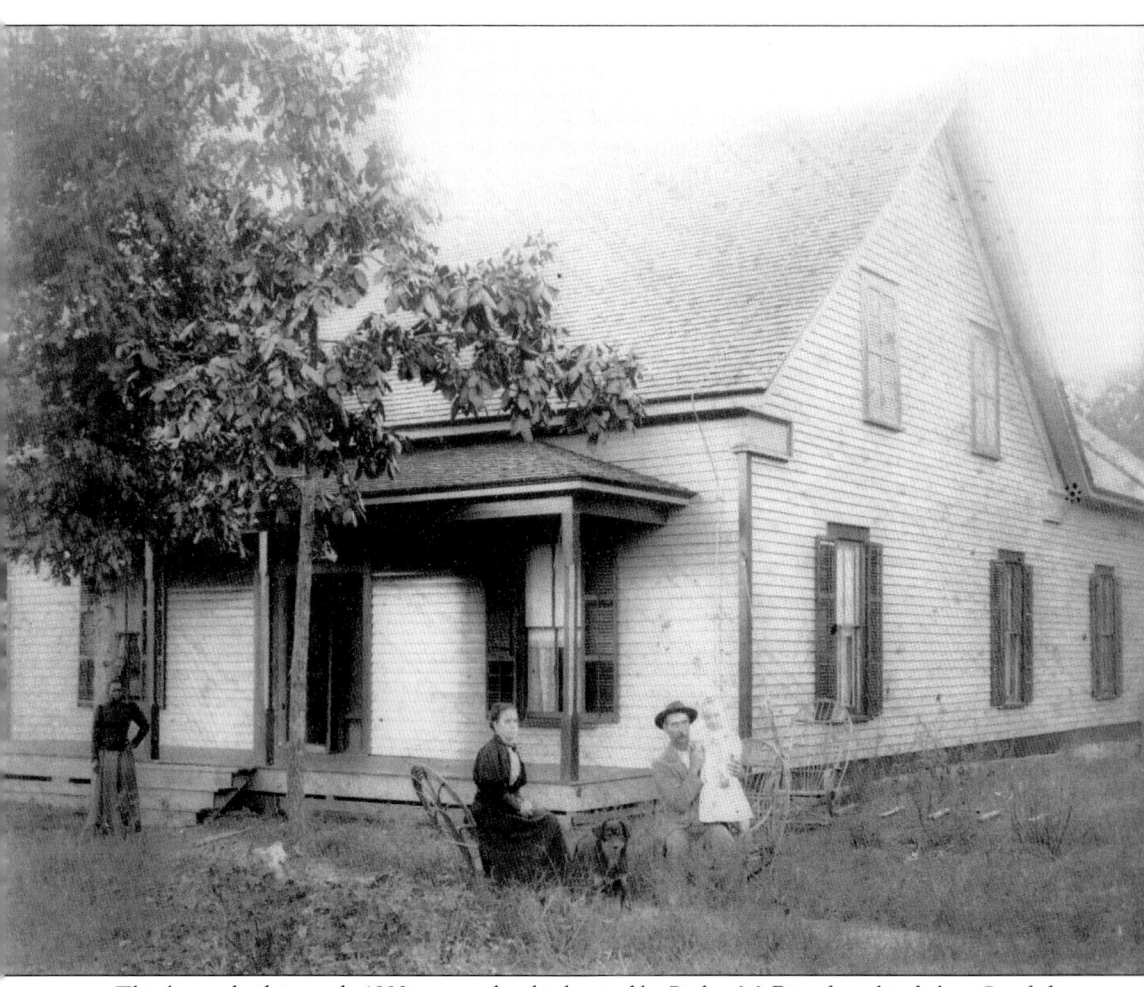

This home, built in early 1892, was on land inherited by Parker M. Rice from his father, Confederate colonel Solon Z. Rice. Parker Rice and his bride, Blanch Ruff Rice, moved into the house shortly after their marriage on October 29, 1891. The family is shown here with their first child, a family servant, and their dog. At the time, a log cabin constructed by the Cherokee Indians was converted to a blacksmith shop. A nearby dirt mound with rocks on it was believed to be the burial place of Cicada Nickajack. The house, sitting on almost 30 acres, was razed in the early 1980s for the construction of an $8.5 million townhouse complex. (Courtesy Parker Lowry.)

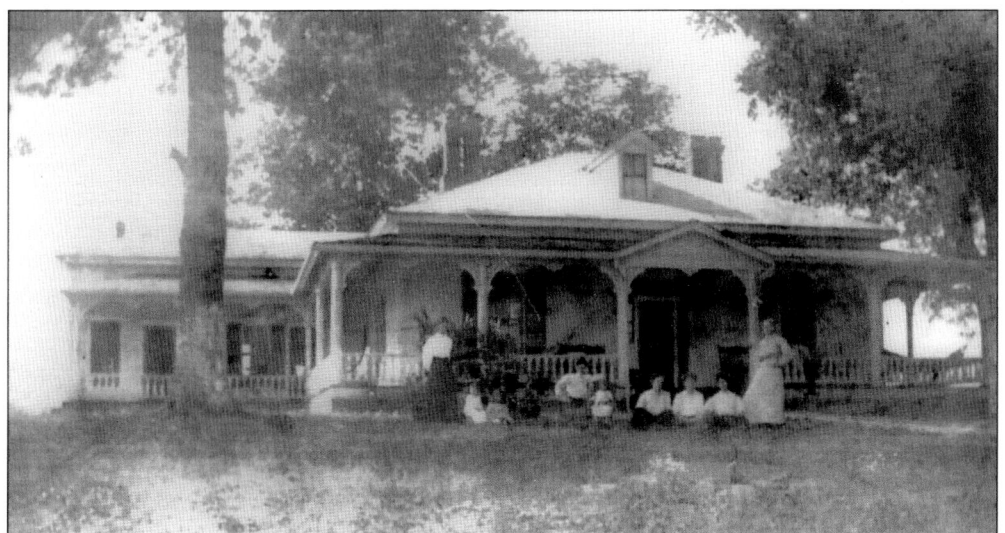

The home of Cobb County's first state senator, John Gann, was constructed in 1841 just west of Nickajack Creek. It may be the oldest house in Smyrna, and it is listed in the National Register of Historic Places. Former Georgia governor Roy Barnes's wife, Marie, lived here at one time. It has also been occupied by S.B. Love, the Hill family, and Smyrna's first mayor, Jake C. Moore. (Courtesy Duke and Pat Torbert.)

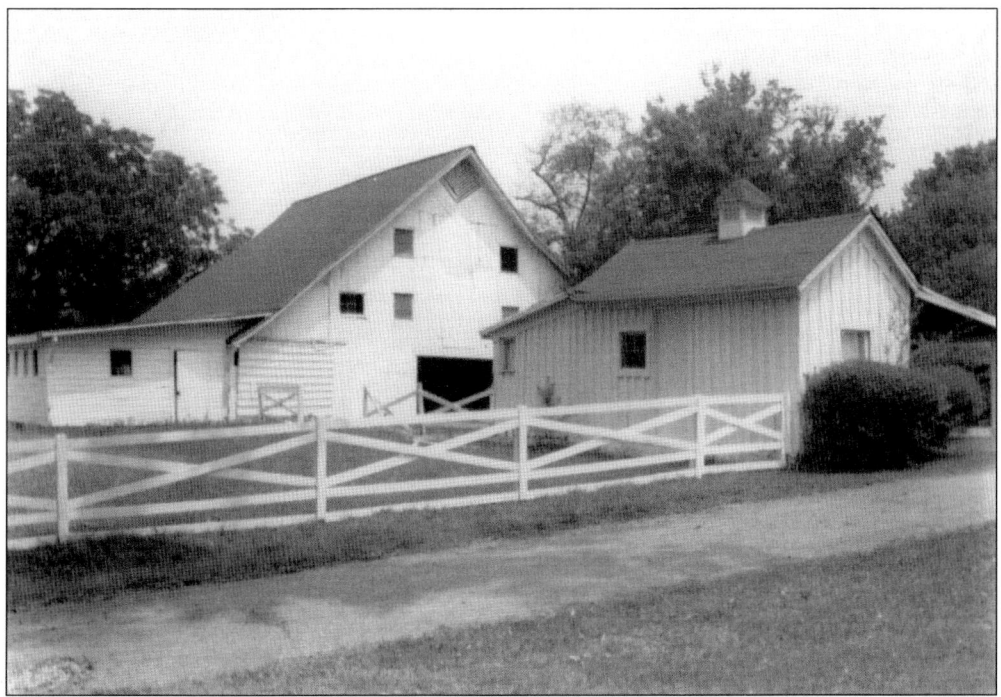

Located in the Concord Covered Bridge Historic District near the Gann House is a barn, attached garage, and storage building composed of vertical timbers. A portion of this former working farm was sold for the construction of the upscale subdivision Mill Grove, a community that had a post office as early as 1837.

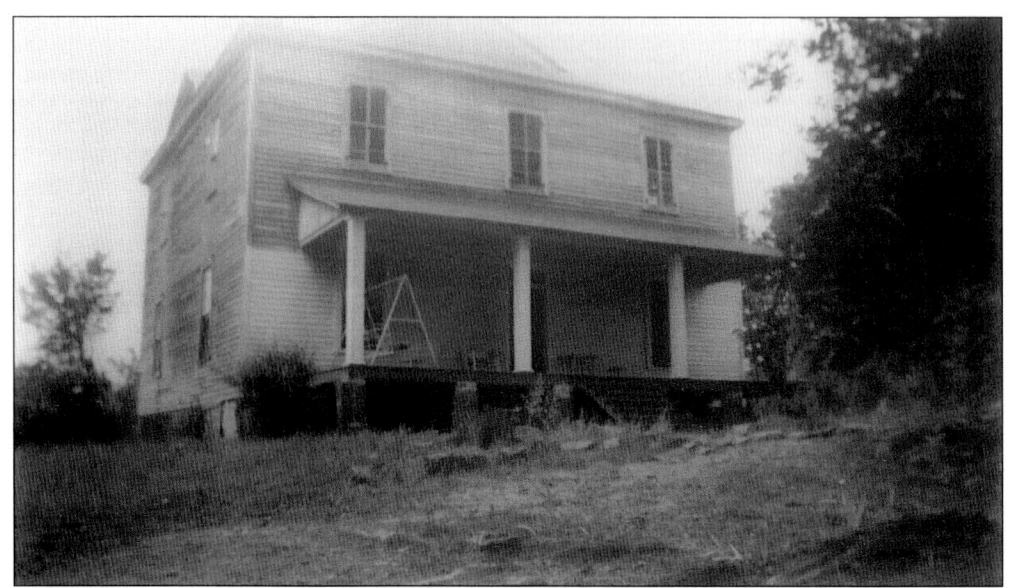

This 1938 photograph shows the antebellum home, built around 1856, of Martin Luker Ruff Sr. Now on Cobb County's historic registry, the property contains the main house, barn, and carriage house, all still intact. The home changed ownership several times, but purchases remained within the Ruff family until 1943. It is currently occupied by Phillip Ivester, Smyrna Historical Society member, and his family. (Courtesy Carolyn Ivey.)

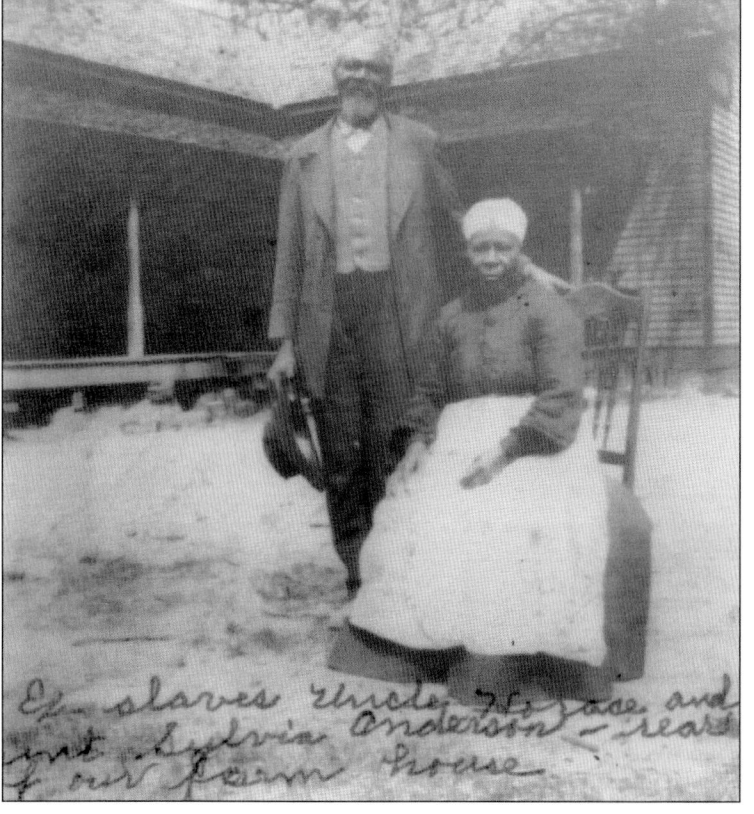

Known as "Uncle Horace" and "Aunt Sylvia," the Andersons were former slaves of Martin Luker Ruff Sr. The 1860 census shows that Ruff owned nine slaves, five female and four male. The Andersons continued to work on the Ruff farm after "The War." They are buried in the Mount Zion Church cemetery, Smyrna's only African American cemetery, located on Hawthorne Avenue. Horace Anderson's grave indicates that he died on September 11, 1917. (Courtesy Parker Lowry.)

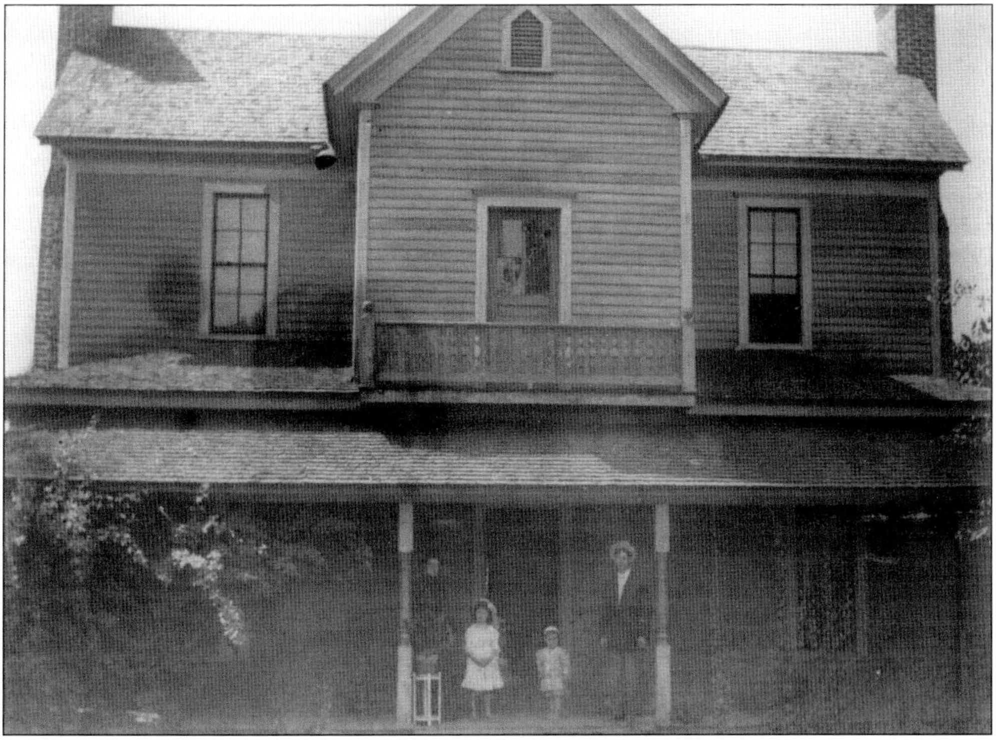

This house, listed in the National Register of Historic Places and Cobb County's historic registry, was the residence of Henry Clay Ruff, son of Martin Luker Ruff Sr. and Smyrna's first miller, until his death in 1907. In 2009, a list of slaves owned by the Ruffs was found attached to a shelf in a closet. Listed were washerwoman Matilda, 40; farmhand Calvine, 17; Yeuda, 11; and Rhoda, 7. This home was built around the 1850s. (Courtesy Dr. Robert and Pat Burns Roche.)

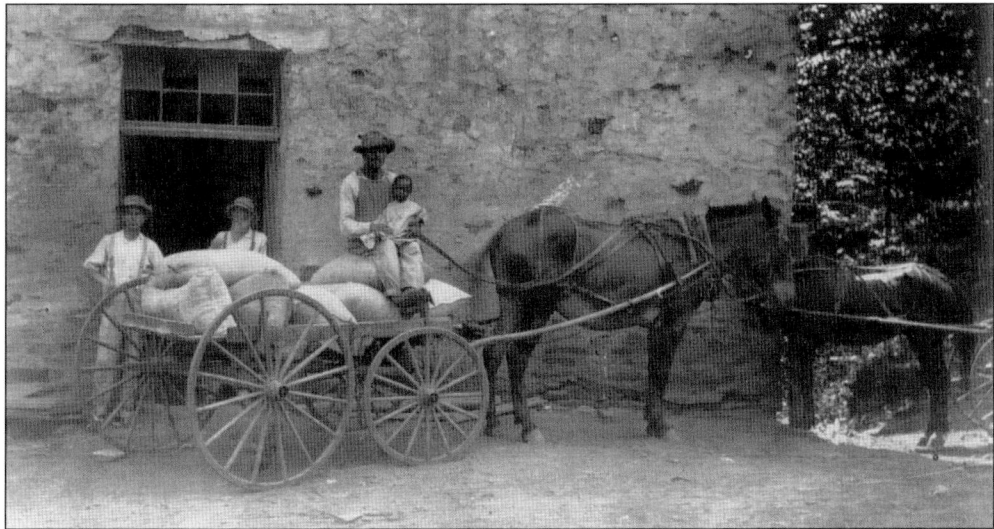

Currently owned by Dr. Robert and Pat Roche, the Daniell/Ruff Grist Mill is located just south of the covered bridge. It was used for grinding corn and making flour. It stayed in operation until the 1920s. Although the date of construction is unclear, an 1847 map shows a settlement in the area with a post office called Mill Grove. (Courtesy Dr. and Mrs. Roche.)

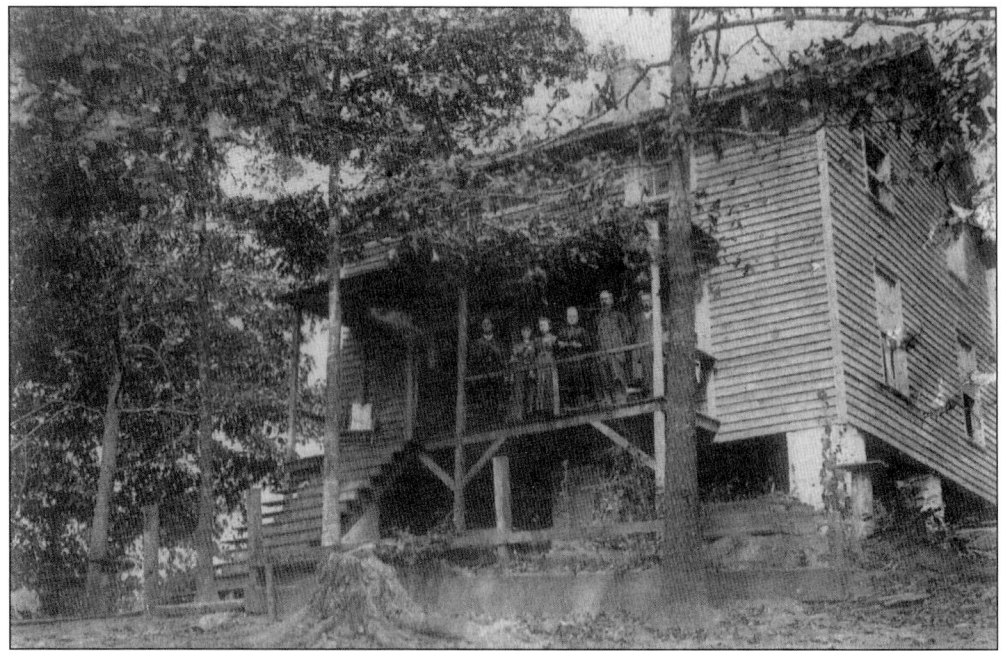

The Woolen Mill superintendent's home, built around 1860, was part of a small village constructed to house the mill's employees. In 1879, machinist James Earnshaw was superintendent and his wife, Lucy, worked in the mill. Their daughter, Mary Ella, married John Wesley Ruff, a carpenter at the mill. In 1899, Elliott Earnshaw moved from Atlanta to live with John Wesley Ruff. (Courtesy Parker Lowry.)

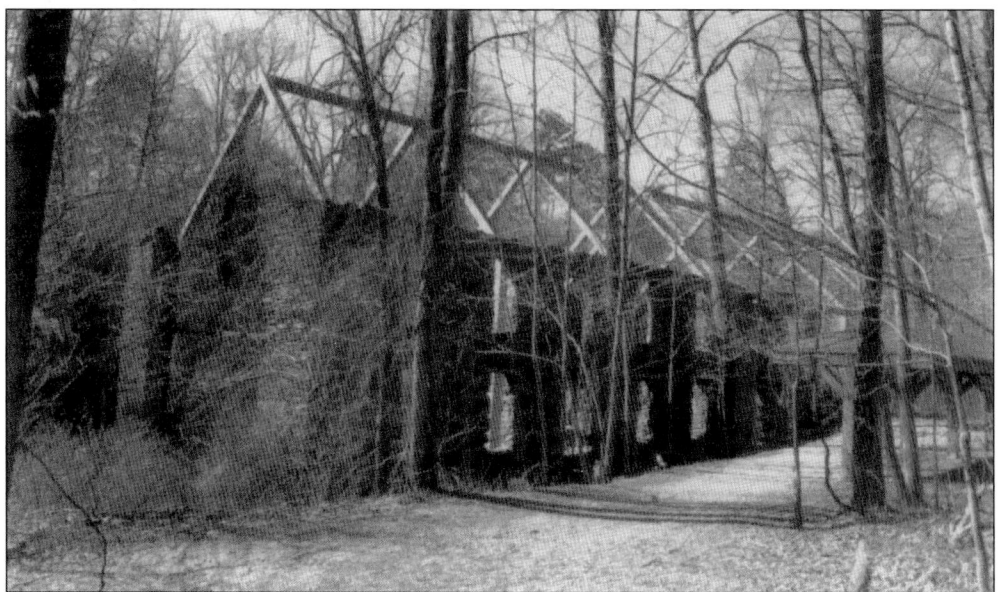

Burned by Sherman's troops on July 3, 1864, the Concord Woolen Mill was one of the first industrial employers in Cobb County when it opened in 1847. During the Civil War, it manufactured Confederate uniforms. Again destroyed by fire in 1889, it was rebuilt and won many prizes for its fine products. Competition from other mills put it out of business in 1910. It is now part of Cobb's Heritage Park.

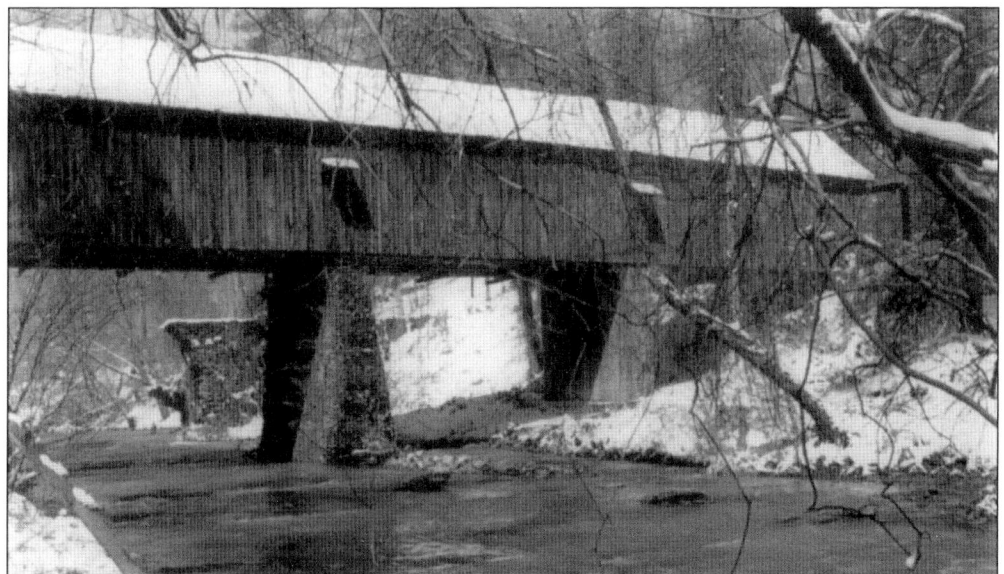

The Concord Covered Bridge, first constructed as a flatbed bridge, was destroyed in the Battle of Ruff's Mill. The cover and a new middle support were added when it was rebuilt. Seen in the background are the broken remains of a dam that backed up the waters of Nickajack Creek, creating a recreational lake for Smyrna residents. (Courtesy Smyrna History Museum.)

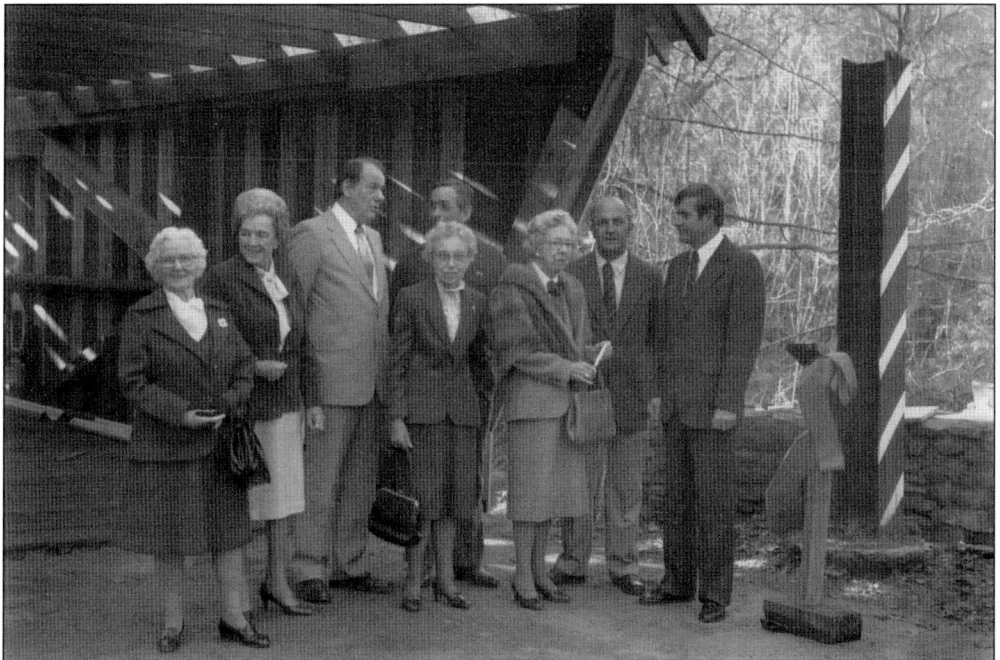

A ribbon-cutting ceremony was held on December 17, 1983, for the reopening of Concord Bridge after repairs. Gathered here are, from left to right, Ethel Turner; Mrs. Reese Landers, granddaughter of Robert Daniell; Harvey Paschal, Cobb County commissioner; Frank Johnson, Georgia state representative and former Smyrna mayor; Blanch Rice Brawner and Judith Rice Lowry, sister and great granddaughters of Henry Clay Ruff; Butch Thompson, Cobb commissioner; and congressman George "Buddy" Darden. (Courtesy Col. James G. Bogle.)

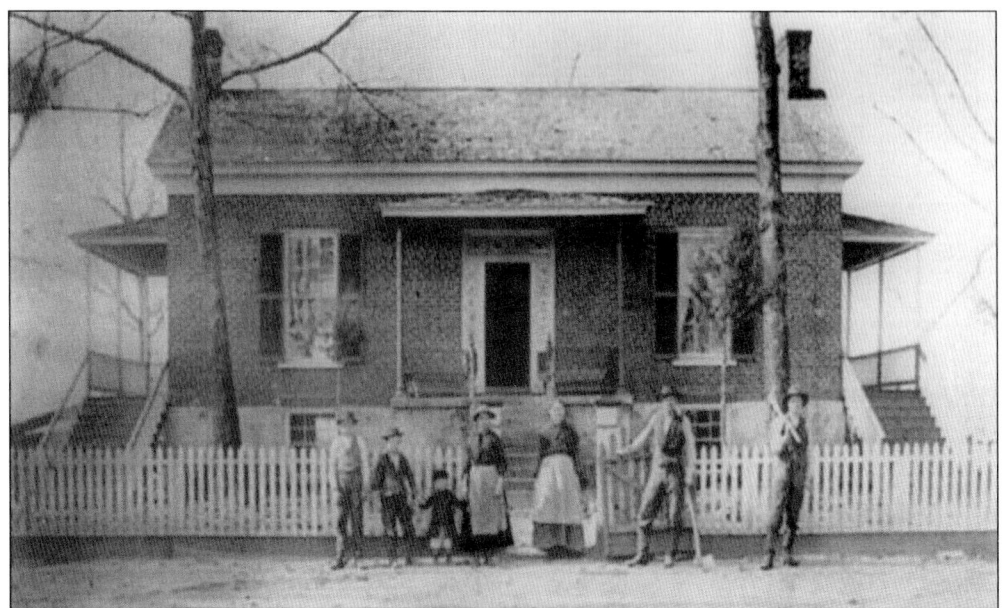

This 1885 photograph shows the home of Robert Daniell. It was constructed around 1872. Shown here are, from left to right, Ed Dewes, Jessie Daniell, Jennie Daniell, Mary Daniell, Fannie Daniell, Putman Daniell, and Pliny Frank. Robert Daniell and Martin Luker Ruff Sr. founded the industrial community along Nickajack Creek in the 1840s.

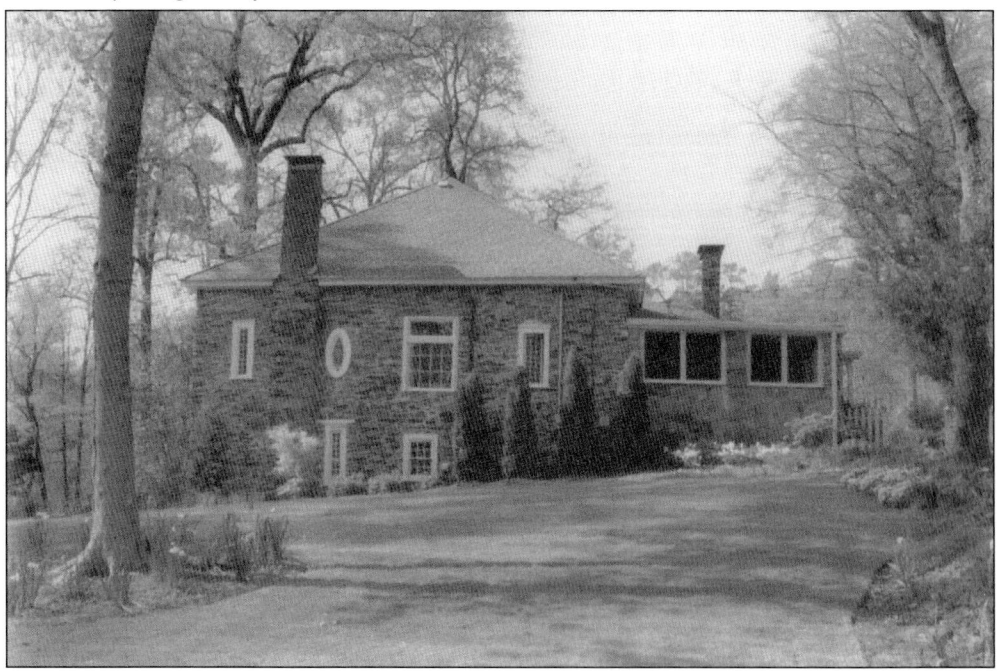

The John W. Rice summer cottage, also known as the "Rock House," was constructed around 1899 of fieldstone held in place by thick mortar joints. It is situated above Nickajack Creek, overlooking the ruins of the dam that once served the Ruff-Daniell industrial site. Originally, no two windows in the structure were alike. It is listed in the National Register of Historic Places and the Cobb County historic registry. (Courtesy Dan Hopwood.)

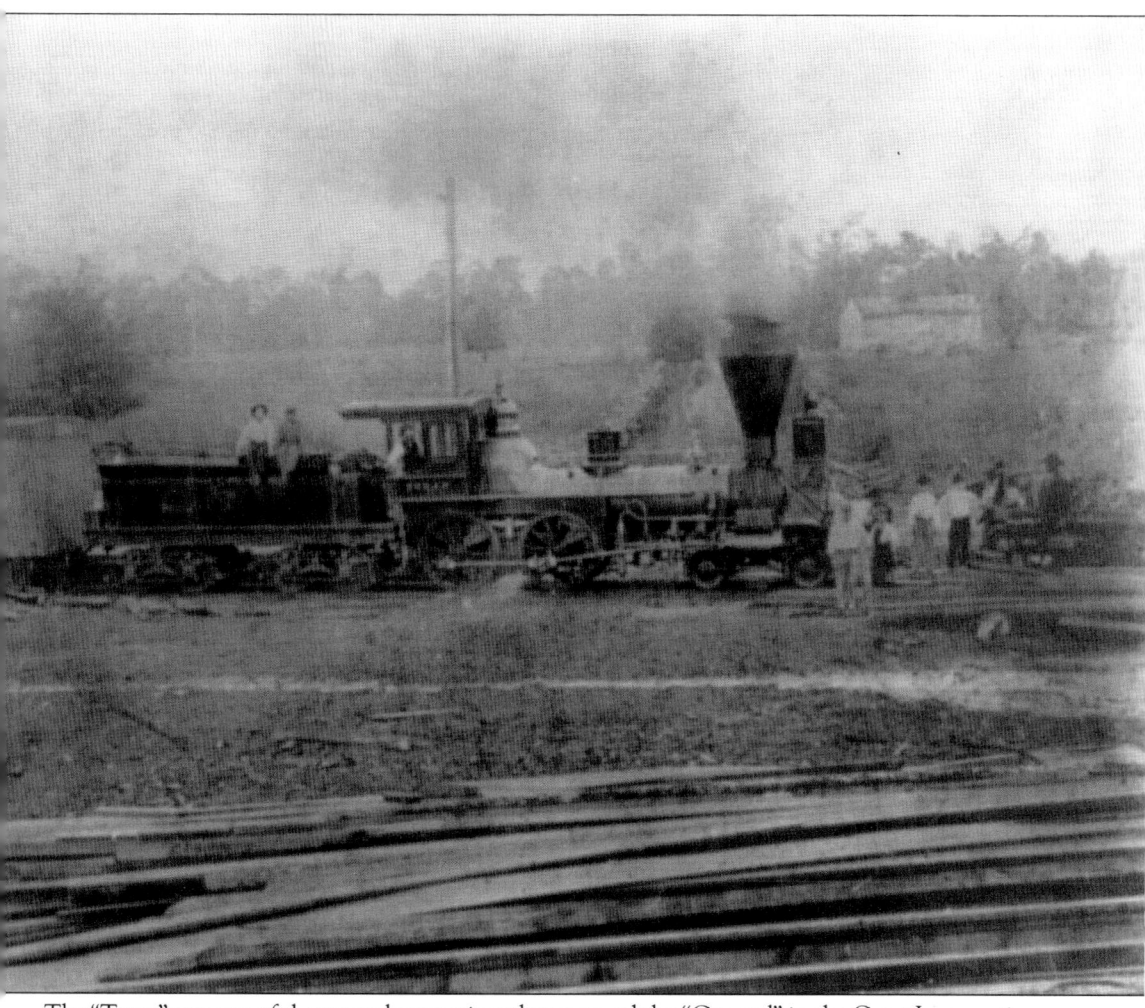

The "Texas" was one of the steam locomotives that pursued the "General" in the Great Locomotive Chase, a true story made into a Disney movie. The Western & Atlantic Railroad, which still runs through Smyrna, became famous on April 12, 1862, when James Andrews, a civilian Union scout, commandeered the Confederate steam locomotive General. W.A. Fuller, a resident of Smyrna at the time, was engineer of the General. He had stopped at Big Shanty (now Kennesaw, Georgia) to let the passengers enjoy lunch at the Lacy Hotel. While they were eating, Andrews's raiders stole the General and traveled north toward Chattanooga, destroying tracks, water towers, and stations behind them to cut off the Confederate supply lines. There was no telegraph station at Big Shanty to warn other stations about the theft of the train. Fuller and his men first chased them on foot, then with handcars, and finally with other steam locomotives, like the Texas. Andrews and his men encountered a number of problems, and, eventually, about 18 miles from Chattanooga, they ran out of fuel. The raiders scattered throughout the countryside, but within two weeks, all of them were captured. Some were sent to prison, and others were exchanged for Confederate prisoners. James Andrews was found guilty, sent to Atlanta, and hanged on June 7. In addition, seven others were convicted as spies in Knoxville, sent to Atlanta, and hanged. They were buried in unmarked graves in Atlanta, but were later reburied in the National Cemetery in Chattanooga.

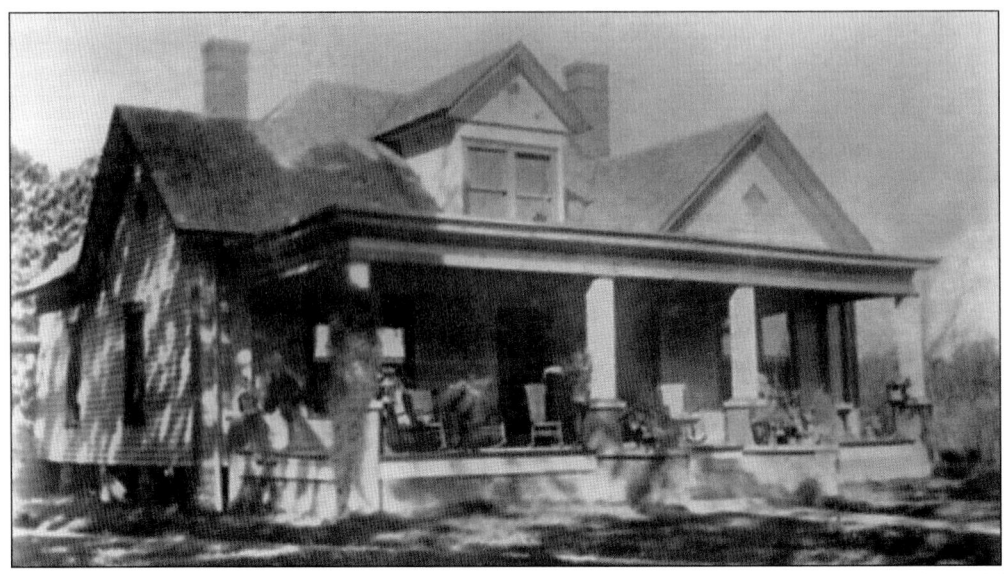

Shown here is the home of Rufus Alexander Eaton Jr. and Myrtice Parnell Eaton, parents of Gerald Eaton. It is similar to the home of Alexander Eaton Sr., which was used during the Civil War as headquarters of Hood's Corps, commanded by Confederate general John Bell Hood. From July 3 to 5, 1864, Hood directed his troops in the Battle of Ruff's Mill from this house.

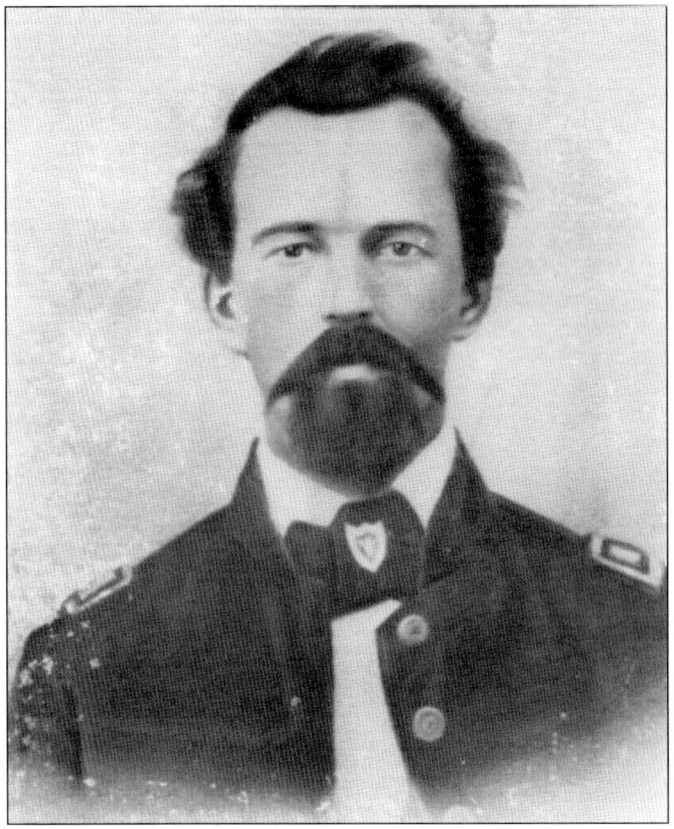

Solon Zachariah Ruff was born in 1837, the son of Martin Luker Ruff Sr. and Susan Volumnia Varner. Susan died in childbirth with son Matthew Varner Ruff on September 15, 1858. A math professor and drill instructor at the Georgia Military Institute, Solon was elected lieutenant colonel in the Fourth Brigade, First Division Georgia Volunteers in 1861. He was killed in action on November 29, 1862, while leading an attack on Fort Sanders in Knoxville, Tennessee.

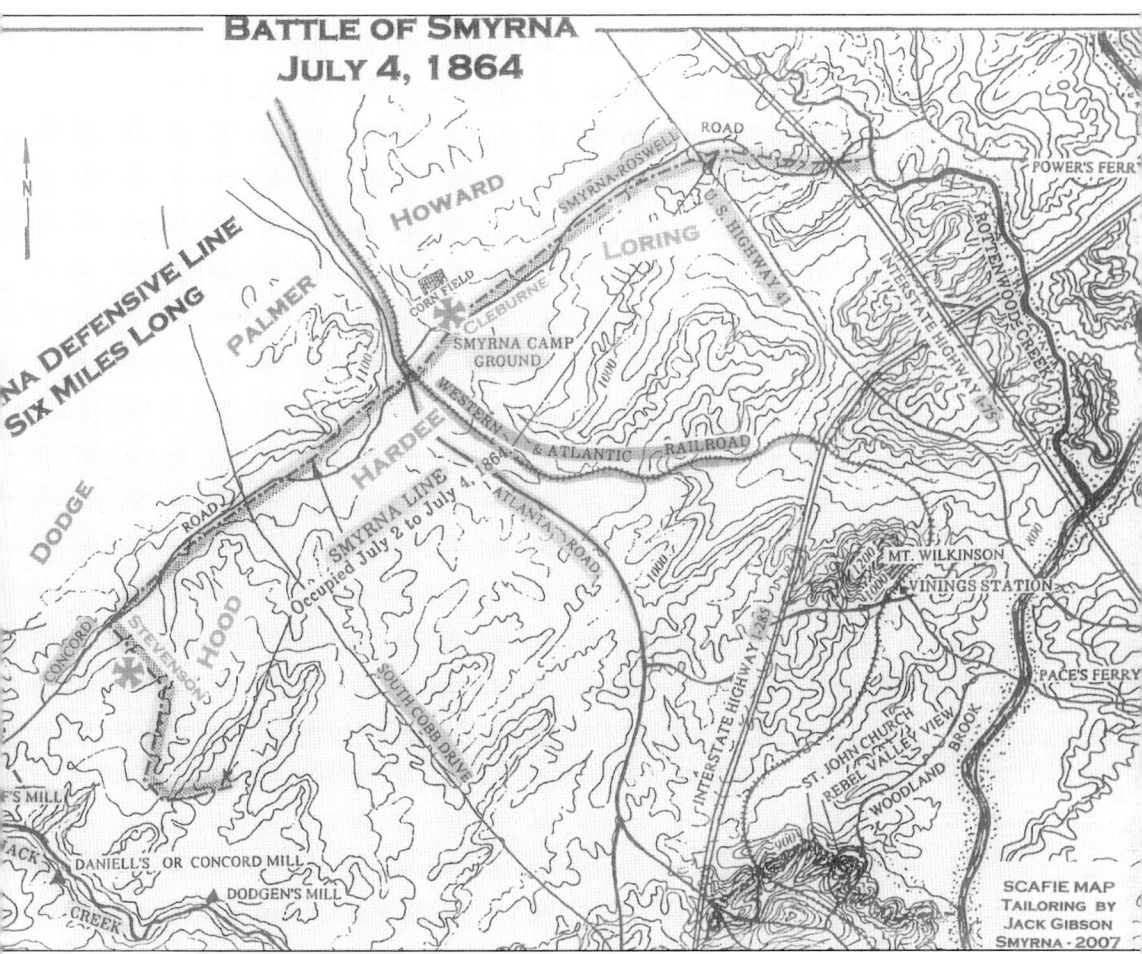

In July 1864, two Civil War battles occurred in Smyrna: the Battle of Smyrna Camp Ground, on July 3, and the Battle of Ruff's Mill, on July 4. In the days following, Sherman's troops encountered approximately seven miles of shoupades, a unique, arrowhead-shaped infantry fort built along the Chattahoochee. Rather than fight through them, Sherman's troops made their way around them, and the Battle of Atlanta then began. (Courtesy Historic Cobb County.)

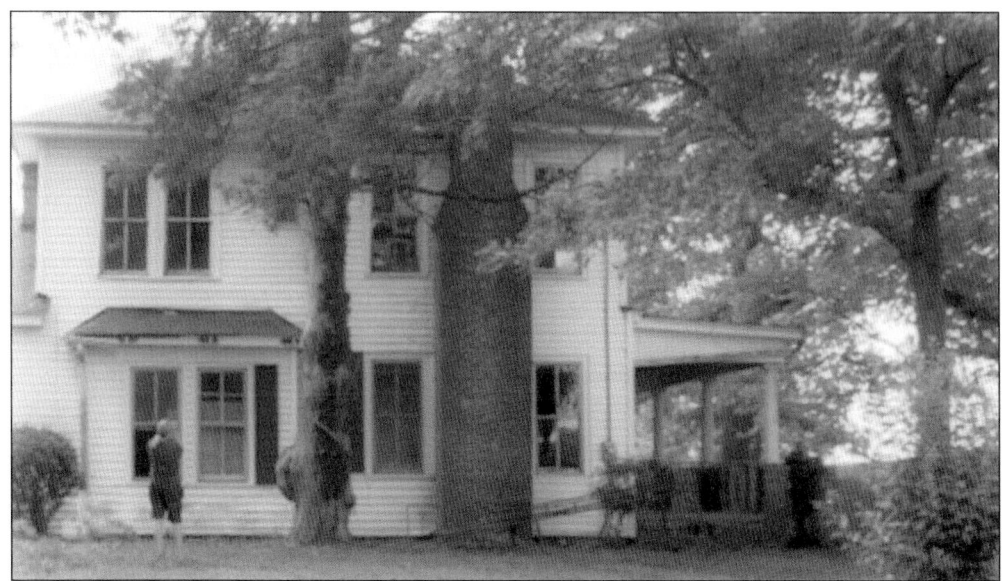

This house on Dixie Avenue is believed to be the place referred to by General Sherman in his memoirs of his visit to Smyrna. The entry reads, "I came very near being shot myself while reconnoitering in the second story of a house on our picket-line, which was struck several times by cannon-shot and perfectly riddled with musket balls." Sherman's bullet-ridden hat is on display in the Smithsonian. (Courtesy Kara Hunter-Oden.)

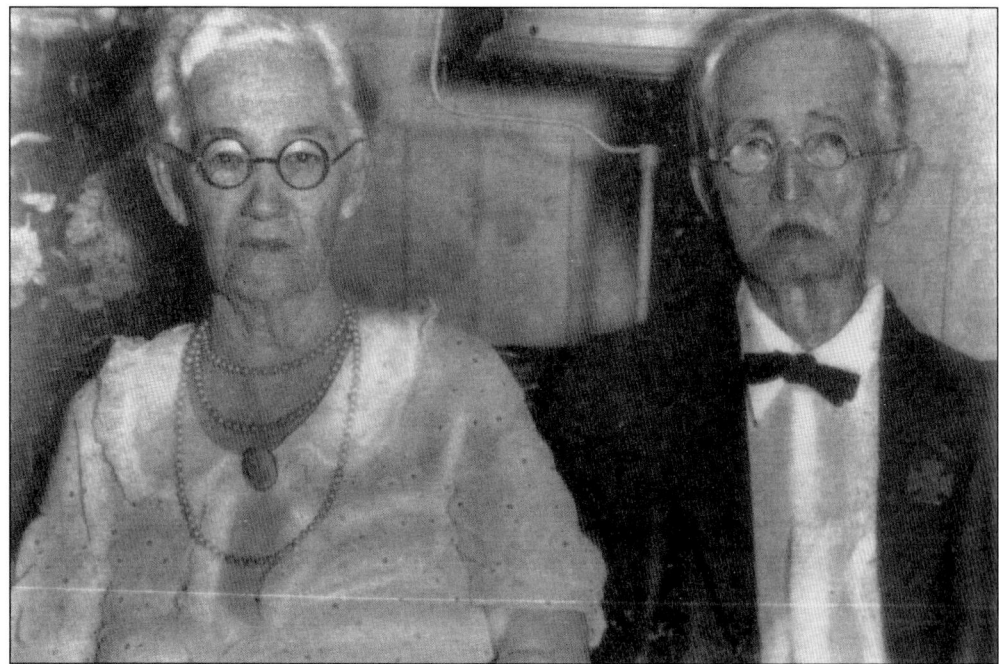

John Gideon "J. Gid" Morris and his wife, Mary, were early Smyrna pioneers. In 1863, at 16, John served with the Confederate army in Wheeler's Cavalry. Gideon was associated with the charter of the Bank of Smyrna (1910) and later Belmont Farms. He was Smyrna's mayor from 1925 to 1927. His family home, located on Atlanta Road, is eligible for inclusion in the National Register of Historic Places. (Courtesy Larry Blair.)

Three
Downtown Smyrna

When Smyrna was chartered in August 1872, the city limits were one mile in every direction from the Smyrna Boys Academy. Then, in 1897, the city fathers reduced the city limits to one-half mile in every direction from the same building, which was by this time the Masonic hall of the Nelms Lodge. The reason for the change in the city-limits extent is not known, as all city records were lost in a city hall fire in the early 1920s. It might have been because the city did not have the resources to provide services to the residents who purchased large tracts of land on the outer edges of the city in the mid- and late 1890s. The population was only about 400 at the time, and the community still had an agricultural economy, with the exception of the woolen mill complex at Concord. The Atlanta-Marietta Road (US Highway 41, Dixie Highway) was not paved until around 1911. Prior to 1905, the available modes of transportation were the W&A Railroad and horse-drawn buggies and wagons. There was also a car or two in the county.

The streetcar line (Atlanta Northern Railway, in operation 1905–1947) improved transportation, but it also encouraged more wealthy Atlanta residents to purchase more land in the area. The economy changed somewhat when the Bell Bomber Plant was constructed nearby and opened in 1943 to build B-29s for the Air Corps during World War II. It closed immediately after the war ended in 1945. By the end of the decade, the population was still about 2,000. Real growth did not come to Smyrna until the mid-1950s, when the Lockheed Corporation reopened the old Bell Plant. In addition, Smyrna developers constructed and opened the South's largest shopping center, Belmont Hills, in November 1954, and the associated Belmont Hills subdivision, originally named Lockheed Heights. When the census was taken in 1960, Smyrna's population had increased to 10,157, and it has not stopped growing yet.

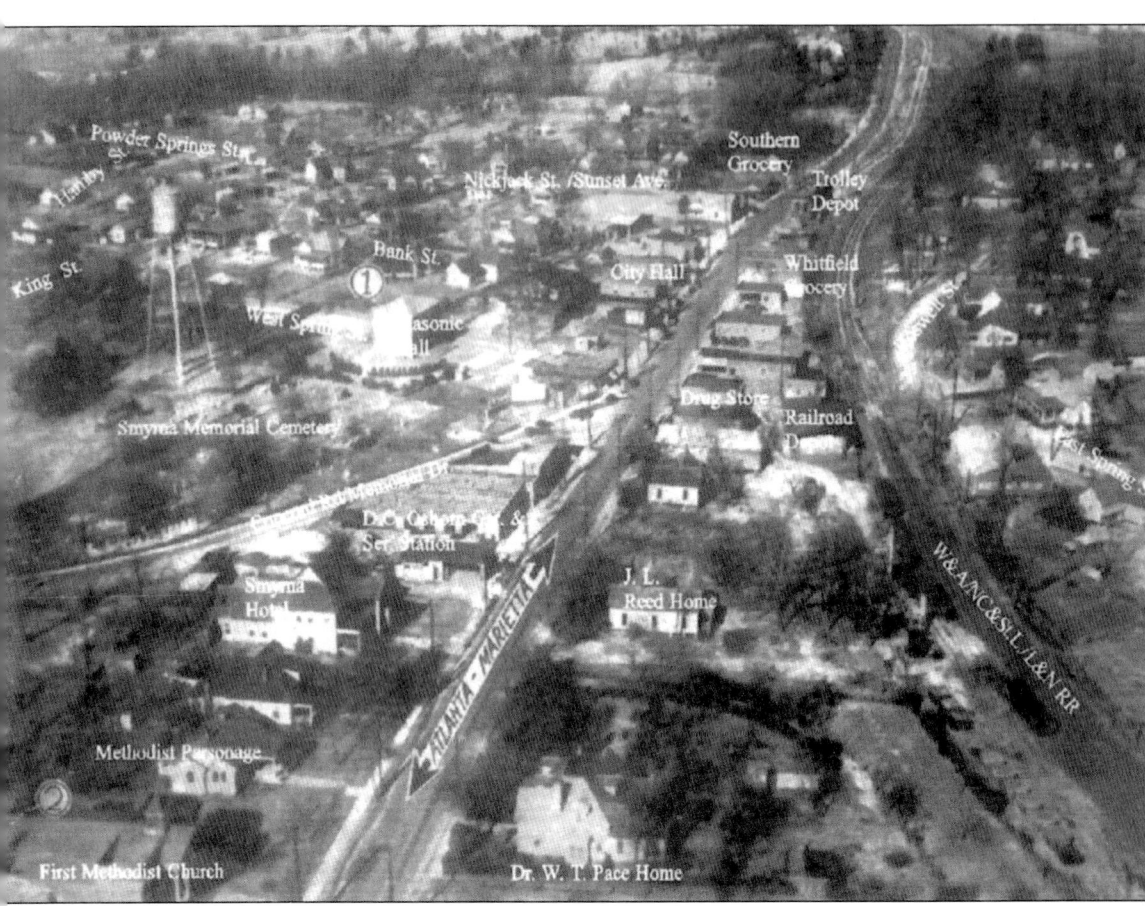

Smyrna in 1936 was typical of many of the smaller towns in Georgia. With less than 1,500 people at the time, the downtown area had a mixture of residences and businesses. The building marked "1" at left center was originally the Boy's Academy and the point from which the first city limits were measured: one mile in every direction. The railroad, at right, was constructed in 1836–1842 and contributed to the permanent location of the city. The Atlanta-Marietta Highway at center was also US Highway 41, better known throughout the country as the Dixie Highway. Practically all of the structures on the west side of the railroad were demolished in the Smyrna Downtown Redevelopment Program that started in the late 1980s. The historic Smyrna Memorial Cemetery and a portion of the 1883 Methodist church building are all that exist today. (Courtesy Rex Pruitt.)

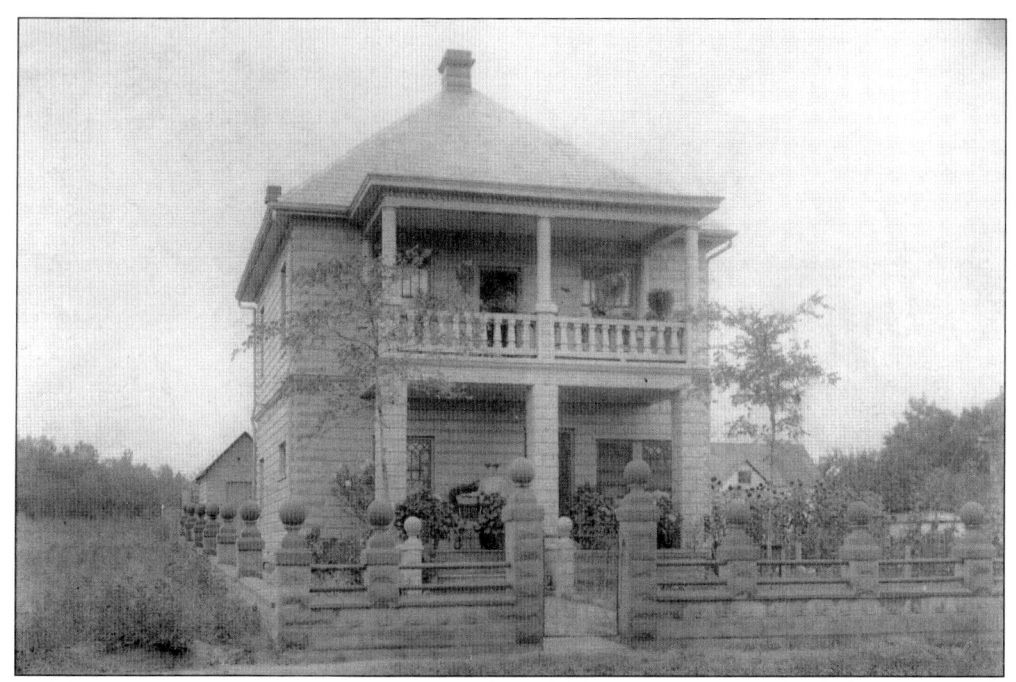

Henry Gautschy came to Smyrna from Germany in the early 1900s to operate a liquor distillery. His home, one of the first in Smyrna with electricity and indoor plumbing, was patterned after a Rhine River manor. The stone look is actually the result of handmade concrete blocks made from molds purchased at Sears-Roebuck. It still stands on Atlanta Road, next to CVS pharmacy. The building has housed a beauty shop, antique store, collectible model automobile store, and clothing boutique, the Honey Bee. (Courtesy Milton Hill.)

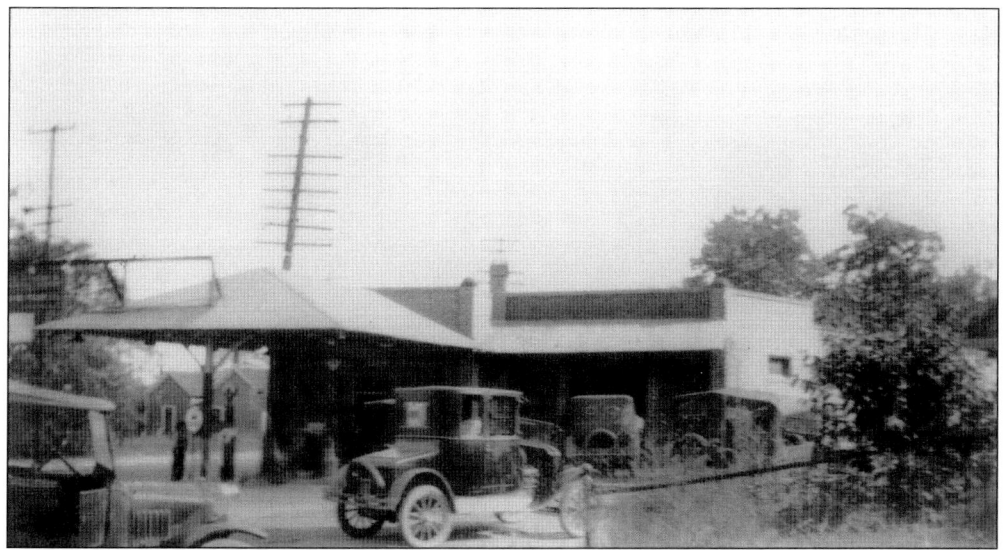

In 1925, the Smyrna Garage, operated by D.C. Osborne, was located at the intersection of Atlanta and Concord Roads. This site was formerly the home of the Anchor Oil service station and several banks. Osborne served as a Smyrna city councilman from 1934 to 1937.

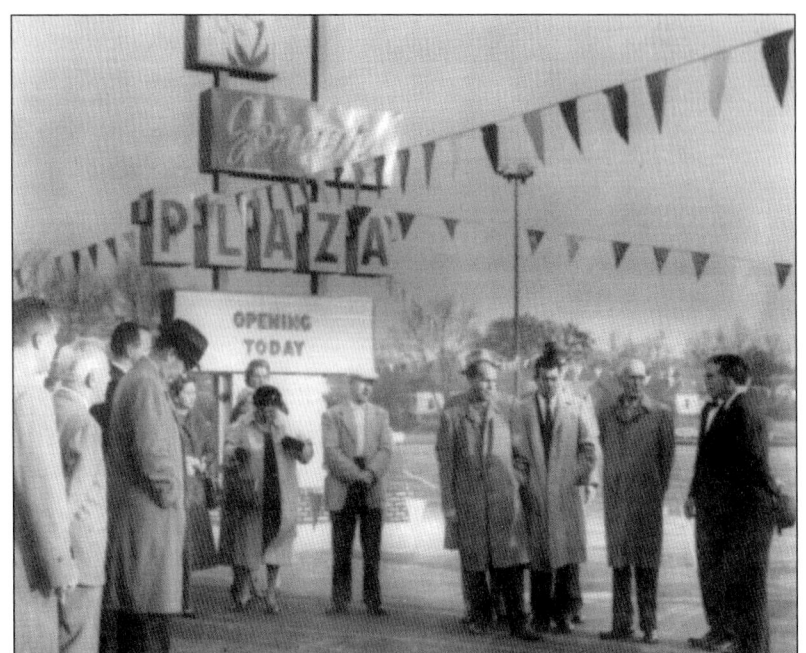

In December 1959, J.D. Daniel's Food Town was the first store to open in the Jonquil Plaza Shopping Center, located on Atlanta Road. Food Town operated from 1959 to 2007, when Jonquil Plaza was demolished to make way for Jonquil Village.

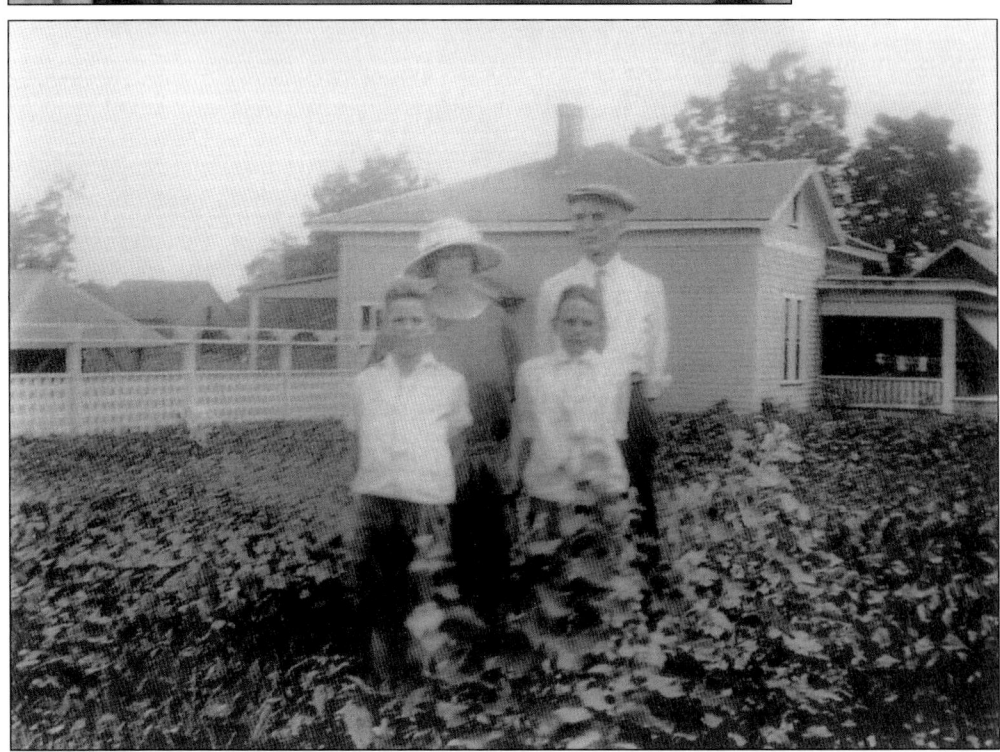

In 1908, Henry Konigsmark Sr. moved to Smyrna and married Alma Reed. The couple is seen here with their twin boys, Henry Jr. (left) and Reed. Henry Sr. served as secretary of Belmont Farms. Alma served as Smyrna's postmistress from 1902 to 1908. The Konigsmark Coal Company was located on the south end of this property, adjoining the residential property of Dr. W.T. Pace. The Konigsmark and Pace Properties were sold to the developers of Jonquil Plaza. (Courtesy Ann Konigsmark Johnson.)

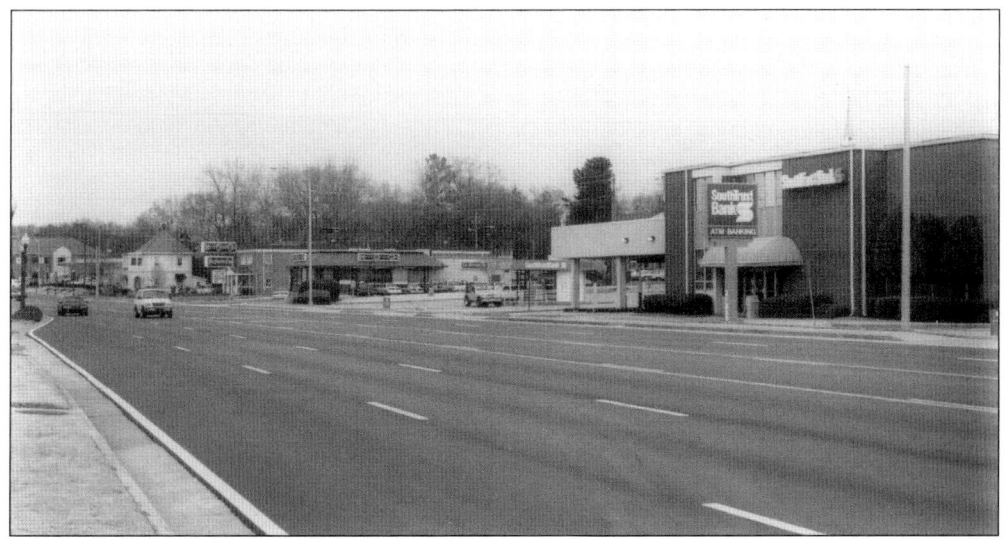

Located on the southwest corner of Church and Atlanta Streets, Ken's Corner Grill occupies the land that was the home of D.J. and Carol Reed Ray in the 1940s. The Gautschy house is seen on the far left, just past Ken's Corner Grill. The Nash family lived just north of the Gautschy house. The location of the drive-up windows of the SouthTrust Bank was the former site of Smyrna First Methodist Church. (Courtesy Harold Smith.)

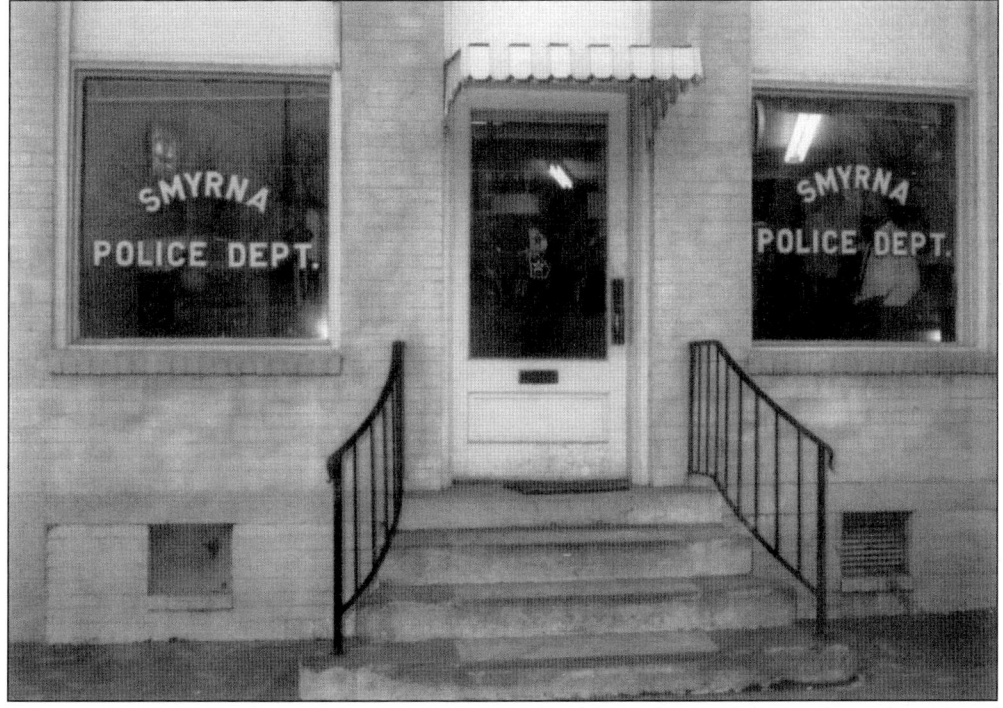

In 1958, the Smyrna Police Department took over the old Smyrna Bank located at Atlanta Road and Bank Street. The bank's former vault was used for records and evidence storage. The attic was used as the officers' locker room. In 1970, the structure was demolished. The cornerstone from the building can now be found in the rock wall that surrounds a burial plot in Smyrna Memorial. (Courtesy Harold Smith.)

41

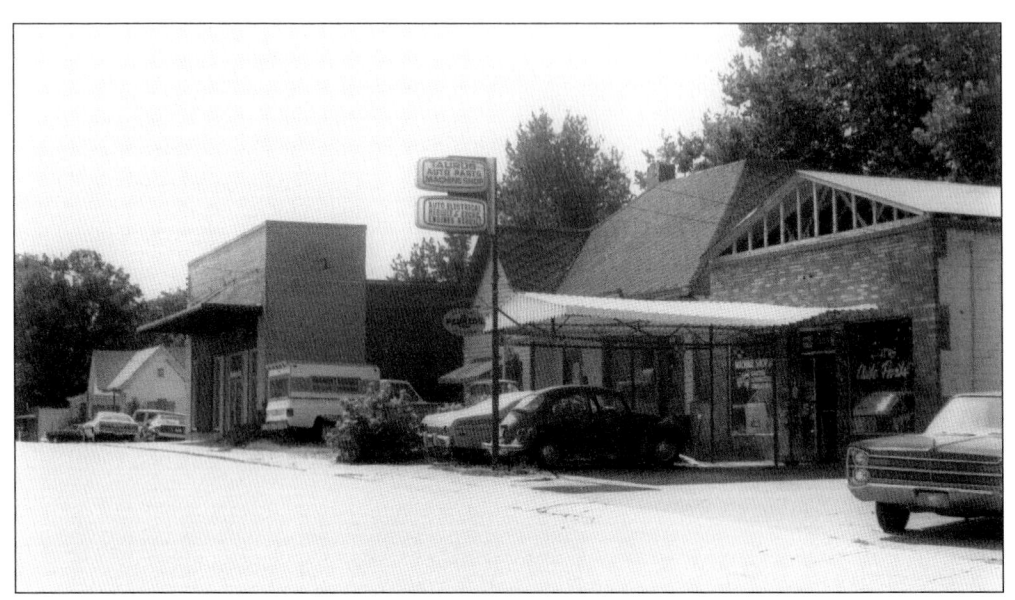

Colonial Store Supermarket (left of center) opened in 1951, replacing the Rogers store on Atlanta Road. It was later owned by Southern Acceptance Company before being sold to the city of Smyrna for its Parks and Recreation Department. It was later used as the judicial building. The unfinished building on the right, constructed to house Howard's Hardware, later housed the printing department for the *Smyrna Herald* newspaper.

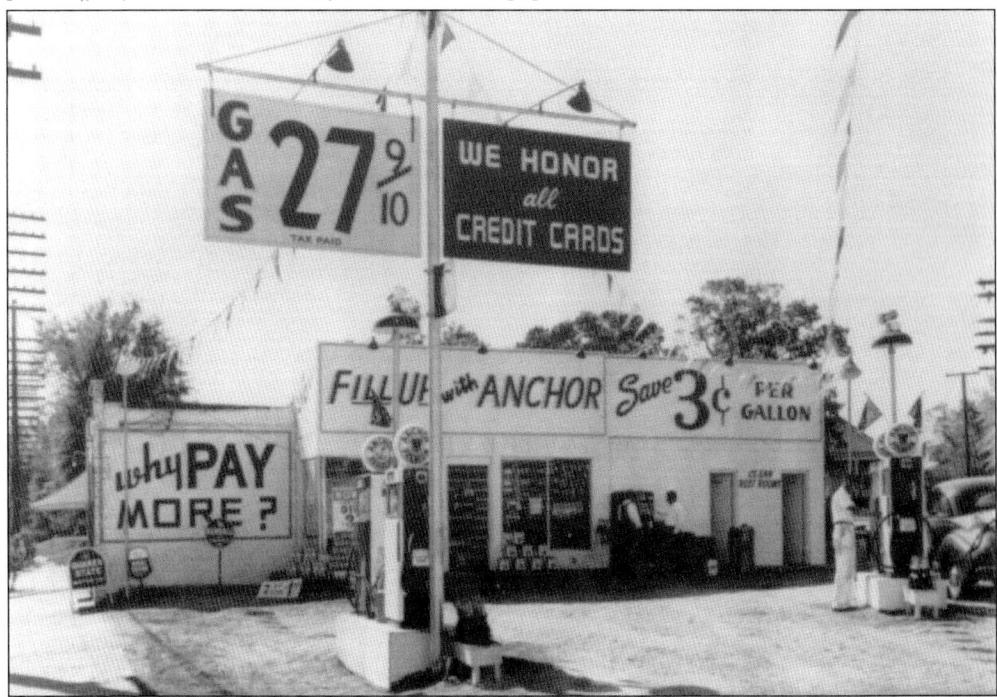

Owned by Joe Wine, the Anchor Oil station was located in the triangle created by Atlanta Street and Memorial Drive. This was a prime location for several garages and service stations over the years. Fill-ups at the station often included premiums such as Depression glass dinnerware pieces. "Gas wars" kept prices low. Wine owned stations in Fair Oaks, Oakdale, and at another Smyrna location.

J.D. Daniel's Red Dot Store was located on the corner of Atlanta Road and East Spring Street. The building had previously housed a number of other grocery stores. In 1959, Daniel relocated to the new Jonquil Plaza Shopping Center, opening his store as Food Town. The Smyrna Railroad depot can be seen at the left.

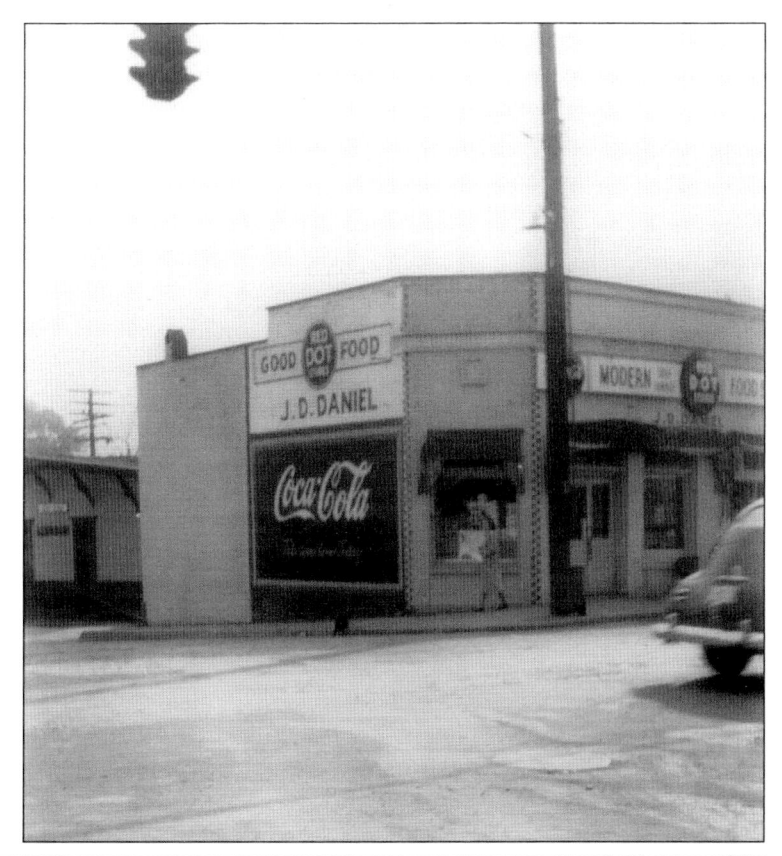

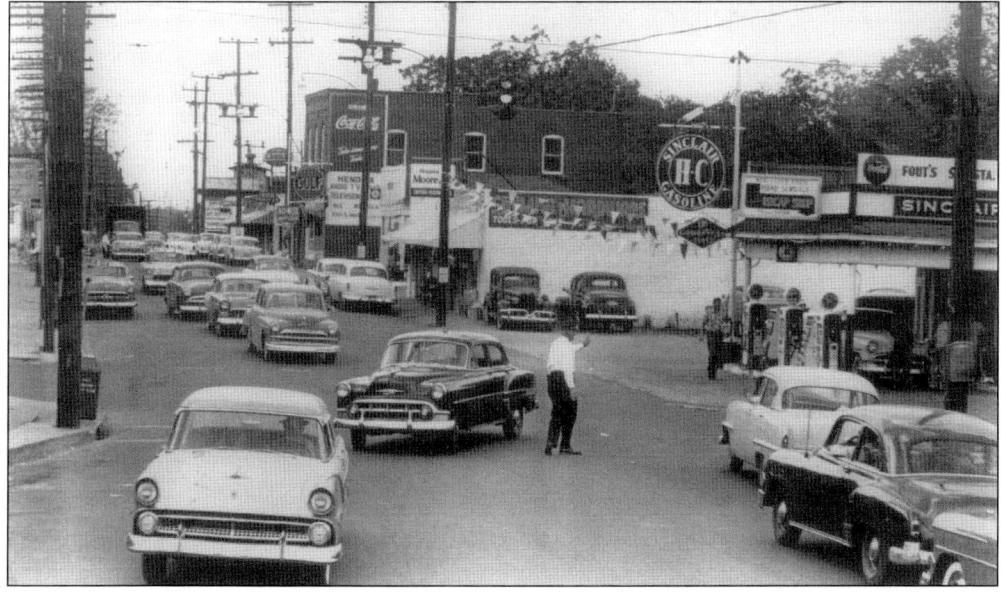

Downtown Smyrna is seen here in 1956, two years after the opening of Belmont Hills Shopping Center. Every building in this photograph was demolished in the downtown redevelopment program of the late 1980s and 1990s. Today, this is the location of the entrance to Market Village, city hall, the library, community center, and other government facilities. (Courtesy Becky Nash Paden.)

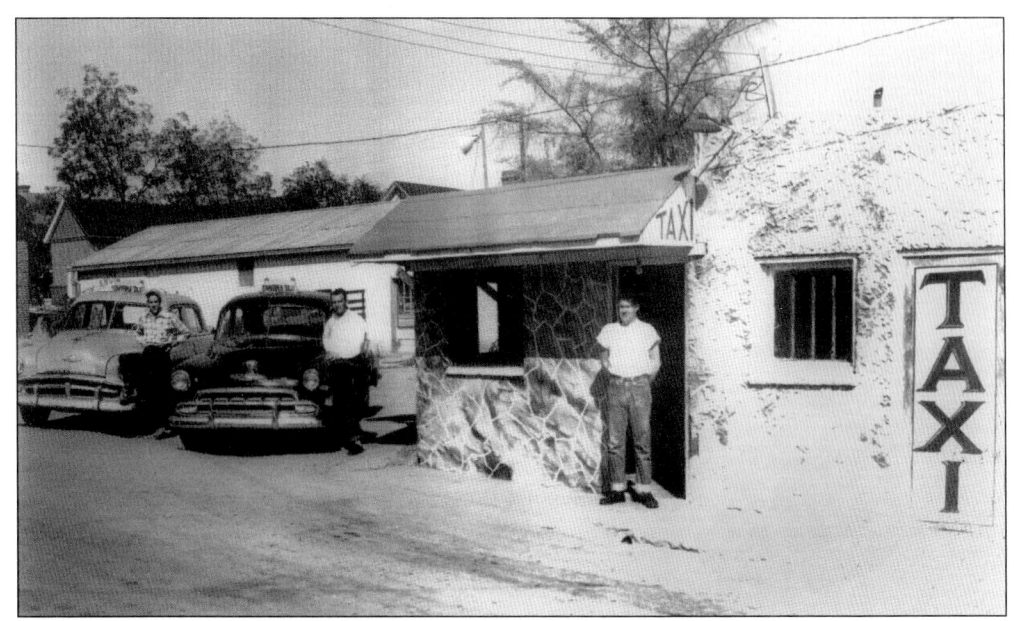

The entrance to Smyrna's Market Village, at Atlanta Road and West Spring Street, has been the location of many businesses, including Brooks Brothers Taxi, Smyrna Taxi, and Hasty Grill. A memorial park was then constructed in honor of Smyrna's railroad stationmaster, John Tatum, who was also Smyrna's mayor from 1941 to 1942. He resigned as mayor due to additional railroad work brought on by World War II.

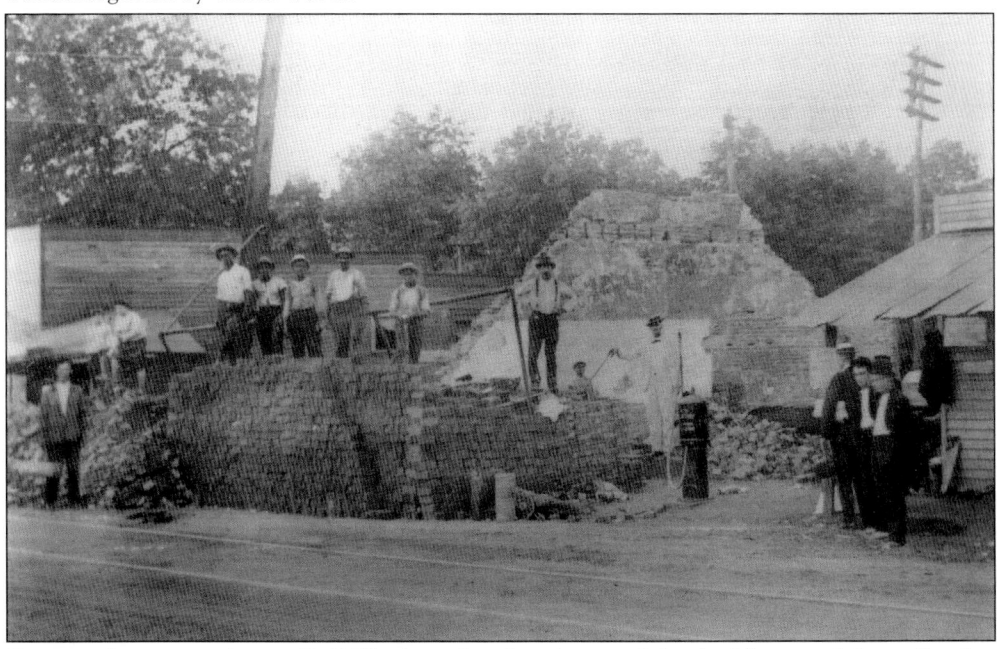

Citizens clean up on August 7, 1915, after a fire that destroyed this building on Atlanta Road at Spring Street. The building's tenants had included Dr. William Pace's office and drugstore, the Presbyterian Church Sunday school, Smyrna's city council room, and P.M. Rice's real estate office. Smyrna's first concrete sidewalk was installed in front of Dr. Pace's store, which he operated until his death in 1932.

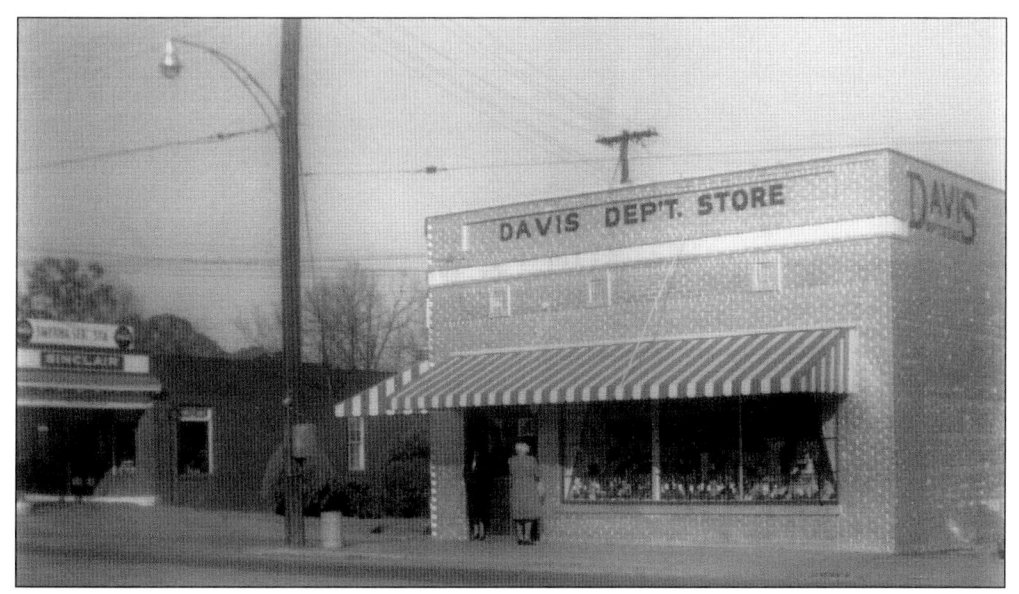

Davis Department Store, which operated from 1951 to 1959, was said to be the region's first "department" store outside downtown Atlanta. Owner Harold Davis was a volunteer fireman and commander of American Legion Post 160. Many businesses had come and gone at this location on the corner of Atlanta Road and Spring Street, including Sur-Way Dry Cleaners and Laundry, operated by A.B. Ware. The cleaners was demolished for the Atlanta Road widening in 1988–1989. (Courtesy Harold Davis.)

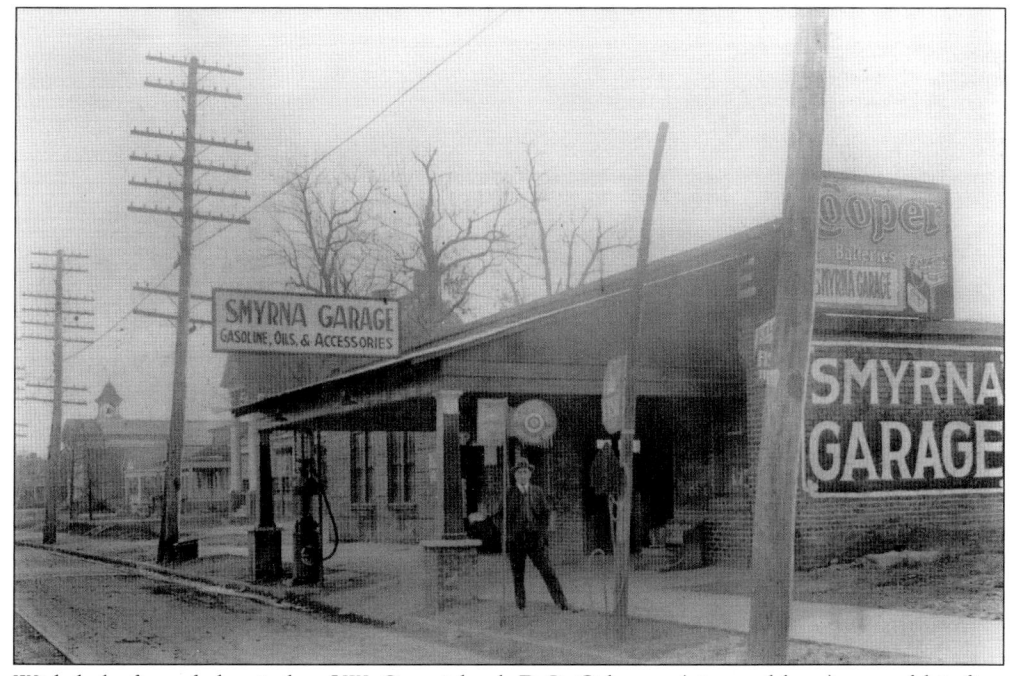

With help from father-in-law J.W. Carmichael, D.C. Osborne (pictured here) started his first service station in Smyrna. It operated from the 1920s to the early 1950s. Osborne was active in many organizations, including First Methodist Church (far left). The Smyrna Boardinghouse/Hotel is directly behind the station. (Courtesy Bill Mortin.)

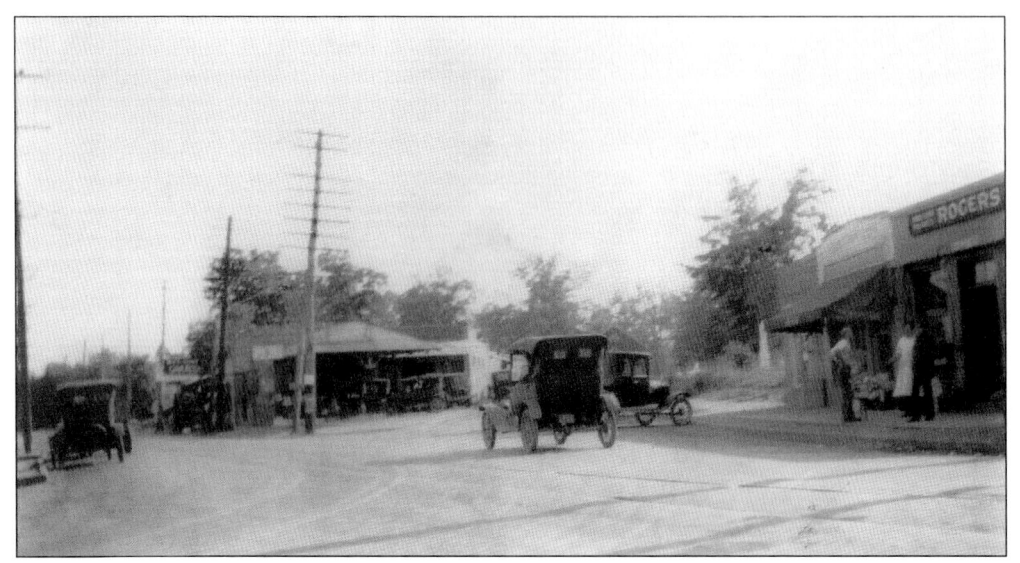

Rogers Store was located on Atlanta Road from around 1898 to 1951. In 1949, Henry Duncan was the manager, "Bill" Scoggins was the assistant manager, and Clarence Newton was the butcher. Harry Lovingood succeeded Duncan as manager later in 1949. Other Smyrna residents who worked at Rogers Store were Wendell Anderson and a Mr. Green, the produce manager.

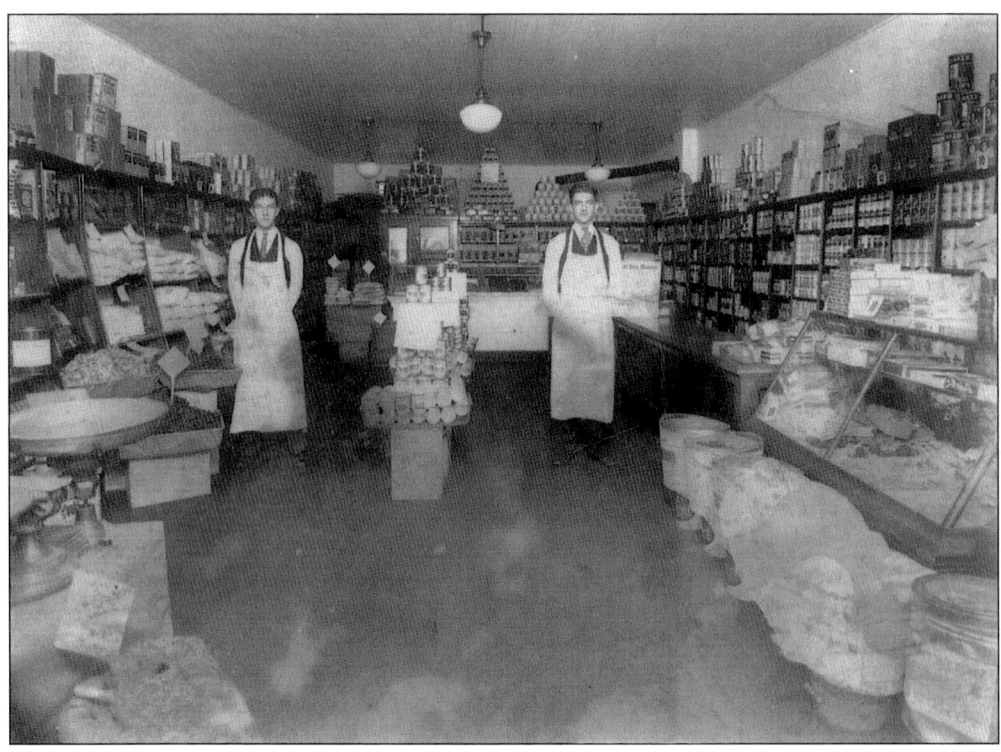

This interior is typical of the numerous grocery stores located in Smyrna in the 1920s, 1930s, and 1940s. Rogers Grocery Store was located on Atlanta Street in downtown Smyrna when this photograph was taken in the 1930s. On the left is Ben Worley, who grew up on Church Street. (Courtesy Jane Walker Wood.)

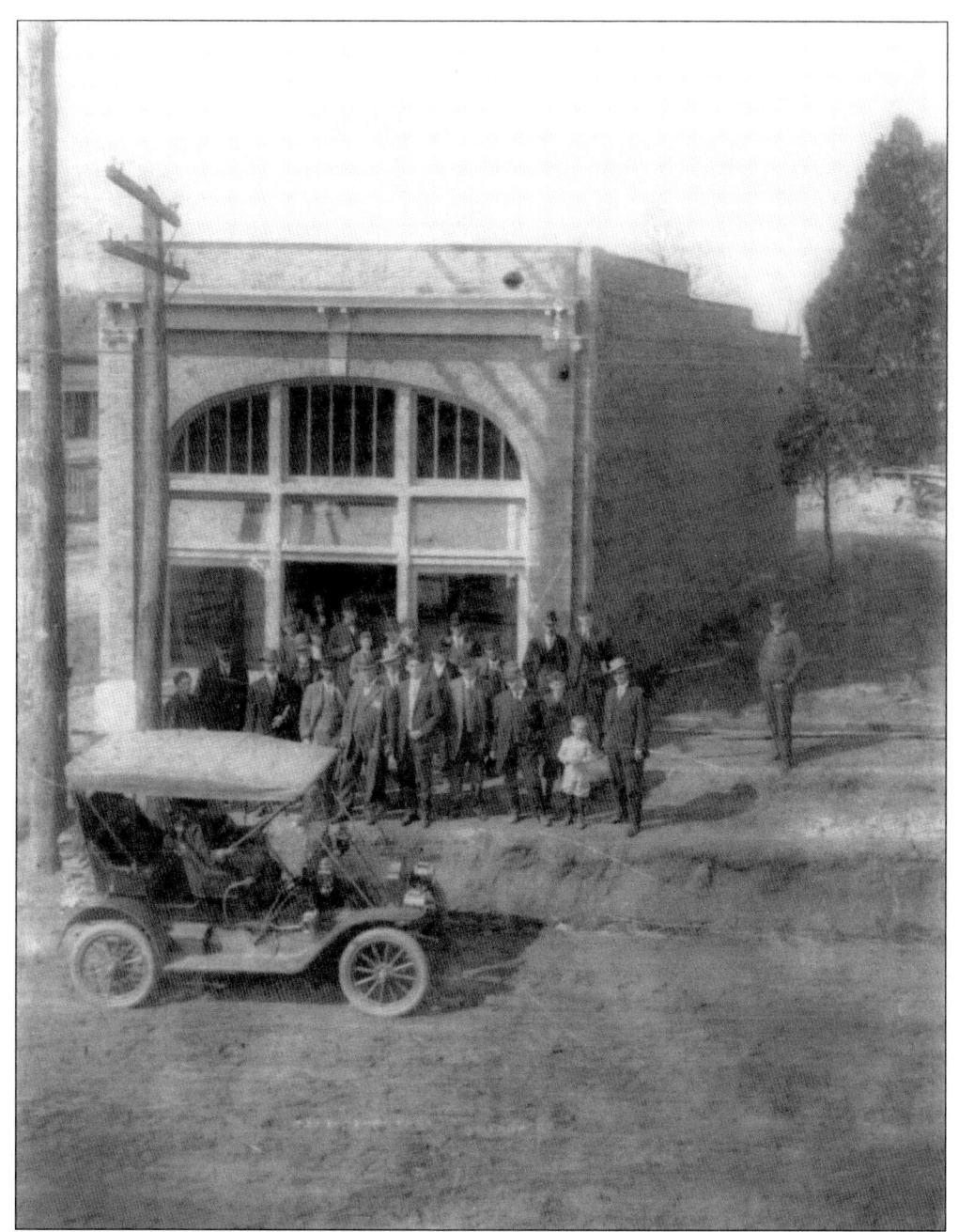

The Bank of Smyrna was officially dedicated on March 10, 1911. Pictured here are, from left to right, (first row) Brant Eidson (boy), Dr. William Tatum Pace, Georgia Knott, Newt Dodgen, W.E. Walker, bank president Parker M. Rice, unidentified, Loring Brown, two unidentified, ? Ireland, Hubert Ireland, and W. Norris Pace. The Ireland boys were sons of Sam J. Ireland, Smyrna's postmaster from 1895 to 1902 and the owner of a grocery store next to the bank. (Courtesy Parker Lowry.)

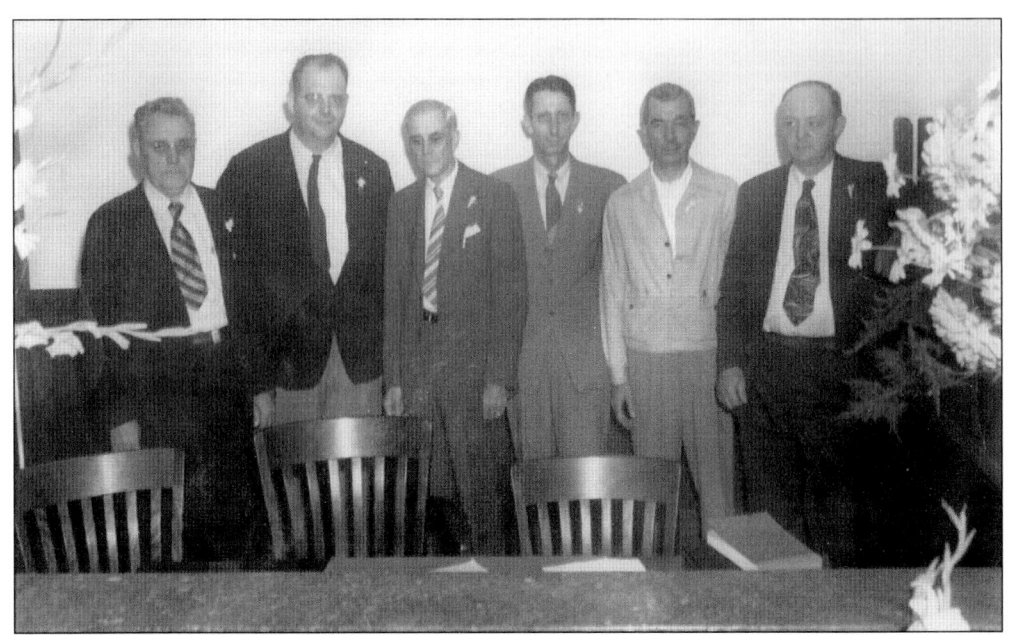

The first Bank of Smyrna failed in the 1920s. On August 5, 1947, the second Bank of Smyrna opened near the same location. Opening capital stock was $55,000, with $15,000 surplus. The bank's officials were, from left to right, W.P. Gresham (president), B.F. Reed Jr. (vice president), and directors Grover Cleveland Green, James W. Nash, Walter T. Crowe Jr., and D.C. Landers. Not pictured is W.C. Patterson, cashier. (Courtesy Becky Nash Paden.)

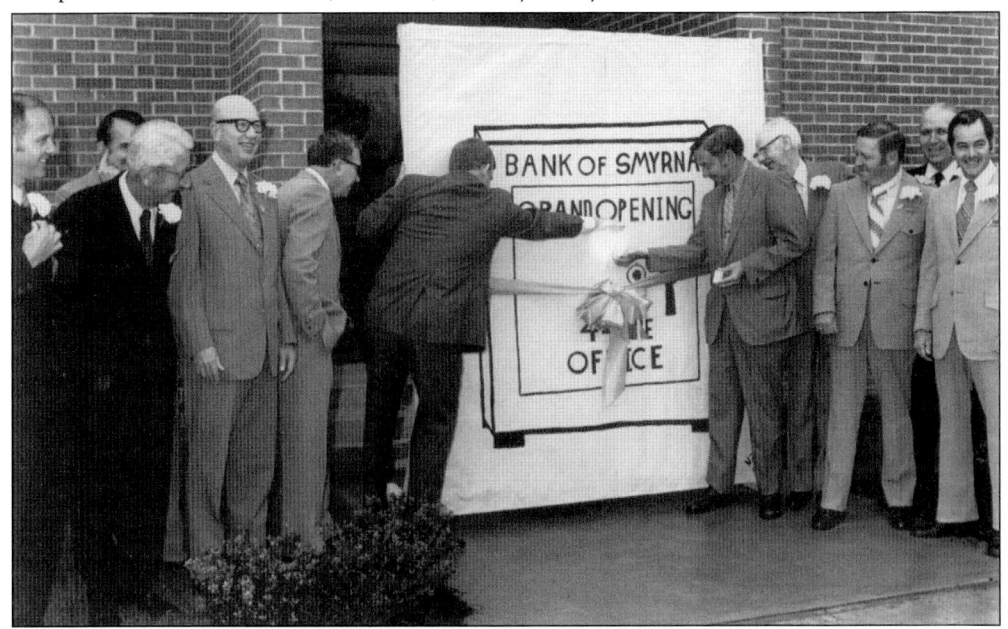

A ribbon-cutting ceremony was held at a new building of Bank of Smyrna on the four-lane highway on May 13, 1972. Among the dignitaries shown here are, from left to right, (bank officials on left) unidentified, Roy Simmons (in back), James Nash, Gardner Potter, Harry Holliday, and unidentified; (on right) Mayor John Porterfield, Lex Jolley (in back), Frank Lee, Winston Burger (in back), and Pete Waddleton. (Courtesy Harold Smith.)

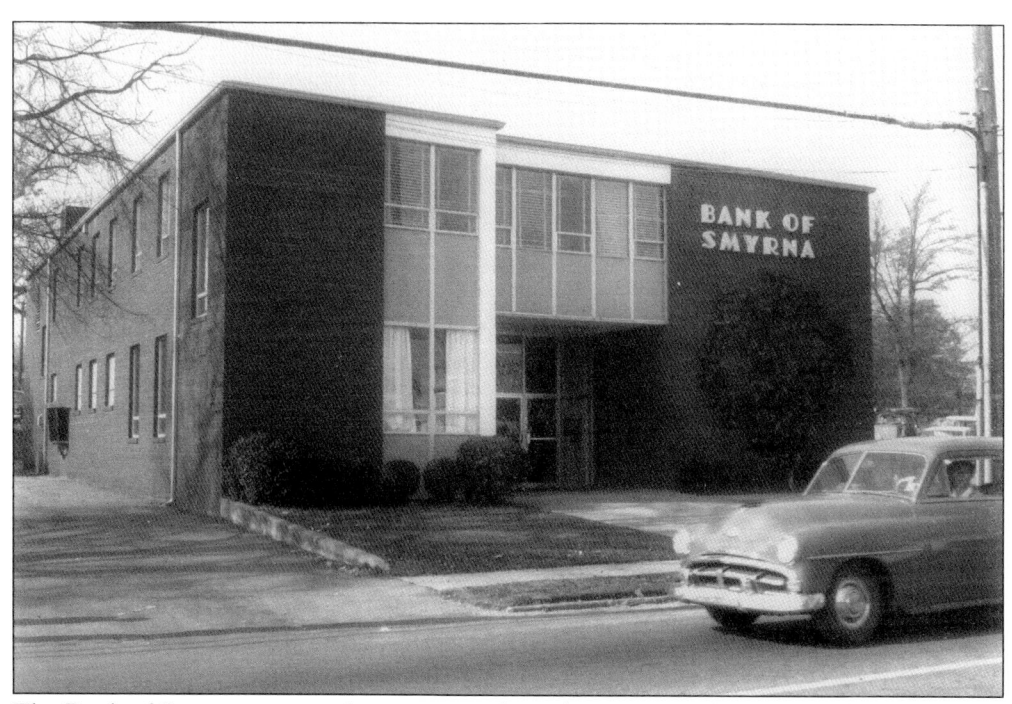

The Bank of Smyrna remained at its original site from August 5, 1946, until December 19, 1956, when it moved into this new location, where a number of Smyrna's historic structures had previously stood. Among the bank's predecessors were The Smyrna Hotel, D.C. Osborn's service station, the Smyrna Boarding House/Hotel, and several residences.

In this 1953 photograph, Barbara Adams Porter poses on the north side of Bank Street. Behind her are, from left to right, the homes of Eunice Groce, George Neese, and former city councilmen Roy and Charlie "Pete" Wood. The Adams family lived across the street, on the south side. (Courtesy Barbara Adams Porter.)

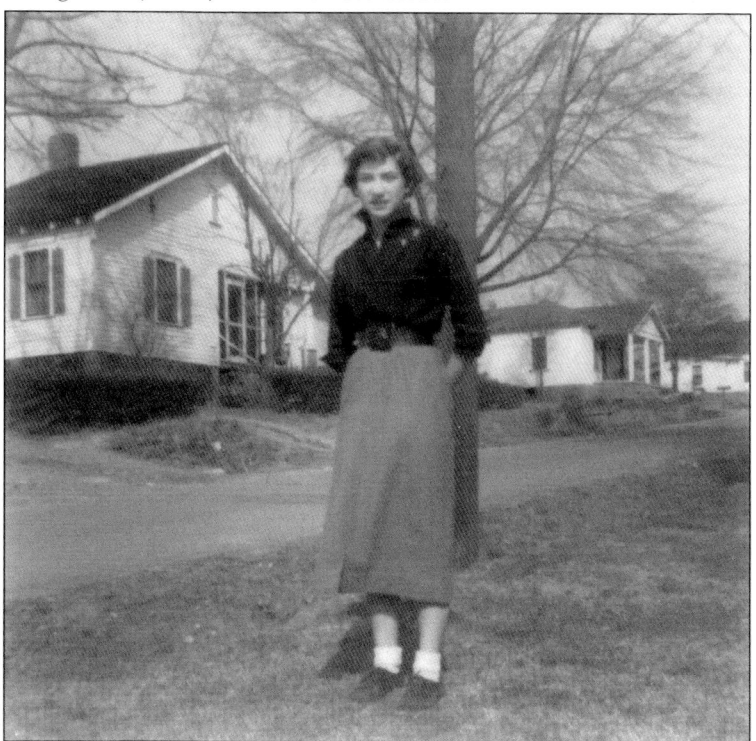

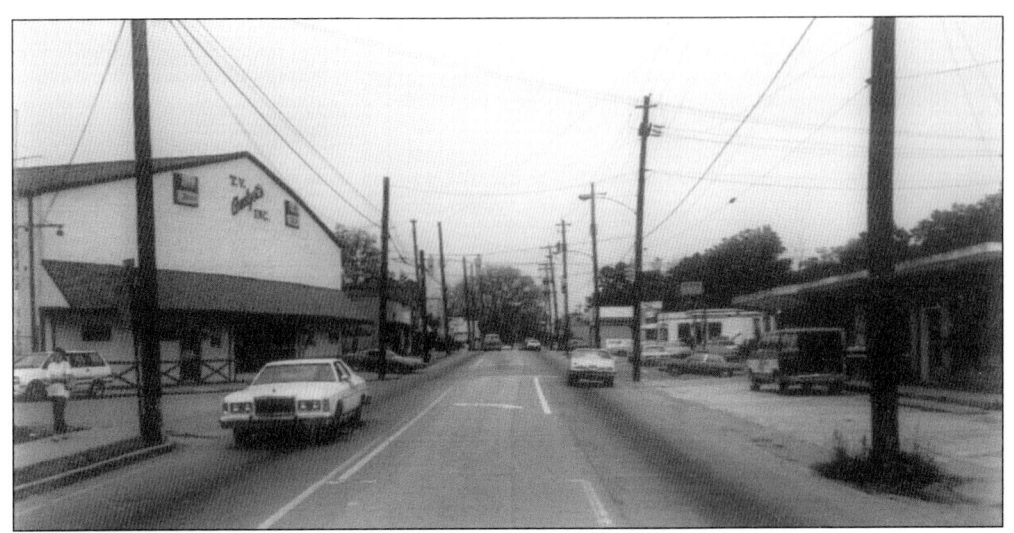

In this 1982 photograph, T.V. Analysts (left) and the former location of Smyrna Drug Store (owned by Dr. D.C. Landers and his son Bob) occupy the present entrance to Market Village. When T.V. Analysts purchased the store, the company added it to four adjoining buildings it owned. A second floor was constructed over all five buildings to make one large structure. (Courtesy Harold Smith.)

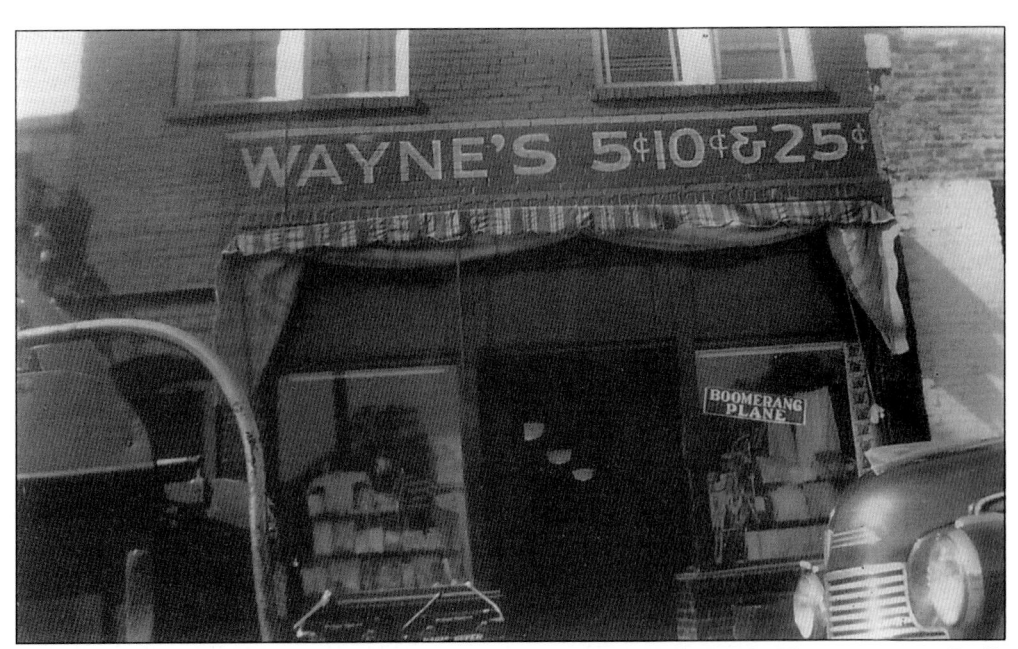

In the late 1940s, Hurbert and Frances Colquitt opened Wayne's 5¢ 10¢ & 25¢ store next to Saul's Department Store. Due to the growth in the city in the early 1950s, the Colquitts changed the store's location a number of times, including on West Spring Street in the first floor of the Masonic lodge building. In 1958, they relocated to Dickson Shopping Center on South Cobb Drive.

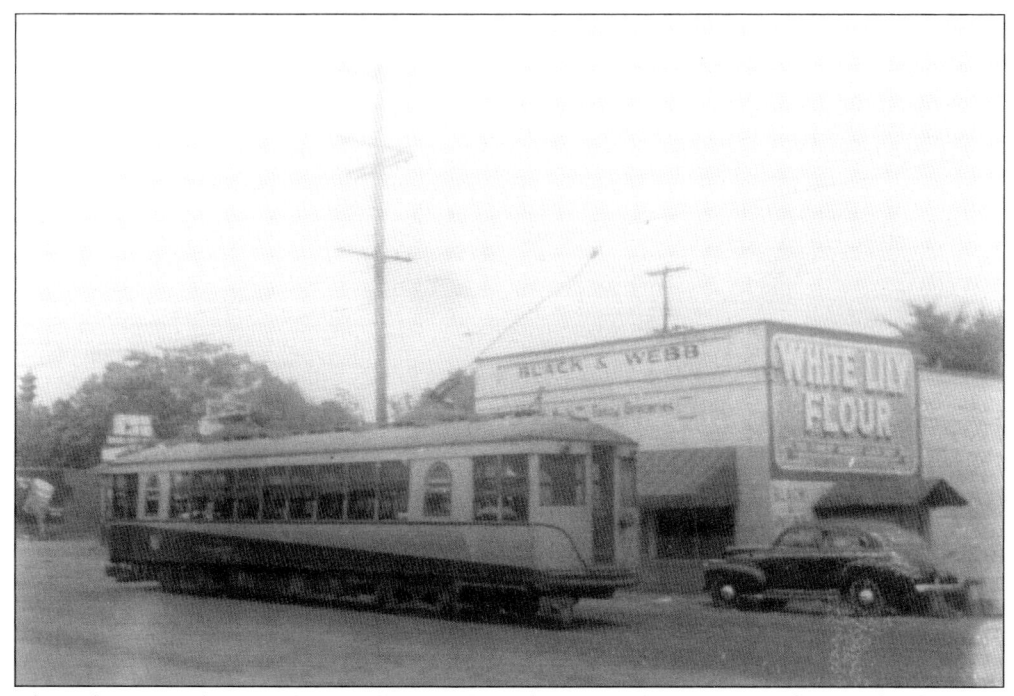

The Atlanta Northern Railway trolley ran through Smyrna from 1905 until it was discontinued in January 1947. It was said to be the "largest interurban electric railway in the South." The tracks ran from the Marietta square to downtown Atlanta. Here, the trolley passes by the Black & Webb Grocery Store, owned by Harry Black and Sam Webb.

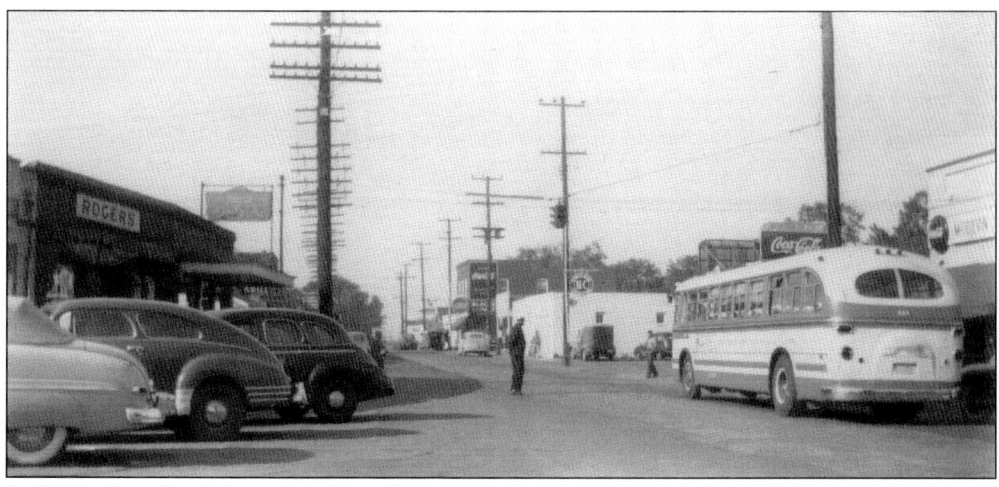

In 1947, when the Atlanta Northern Railway discontinued service through Smyrna, Greyhound Bus Lines used public roads, rather than the private right-of-ways used by the trolleys, keeping with the same routes. Bus fare from Marietta to Atlanta was 35¢. For shorter trips, the fare was based on the number of stops. (Courtesy Smyrna Woman's Club.)

51

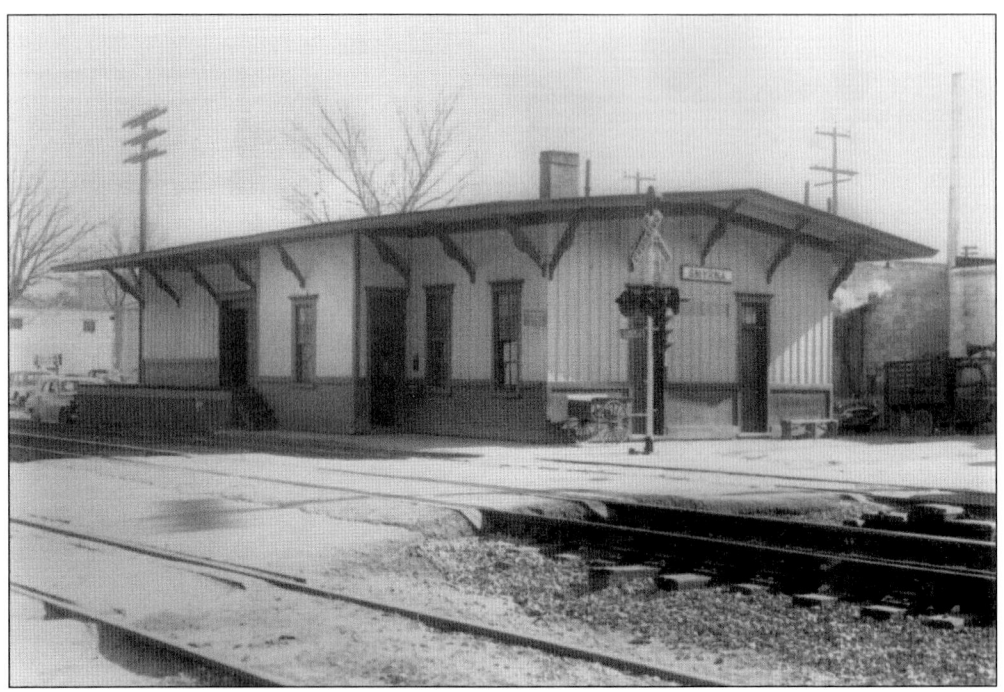

Constructed in 1888, the Smyrna depot, at Spring and Atlanta Streets, served the early railroads. When it was demolished in 1959, Emory Paris obtained the Smyrna sign, which remained on his utility building until his death. Robert Baldwin made several items from the building's cedar and gopher wood. The siren that alerted volunteer firemen to action was mounted atop the depot. The Smyrna Museum replicates the old depot. (Courtesy Smyrna Woman's Club.)

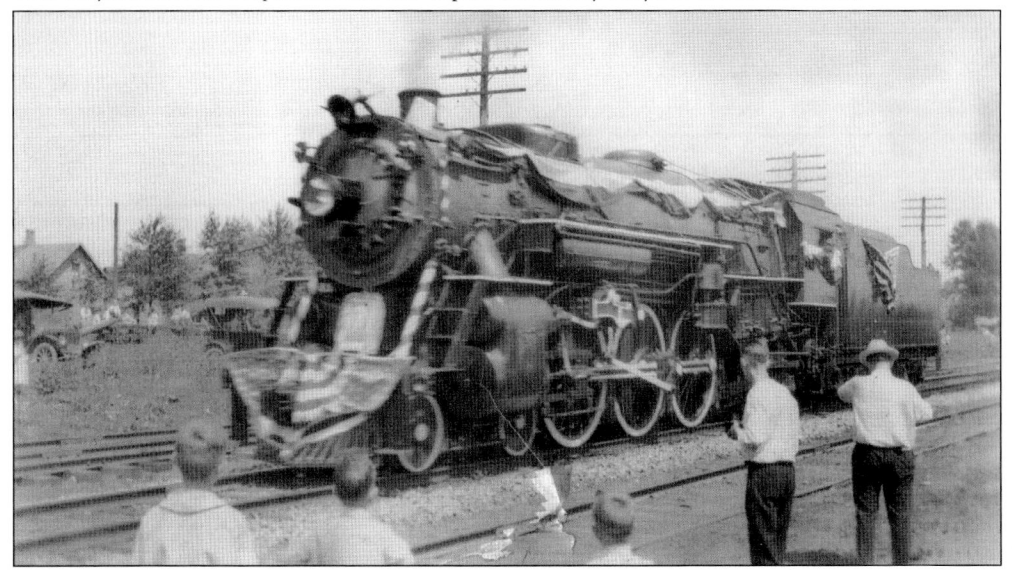

The "Superb," built in 1911, was the second-oldest steel Pullman railroad locomotive in existence. It served as the personal car of Pres. Warren Harding during his 1923 cross-country tour. After Harding's untimely death on August 2, 1923, in San Francisco, the Superb returned his body to Washington, DC. Here, the Superb travels through Smyrna in August 1923. The engine currently resides in the Southeastern Railway Museum in Duluth, Georgia.

Brothers C.J. and Jerry Fouts came to Smyrna in 1948. They owned and operated this Sinclair service station until 1963. It was later owned by Ralph Grady, and the city eventually bought it in the 1990s as part of the downtown redevelopment project. The brothers built an auto repair and service station where the present Smyrna fire station stands. In 1969, they opened a Datsun dealership.

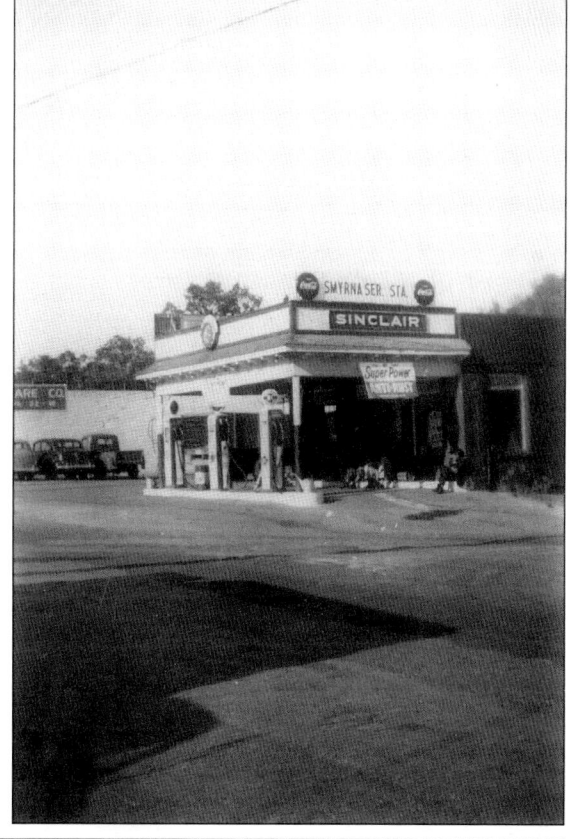

The City of Smyrna installed and dedicated a bronze plaque and a garden to C.J. Fouts (right, with cane) on May 25, 2006, for his long service to the city through a variety of civic and service organizations, including the Smyrna Downtown Development Authority. Fouts passed away less than a month later, on June 13, 2006.

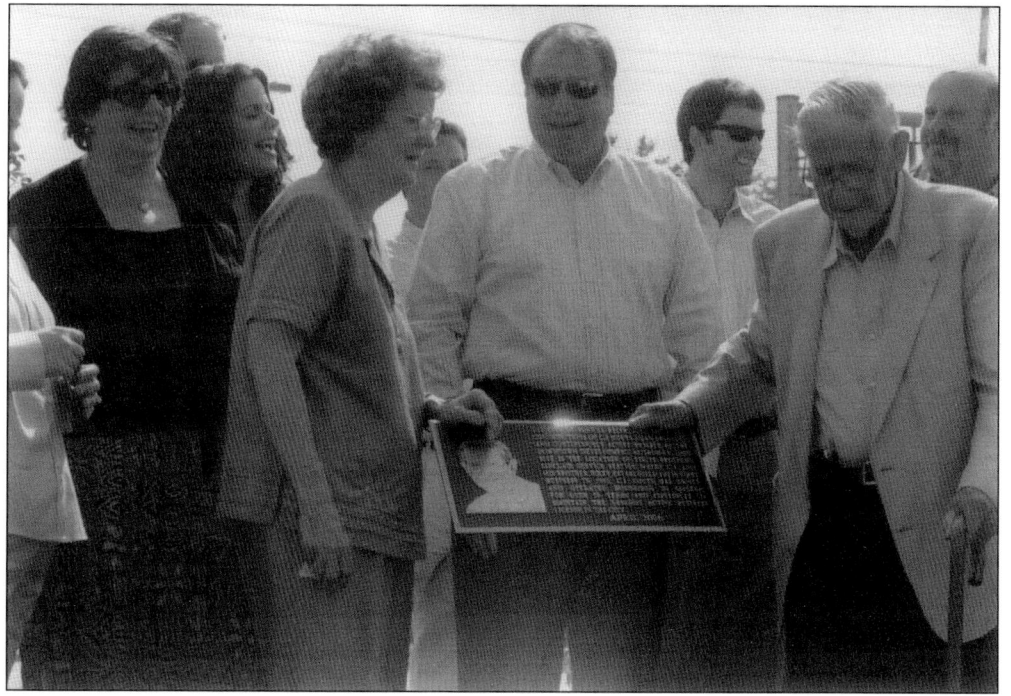

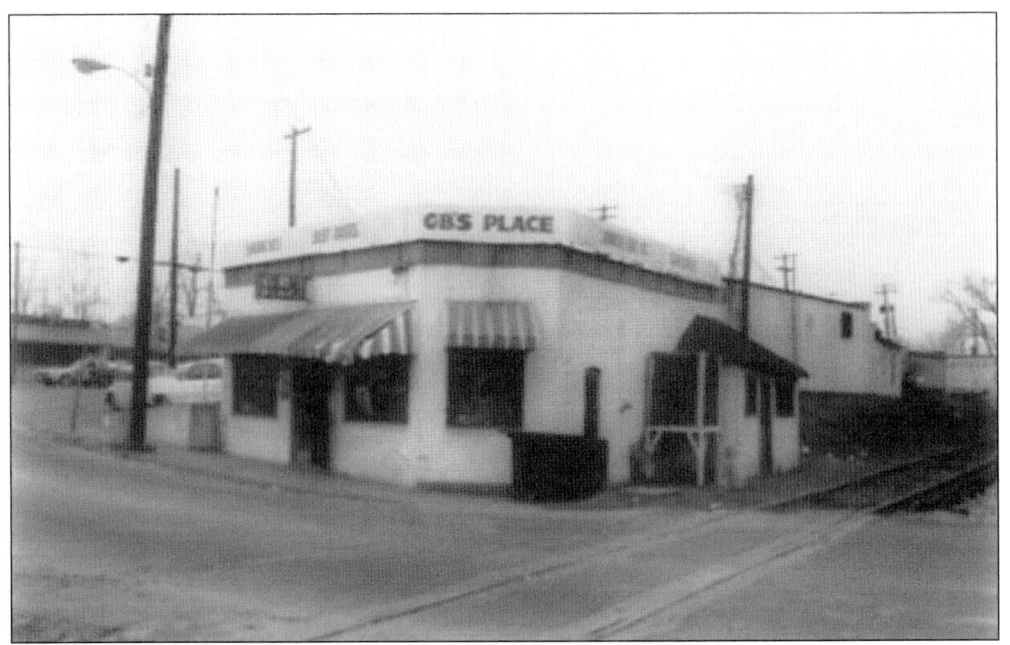

The popular GB's Place opened in 1937. Located behind the Fouts service station facing Spring Street, its main fare consisted of burgers and dogs, but it also served as a convenience store. Many teenagers worked there, including future mayor Max Bacon. It was Smyrna's first establishment with a drive-up window, which served the passengers on trains that stopped at the depot. (Courtesy Keith Dunn.)

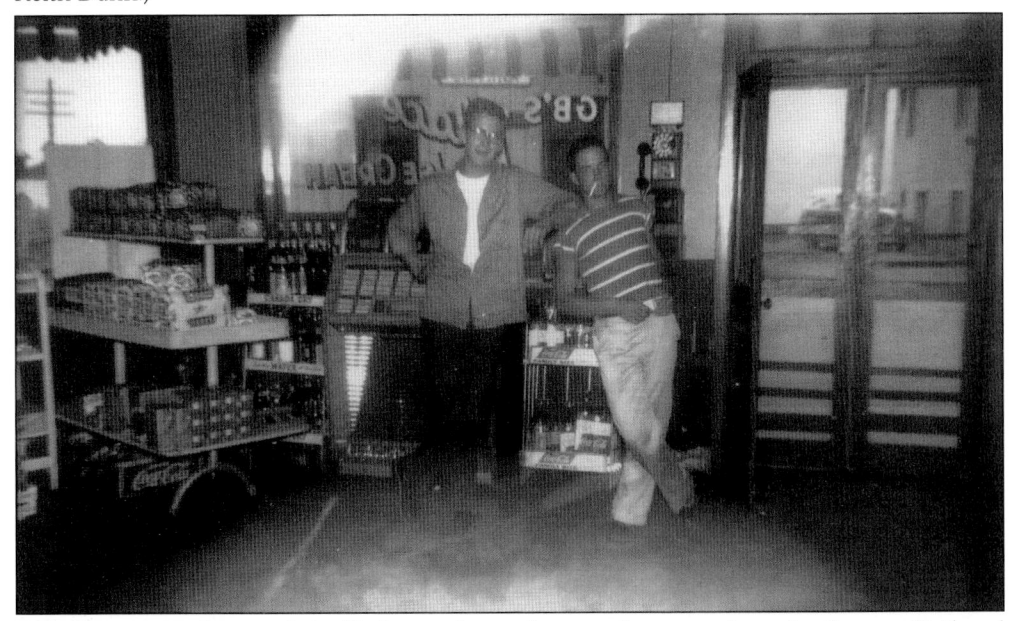

GB's Place was a five-stool establishment located across the street from the Smyrna Railroad depot. In this photograph taken inside the restaurant are Randy Shepherd (left) and Stanley Wilmont, two of the young men employed at GB's. The burgers and dogs were covered with some of the best chili around, said Smyrna mayor Max Bacon. GB's closed in 1974. (Courtesy Betty and Frank Crane.)

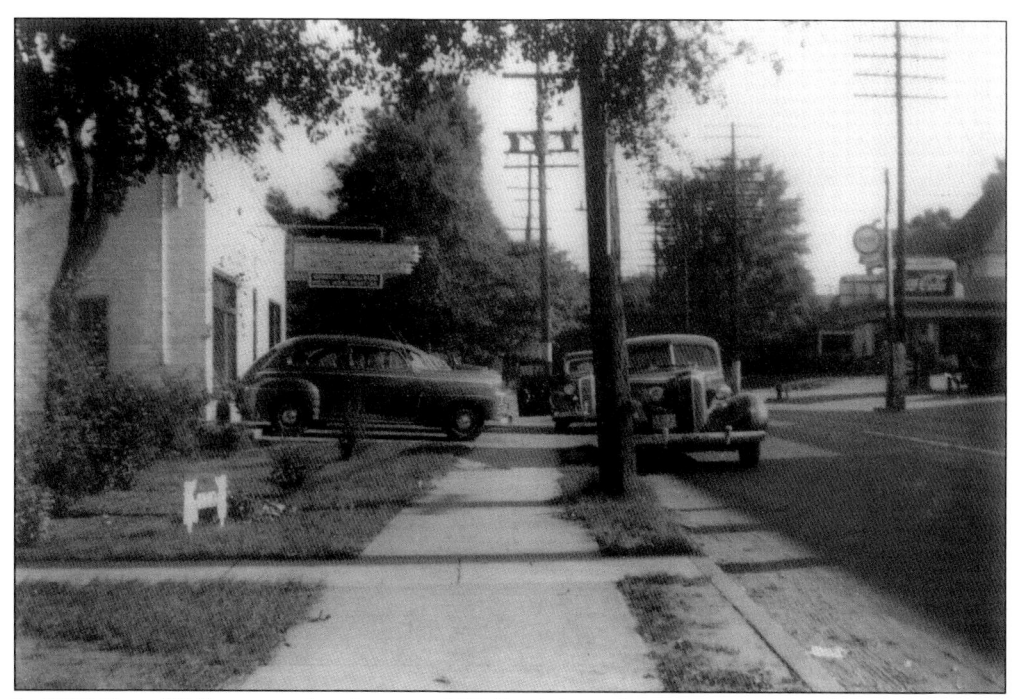

In 1948, Buna Walker owned and operated Walker Motor Company, an automobile repair garage and used-car lot. The business was located on Atlanta Street, near the present location of the Smyrna History Museum.

In this 1939 photograph, Dr. G.C. Green (left) and Henry Konigsmark survey a trashy vacant lot just north of the Smyrna Memorial Cemetery as a cleanup project for the Smyrna Men's Club. The Glover service station, at left, is the same building shown above when it was occupied by the Walker Motor Company. The building is near the current location of the Smyrna Museum and Aunt Fanny's Cabin.

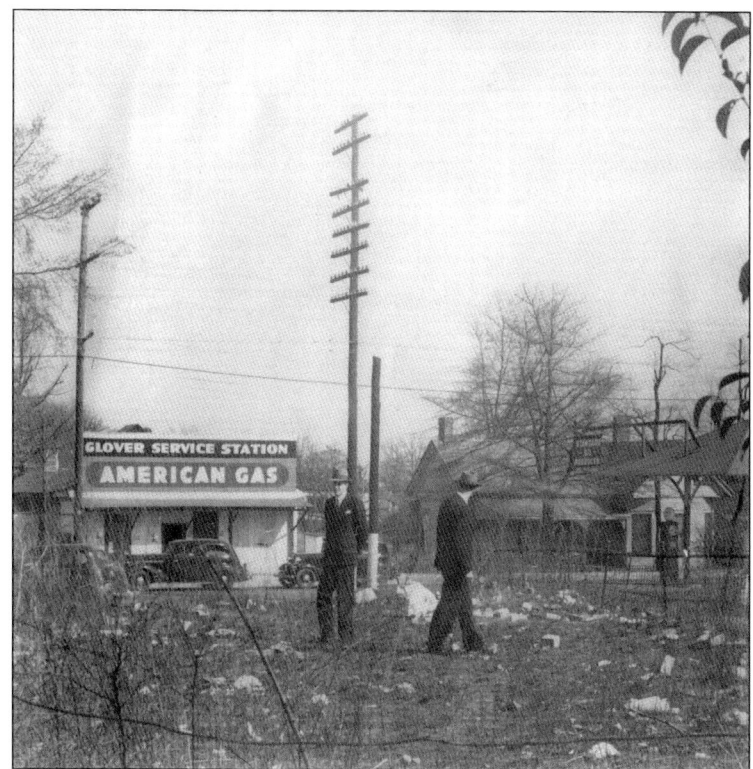

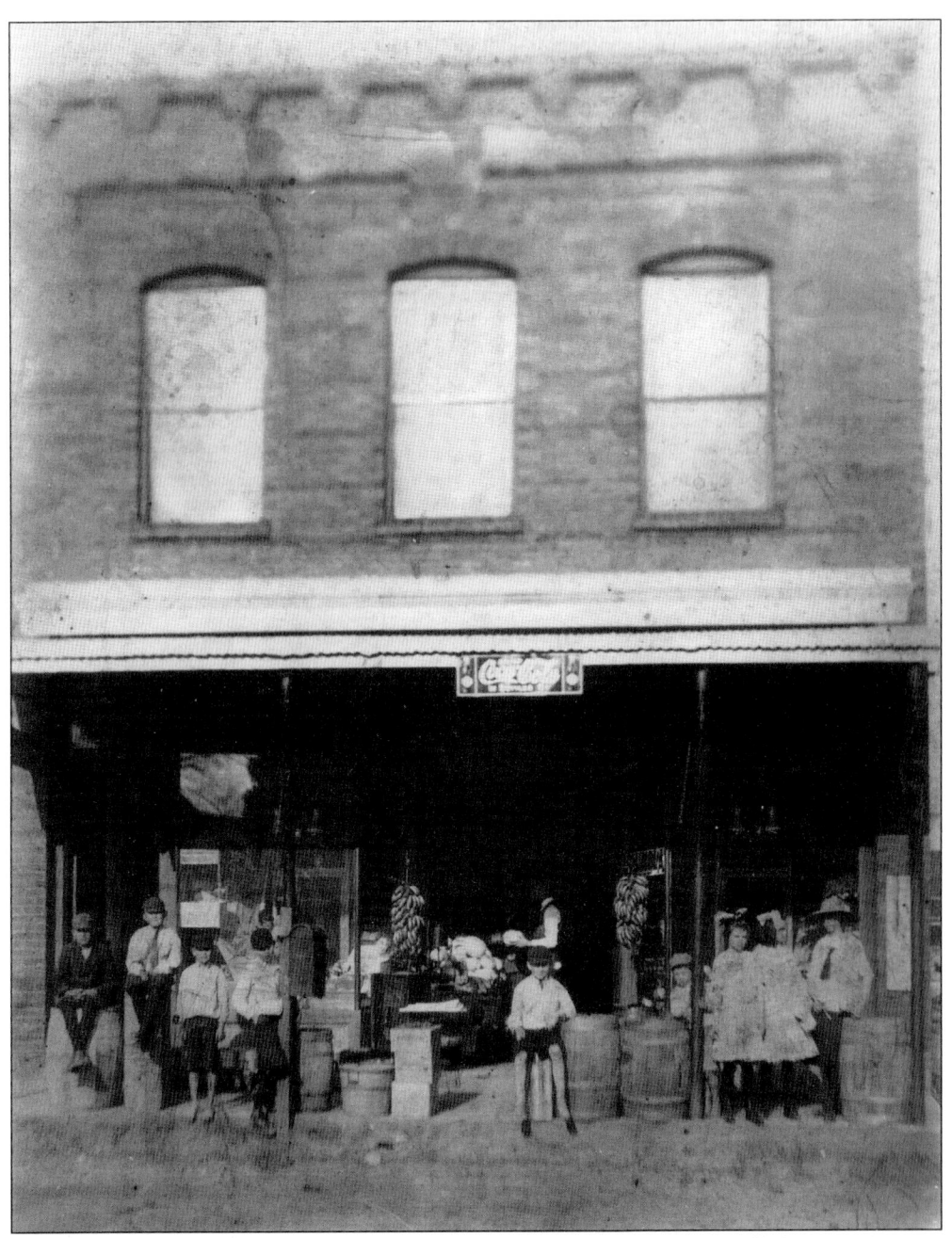

Whitfield Grocery Store, on the northwest corner of Bank Street, eventually became Smyrna City Hall and the police station. Shown here in front of the store are, from left to right, Tom Moss, Albert Ireland, Robert Baldwinh, W.V. Baldwin, Tom Barnes, Jack Thrash, Clara Dunn, Blanch Rice, and Louise Tollerson. Standing in back at center is Bud Whifield, the proprietor of the store. He was Mazie Whitfield Nelson's brother. This photograph was taken in the early 1900s. (Courtesy Robert Baldwin.)

In this 1951 photograph, looking north on the west side of Atlanta Street, future Atkins Drug Store owner and Georgia state representative Bill Atkins poses with future country-and-western songwriter Jean Scoggins. They are standing under the Bob's Tavern sign. (Courtesy Jean and Joan Bennett.)

The Jonquil Theatre (below) was located at Sunset Avenue and Atlanta Road. It was constructed in 1948 by Leonard Branscomb, publisher of the *South Cobb Advertiser*, forerunner of the *Smyrna Herald*. The two-reel movie house was the place to see cowboy movies, chapter serials like *The Lone Ranger* and *Flash Gordon*, and the exploits of a variety of other movie heroes. (Courtesy Jean and Joan Bennett.)

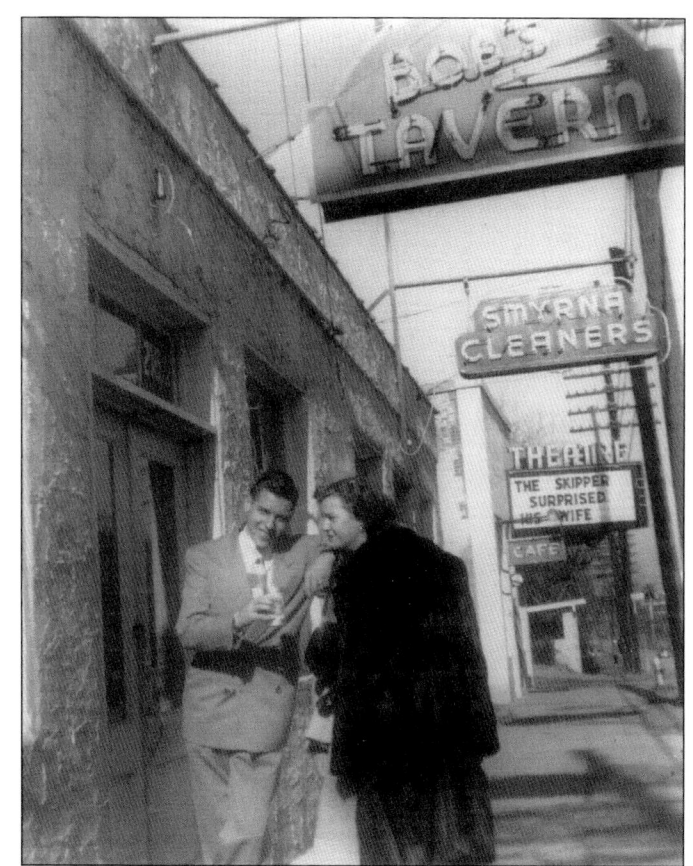

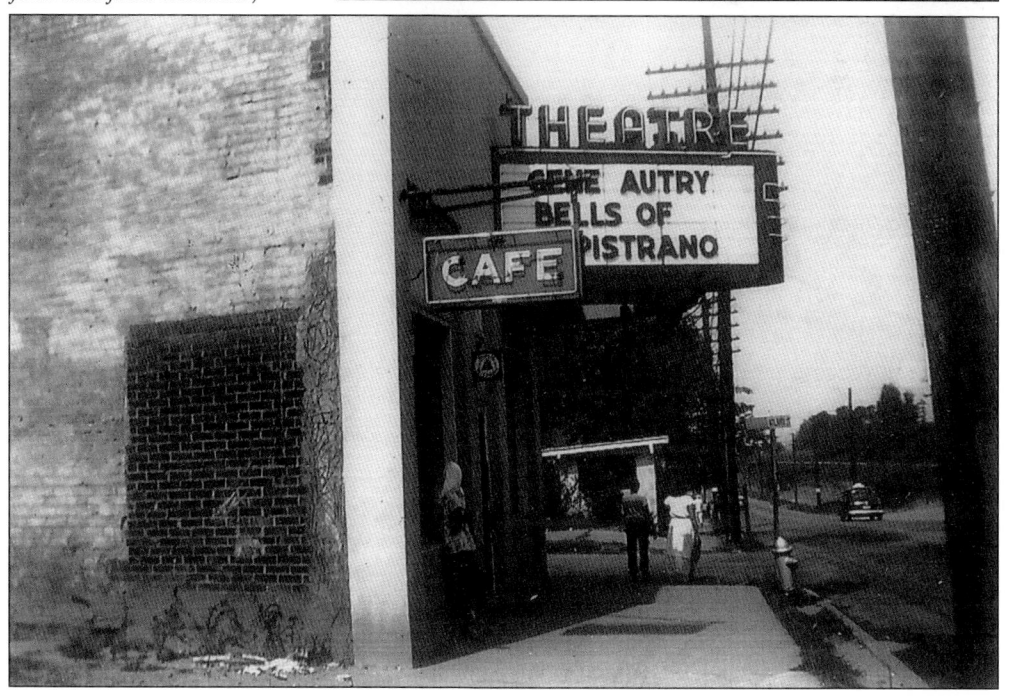

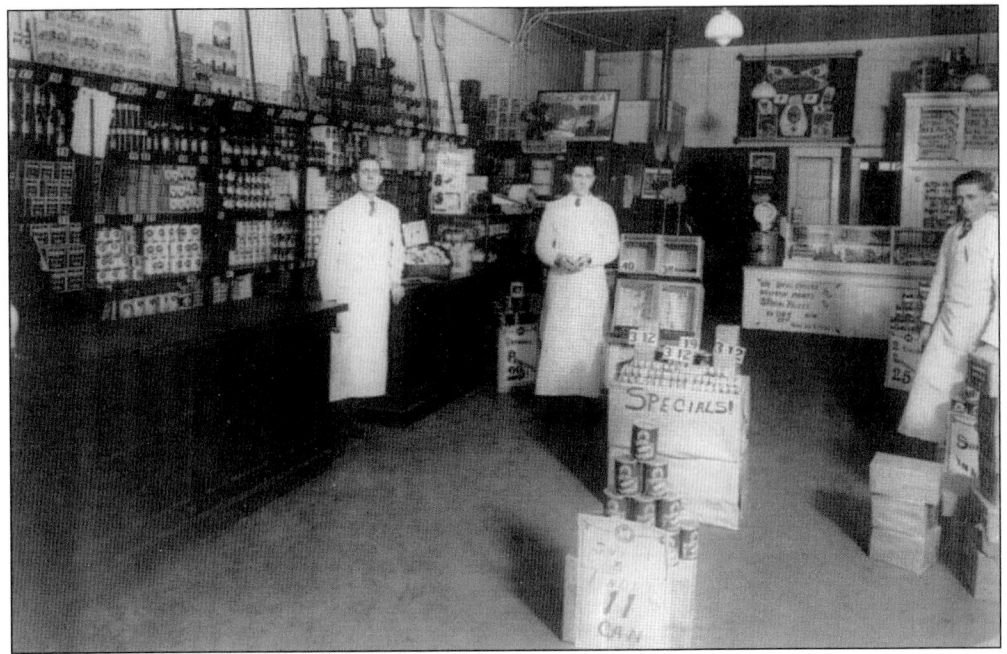

Hill Grocery Store was located at the southwest corner of Atlanta and Bank Streets. The store's operators, the Hill family, lived on nearby Banks Street. Hiram McLarty was also in the grocery business at this location. Throughout the years, the building was used by various retailers. When it was demolished in the downtown redevelopment program, the structure housed the St. Jude's Thrift Store.

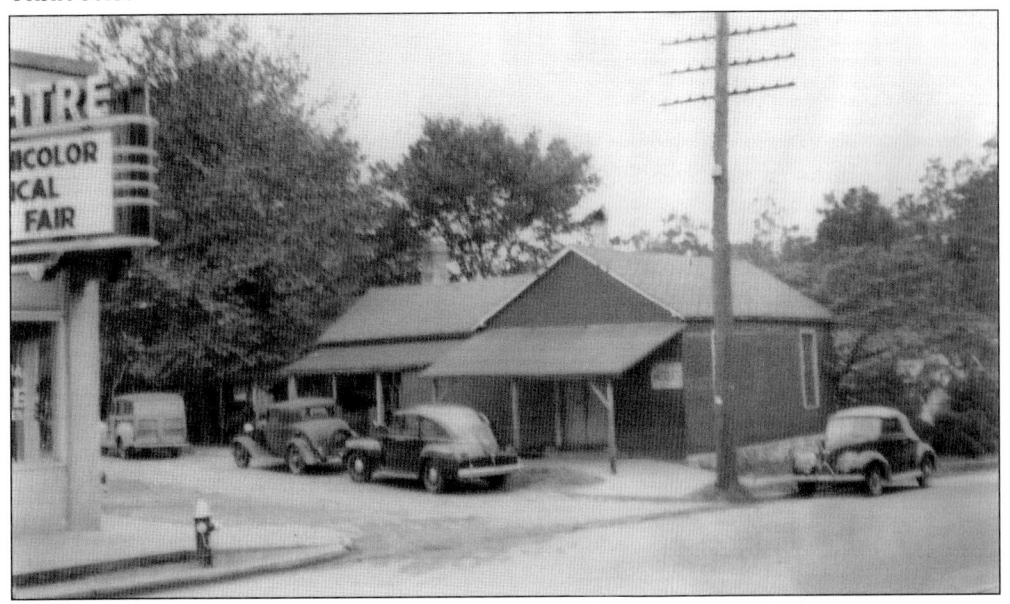

John Stone Grocery, which also housed the post office, was on Atlanta Road at Sunset Avenue. Stone was Smyrna postmaster from 1887 to 1895. He was eventually elected judge of the ordinary, with responsibility for Cobb County's alms (poor) house. History says that Stone Creek was named for him. He and his wife, Lavenia Payne Stone, had two daughters, Mary Ruby and Maude Elizabeth. This building became Dr. W.C. Mitchell's office in 1948. (Courtesy Gennie and Cecil Haralson.)

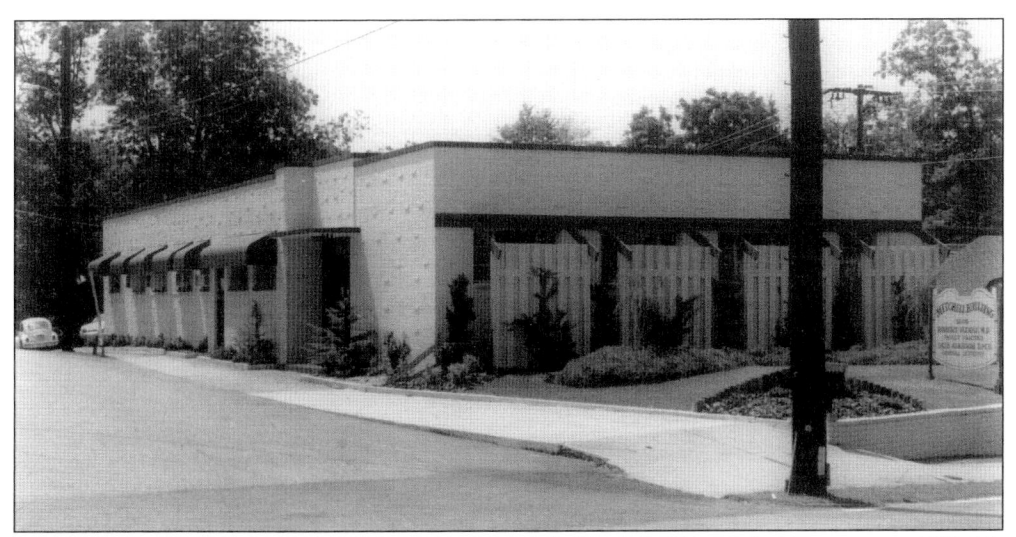

Smyrna's most remembered physician, Dr. W.C. Mitchell, opened his medical practice in 1933. He practiced for 48 years until he retired in 1981. In 1948, he constructed this medical building on the corner of Sunset Avenue. Shortly after his retirement, the building was sold to Blind & Low Vision Services of North Georgia. It was eventually demolished for the downtown redevelopment. (Courtesy Jennie and Cecil Haralson.)

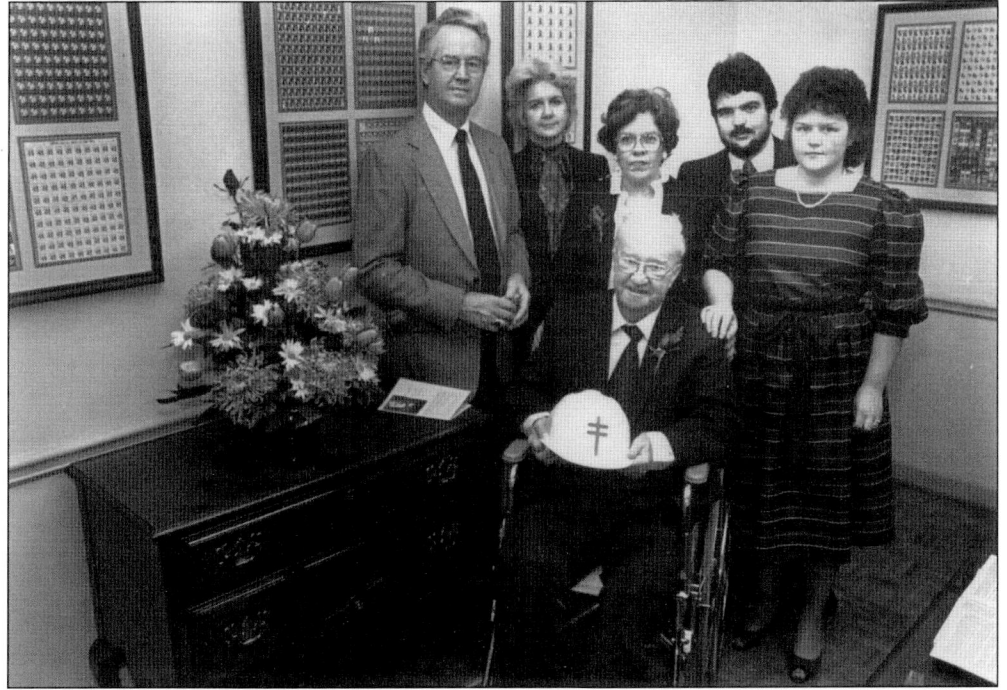

Dr. Mitchell was president of the Smyrna Men's Club, Smyrna Chamber of Commerce, and Smyrna Lion's Club. He served as chairman of the Cobb County Board of Education and was president of the Medical Association of Georgia. He was a lifetime member of the American Academy of Family Physicians. Mitchell (seated) is shown here with, from left to right, son-in-law Harry Evans; daughter Lucy Evans; his wife, "Millie;" son Skip; and daughter Pat. (Courtesy Jennie and Cecil Haralson.)

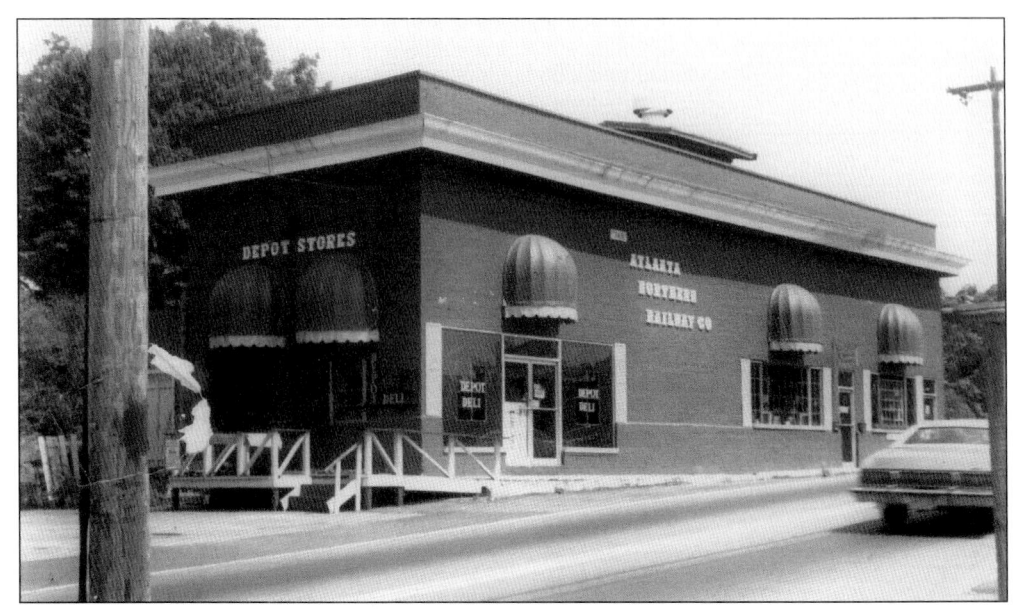

This Atlanta Northern Railway building was often confused with the Western & Atlantic Railroad station by Smyrna's newcomers in the 1950s. Trolleys were powered by electricity through an overhead wire. The rails were located on their own right-of-way between the railroad tracks and the old Dixie Highway. Belmont Farms shipped milk and eggs daily via this trolley to the Kimball House Hotel in Atlanta. (Courtesy Harold Smith.)

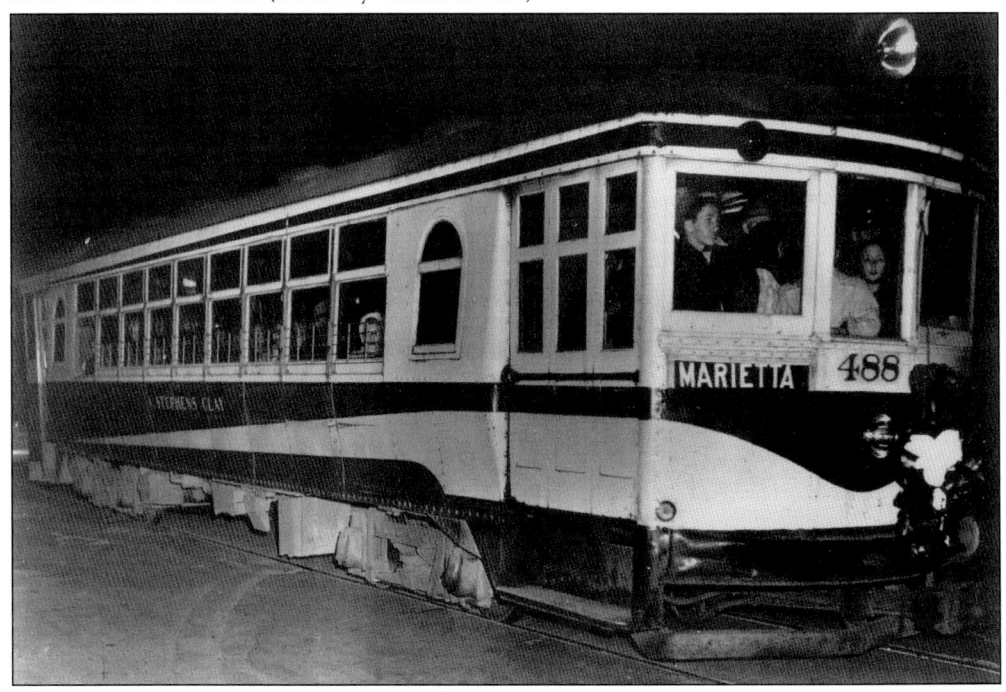

This was the last trip for the trolley car, from Marietta to Atlanta through Smyrna, on January 31, 1947. Its maiden trip took place on July 17, 1905. Following World War II, automobile ownership rose. Trolley ridership dropped so much that the line could not pay its own way. (Courtesy Mazie Whitfield Nelson.)

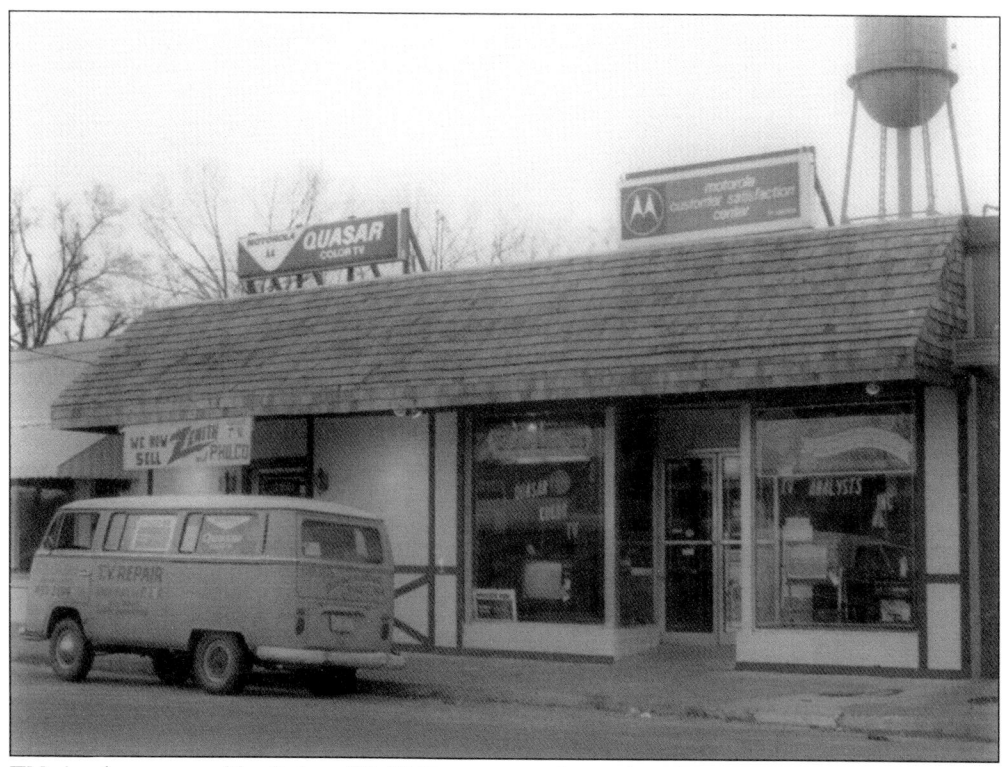

T.V. Analysts, owned by Robert "Bob" Higgins, was located at the intersection of West Spring Street and Atlanta Road. It occupied the former space of four small retail stores: Emma Carter's Antiques, Hubert Johnson's Shoe Repair, Smyrna Florist & Gift Shop, Rogers Grocery Store, and Pro-Graphics Printing Co. The Smyrna water tower, which stood from 1928 to 1984, can be seen behind the store in this 1974 photograph. (Courtesy Robert Higgins.)

Johnson Shoe Shop, owned and operated by Hubert Johnson, was a legendary establishment. Shoes were piled so high that a person had to go through the store sideways. Many people shopped at Johnson's store, as he had a wide variety of styles and colors. Customers could also spend time looking through the collection of "unclaimed" shoes. (Courtesy Harold Smith.)

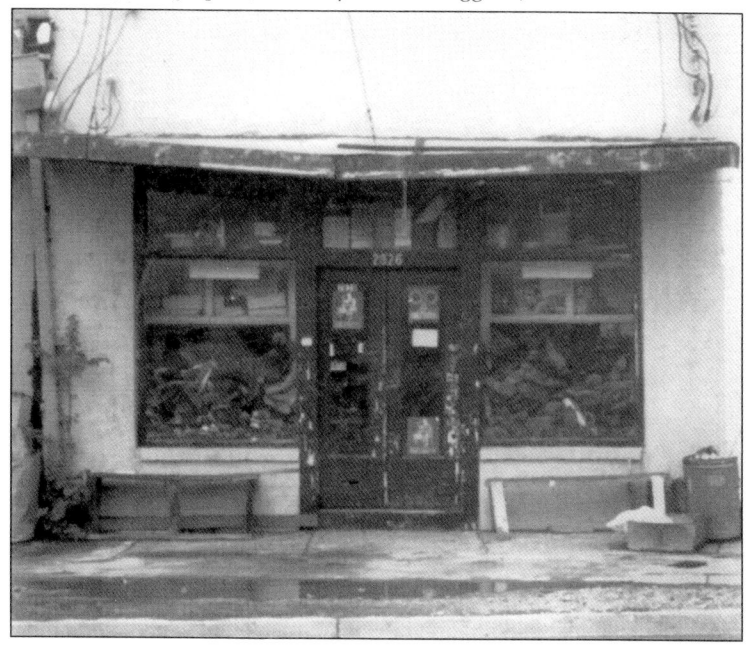

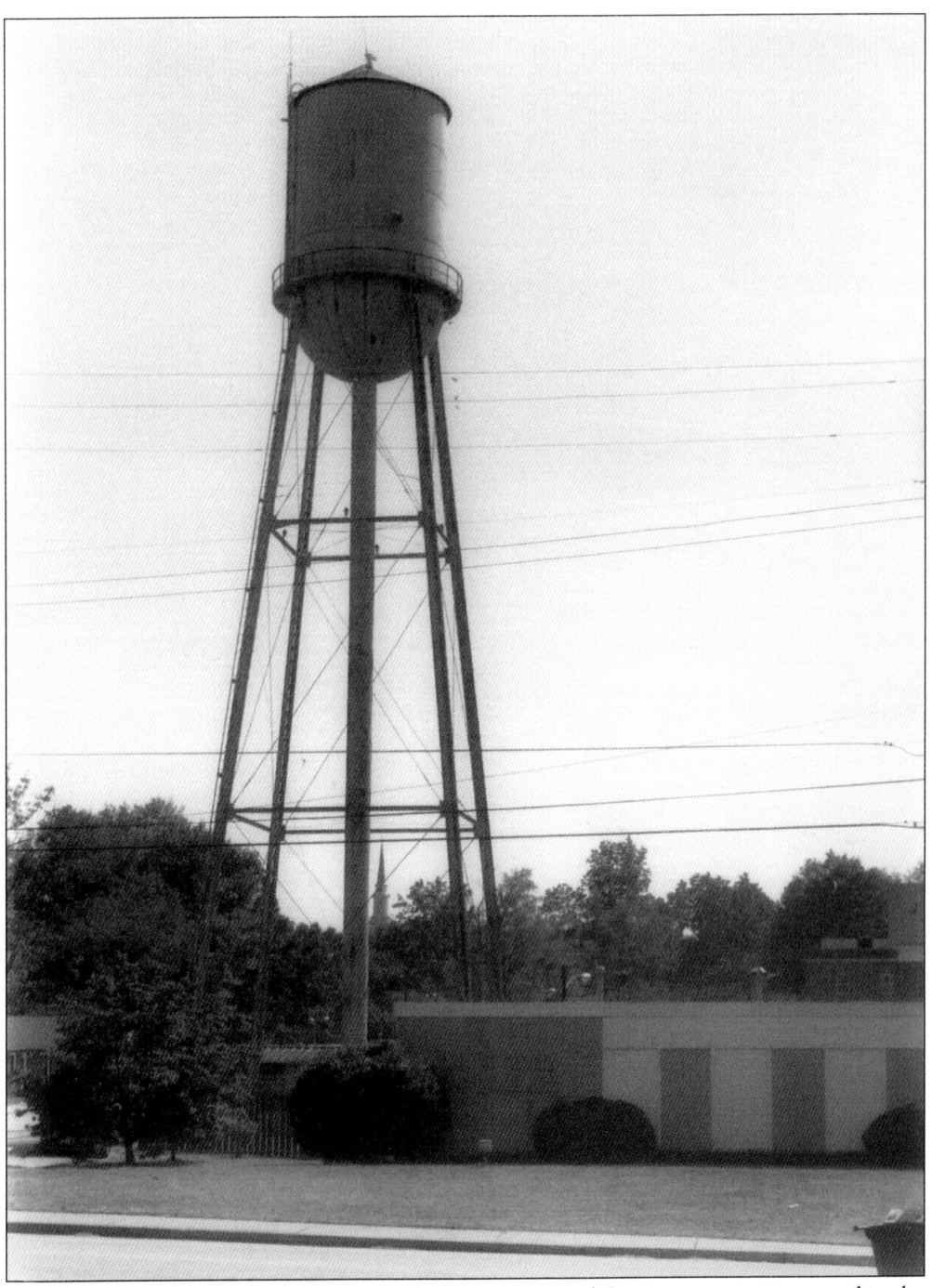

Smyrna's water tank, located at the edge of Smyrna Memorial Cemetery, was constructed in the 1920s and dismantled in 1984. The construction cost of the tower was $2,800, while the cost to dismantle it was $10,500. Also visible here are the Smyrna fire station (foreground), First Baptist Church (behind the fire station), and First Methodist Church (behind the water tower). Some Smyrna residents have fond memories of climbing to the top of the tower and painting or writing school slogans and other graffiti.

Bill Reed stands in the doorway of his realty company office on Atlanta Street in 1955. The row of storefronts backed up to the W&A railroad tracks. A building just south of Reed's office housed the Smyrna city hall (1911–1933). Smyrna's population was growing as a result of the recently opened Belmont Hills Shopping Center.

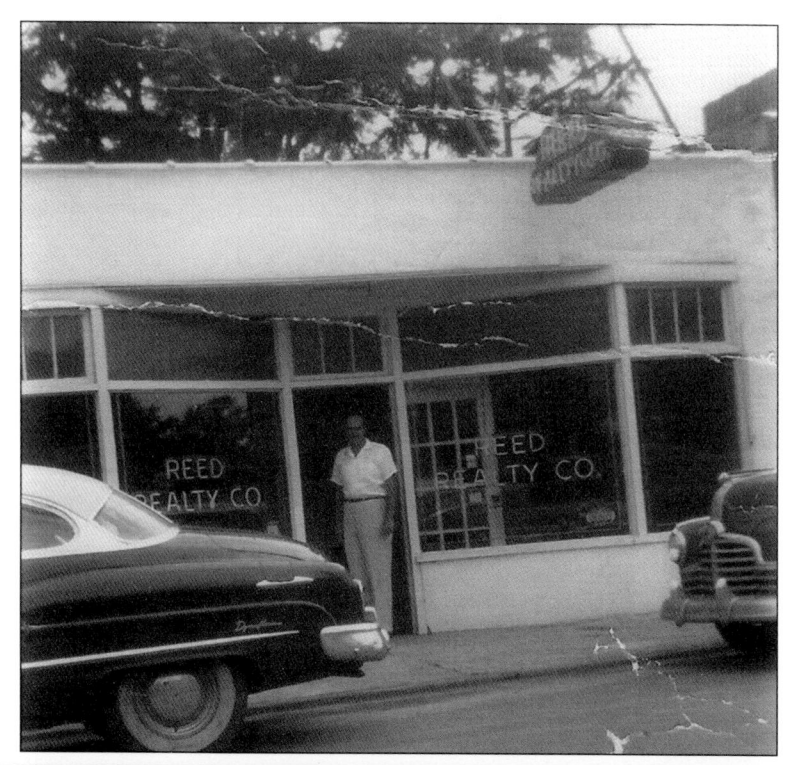

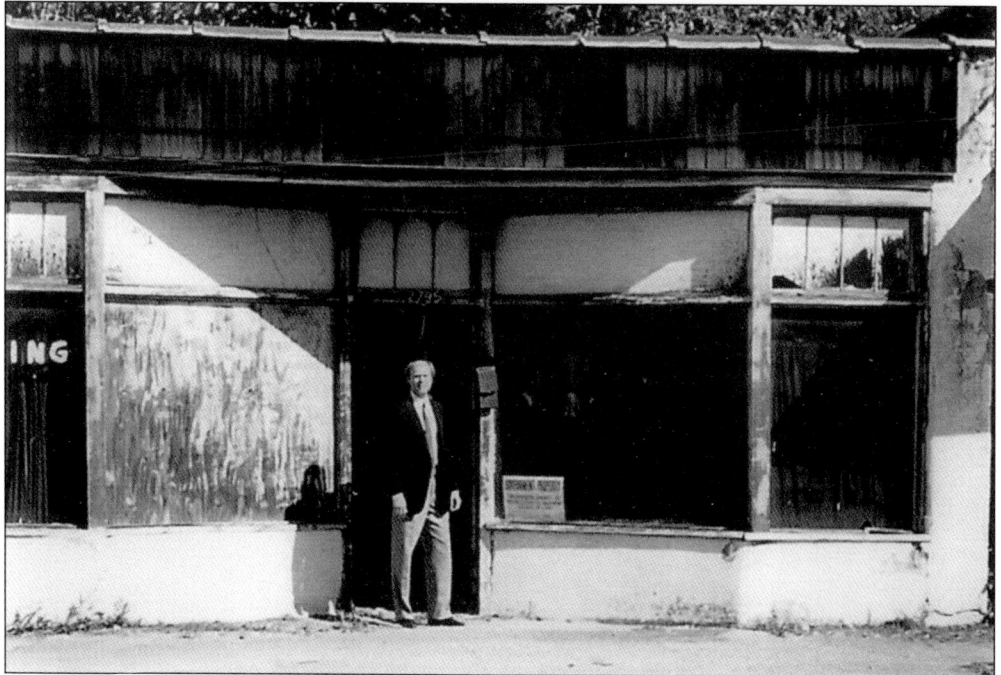

Mark Reed, son of Bill Reed, stands in front of the building that was, in 1955, his father's realty company. This photograph, taken in 1987, depicts the condition of many of the storefronts in downtown Smyrna 30 years after Bill Reed opened his business. Scenes like this brought on discussions about "revitalization." (Courtesy Mark Reed.)

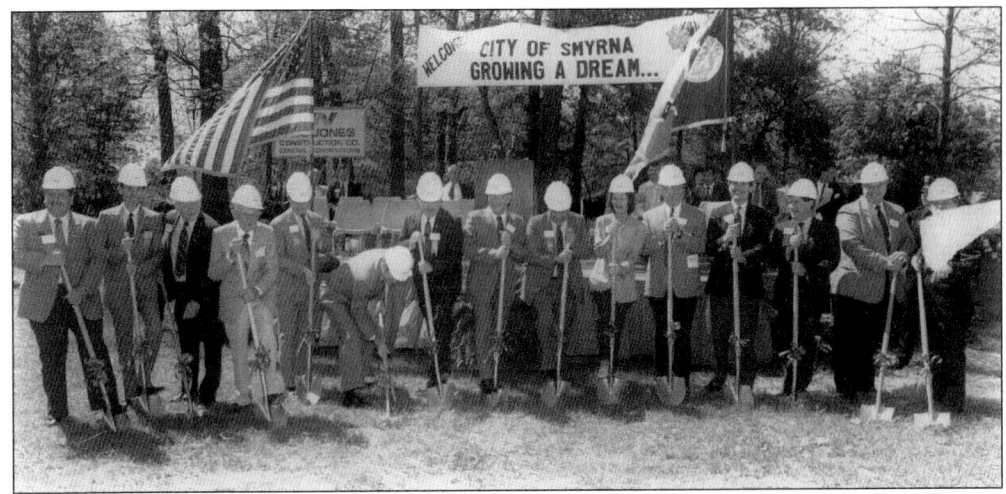

"Growing a Dream" ceremonies for Smyrna's downtown redevelopment were held on April 17, 1990. Pictured here are, from left to right, Councilman Wade Lnenicka, engineer Jim Hudson, former mayors Harold Smith and Mayes Hamby, architect Jeff Floyd, US congressman Buddy Darden, Mayor Max Bacon, Councilpersons Bill Scoggins, Bob Davis, and Kathy Jordan, former mayor Frank Johnson, Dan Atkins, Councilmen Jim Hawkins and Jack Shinall, and master of ceremonies John Delves. (Courtesy Nancy Hancock.)

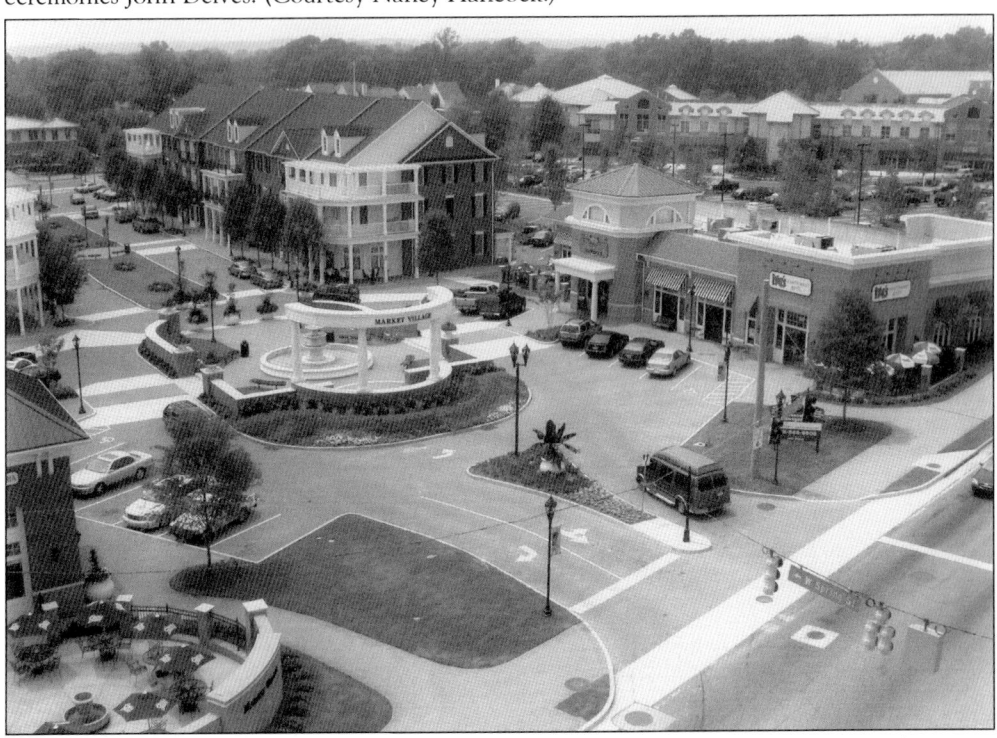

Dedication ceremonies for Market Village were held in October 2002. Plans had started in 1988, after the legislature approved a redevelopment authority for Smyrna. Members of the authority were Hubert Black, Alton Curtis, C.J. Fouts, Dr. Jim Potts, Willousie Spivey, Jimmy Wilson, and Charles "Pete" Wood. Mayor Max Bacon was the chairman. The plans included residential, commercial, civil, judicial, and community projects. (Photograph by Jack Collins.)

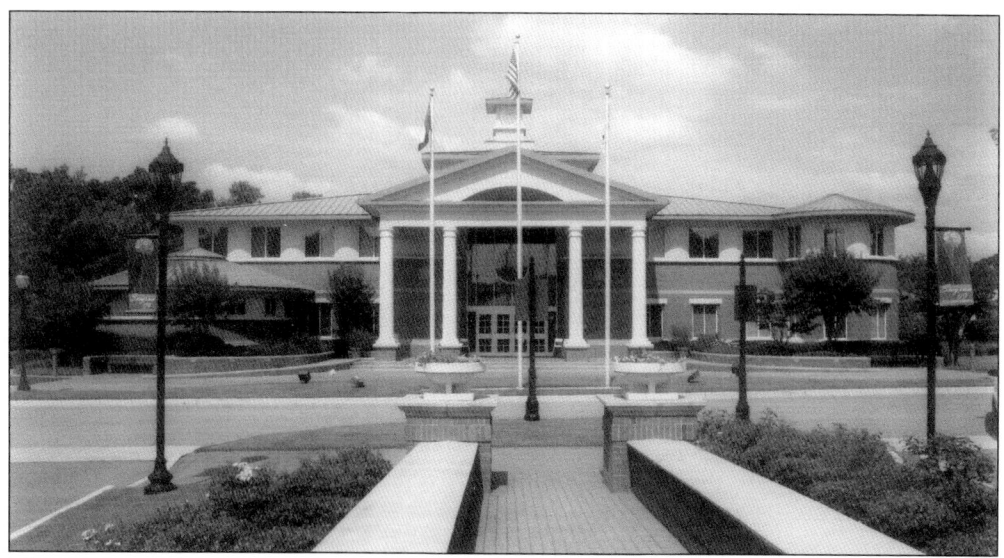

The Smyrna Administrative Services Building (city hall) had its ribbon-cutting ceremony on September 8, 1996. Atlanta Channel 11 news anchor and Smyrna resident Jill Becker was the mistress of ceremonies. More than 300 people were in attendance. The building is located on King Street, the dead end of which, in a few years, would be the main route through Market Village. (Courtesy Harold Smith.)

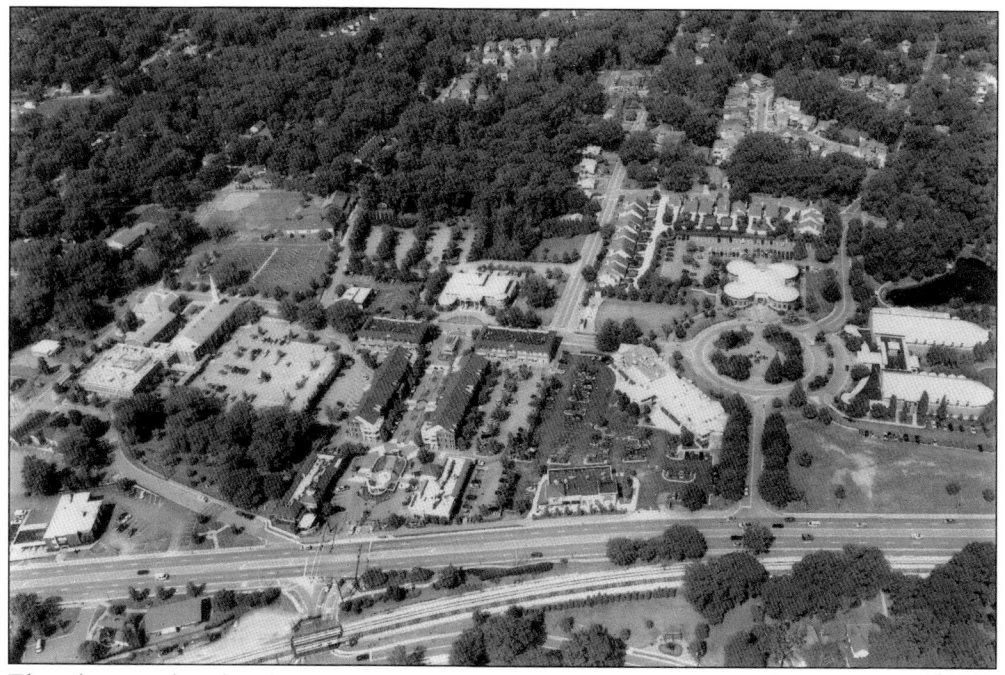

This photograph, taken by retired fireman Jack Collins, shows Smyrna's redevelopment. The welcome center and museum sit along the CSX railroad tracks on the left. Also seen are the bank (lower left), cemetery (in grove of trees at lower left), and First Baptist Church (center left, behind cemetery). In the center is Market Village, which contains a fountain, restaurants, commercial establishments, and condominiums. Village Green can be seen on the right. Around the circle, which has a fountain as its centerpiece, are the library and community center.

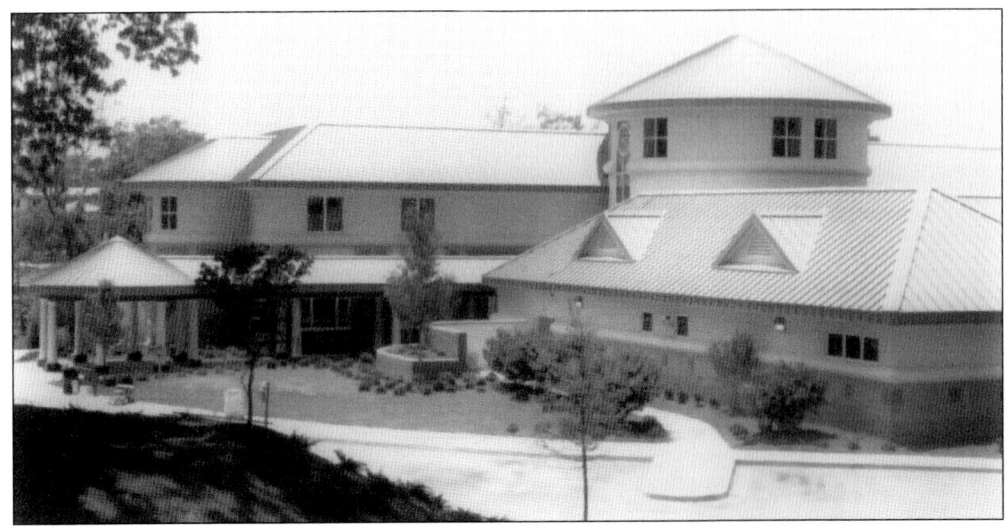

Ribbon-cutting ceremonies were held on August 2, 1997, for the new police station, which was a component of the downtown redevelopment program. Located at 2646 Atlanta Road, the $7.5 million building contains 42,000 square feet and houses administrative offices and the jail, which can accommodate 100 inmates.

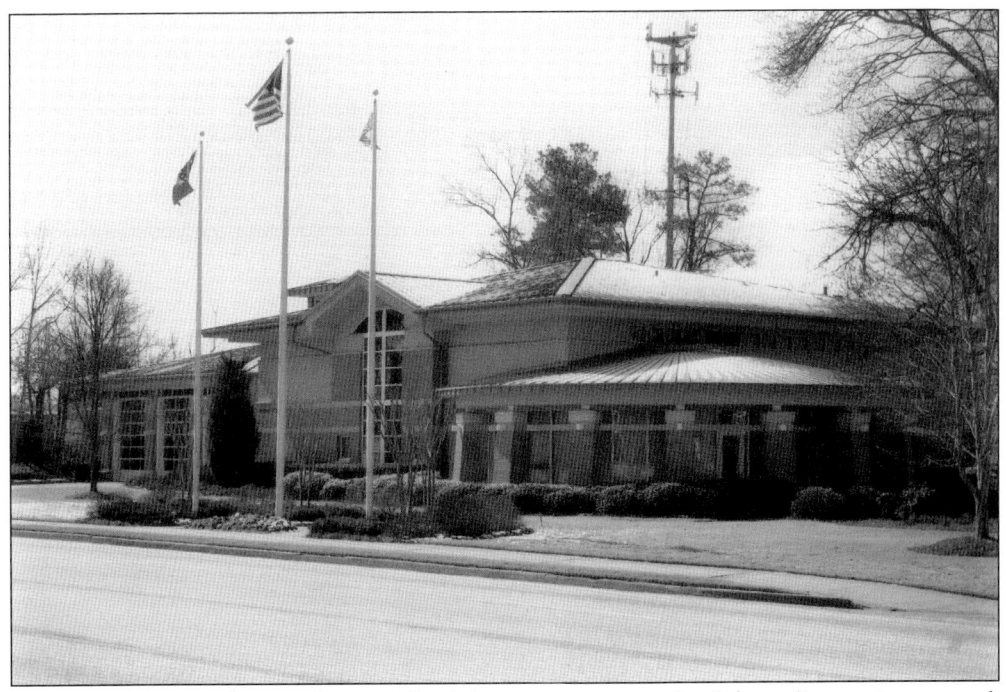

On August 7, 1999, the new Smyrna No. 1 fire station just north of the police station opened. State representative Randy Sauder was the keynote speaker for the opening ceremonies. A typical summer day with temperatures in the 90s greeted the crowd for the outdoor program. The building's cost, $2.5 million, was paid for in cash, according to Councilman Ron Newcomb, who was in charge of the program.

Four

NEIGHBORHOODS

Williams Park is a name that was given to Smyrna's oldest neighborhood when Ron Davis and his wife, Liz, and some of their neighbors decided to organize a homeowners association in November 2004. After much preliminary work, lots of meetings, and investigations, they decided on a name, Williams Park Neighbors, in honor of G.B. Williams. The prominent Smyrna businessman and owner of GB's Place, a popular eating establishment in the neighborhood, had recently died, and the city had dedicated a small park in the area to him. The previously unnamed neighborhood, on the east side of the railroad tracks, became Williams Park in April 2005. According to former city councilman Hugh Marston, the area was Smyrna postal rural route 2 in the 1930s and 1940s. The mayor and council decided to name the streets for some of the early residents: the Gilberts, Marstons, Whitfields, Walkers, Wrights, Matthews, Morrises, Davenports, Pierces, Reeves, Adams, and Reeds.

Smyrna's first city hall was located on what used to be Smyrna-Roswell Road. It burned down in the 1920s. In the late 1940s, the city sold the land to the Southland Ice Company, whose commercial building dominated what is now the entrance to Williams Park, on the east side of the railroad. When refrigerators became available and block ice was no longer needed, the building was converted to a plastic factory. Later, it was bought back by the city and demolished. The town grew, mostly on the west side of the railroad, because of the reopening of the old Bell aircraft factory by the Lockheed Corporation in 1952 and the creation of Belmont Hills Shopping Center in November 1954. Many new neighborhood names were added: Belmont Hills, Rose Garden, Cheney Woods, Forrest Hills, Smyrna Heights, Bennett Woods, King Valley, Smyrna Heights, Green Acres, and The Highlands.

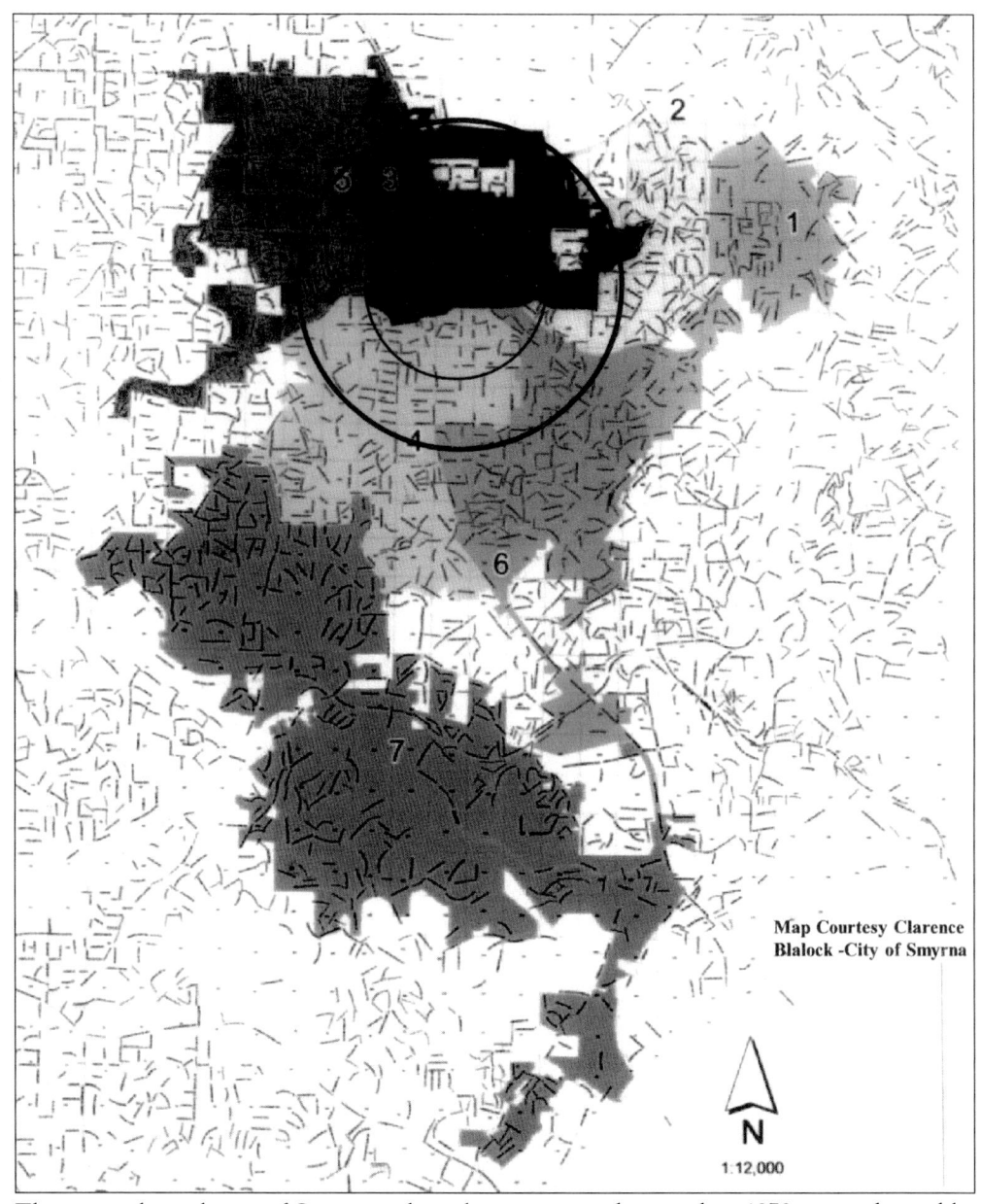

The original city limits of Smyrna, when the town was chartered in 1872, are indicated by the large circle. In 1897, the city reduced the area to the smaller inner circle, one half-mile in every direction from the old Boys Academy building. The first of hundreds of additions was the annexation of the Belmont Hills Shopping Center property in 1951. Smyrna extends north to slightly above Pat Mell Road, east to Interstate 75, south to Interstate 285, and west, in some places, almost to Veteran's Memorial Highway (the former Bankhead Highway). Smyrna has one of the largest and most expensive residential developments in the region, Vinings Estates, along with the independent Whitfield Academy. Both institutions are inside the city limits of Smyrna, but they have Mableton, Georgia, addresses. Most of the neighborhood names came after 1950. (Courtesy City of Smyrna.)

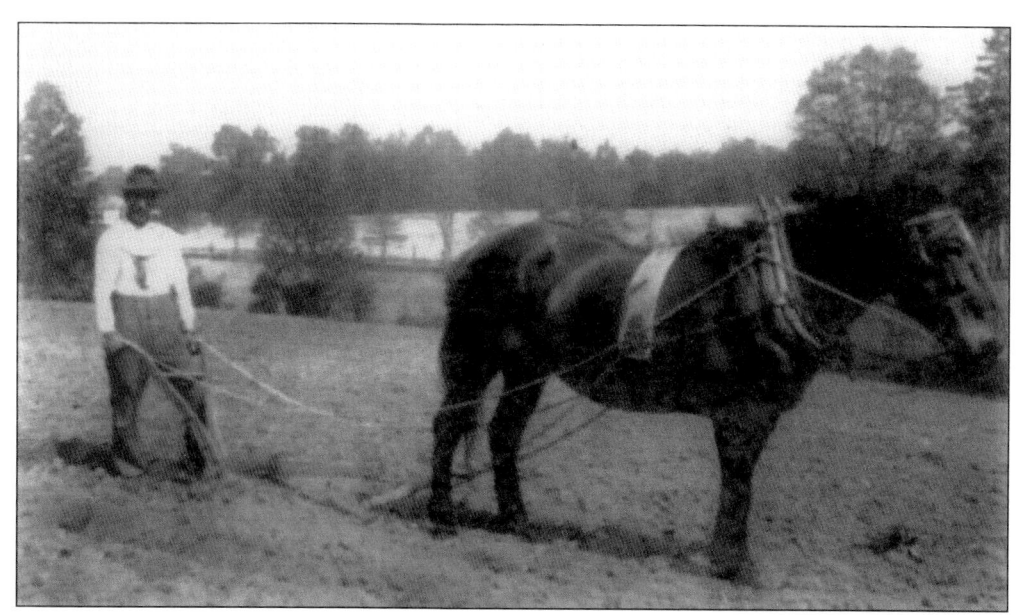

Richard L. Brooks, Cobb County's oldest blacksmith, died on December 3, 1956. He had moved from Cherokee in 1919. He is shown here plowing with Old Fanny on the Belmont Farms property. His blacksmith shop was next door to the cannery, which was later converted to Smyrna's first fire station. He retired in 1946. He and his wife, Adeline, and their 10 children lived on Roswell Street. (Courtesy Martha and Billy Akins.)

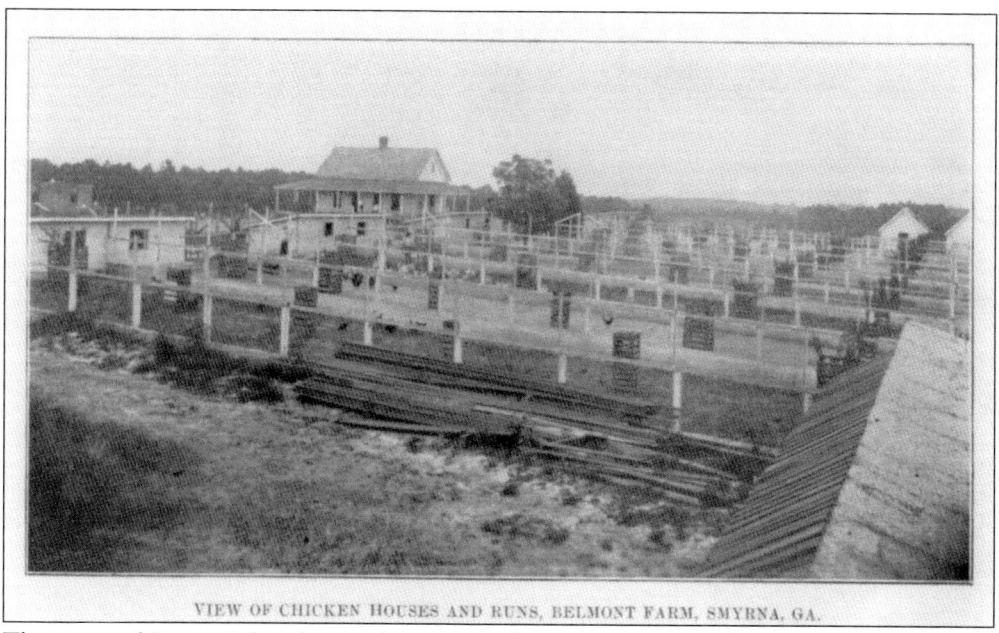

VIEW OF CHICKEN HOUSES AND RUNS, BELMONT FARM, SMYRNA, GA.

The name of Smyrna's best-known business in the early 1900s is still familiar today. Belmont Farms was co-owned by Ed Wight and his son. Loring Brown was the general superintendent. The Wights had moved to Smyrna in 1899. Brown was a well-known Georgia poultry fancier. The operation was described as the largest plant of its kind in the state by the 1900–1901 *Georgia Historical and Industrial Directory*. (Courtesy Ron Newcomb.)

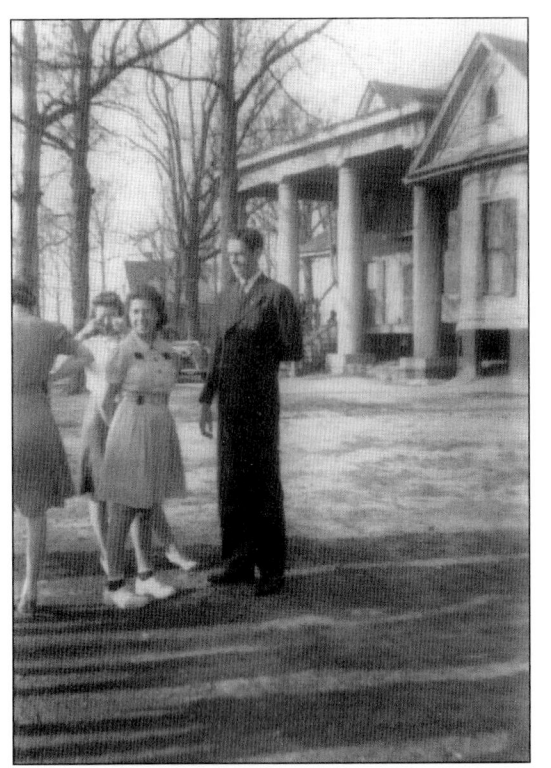

John C. Brooks and his parents, Homer and Nina Brooks, lived in the Belmont house after the farm operations were discontinued. The house had been converted to a multifamily facility, with a number of apartments. Seen here in the front yard are, from left to right, Inez Brooks, Nina Mae Brooks, Betty Cochran, and Homer Brooks. (Courtesy John C. Brooks.)

When Belmont Hills Shopping Center opened on November 18, 1954, it was the largest shopping center in the southeast, boasting 2,500 parking spaces. Its popularity came from many promotions, like the one shown below. "Miss Myrt," a national celebrity because of her phenomenal knowledge of baseball, which she demonstrated in appearances on national quiz shows, came to promote the shopping center. The Belmont House is seen on the left.

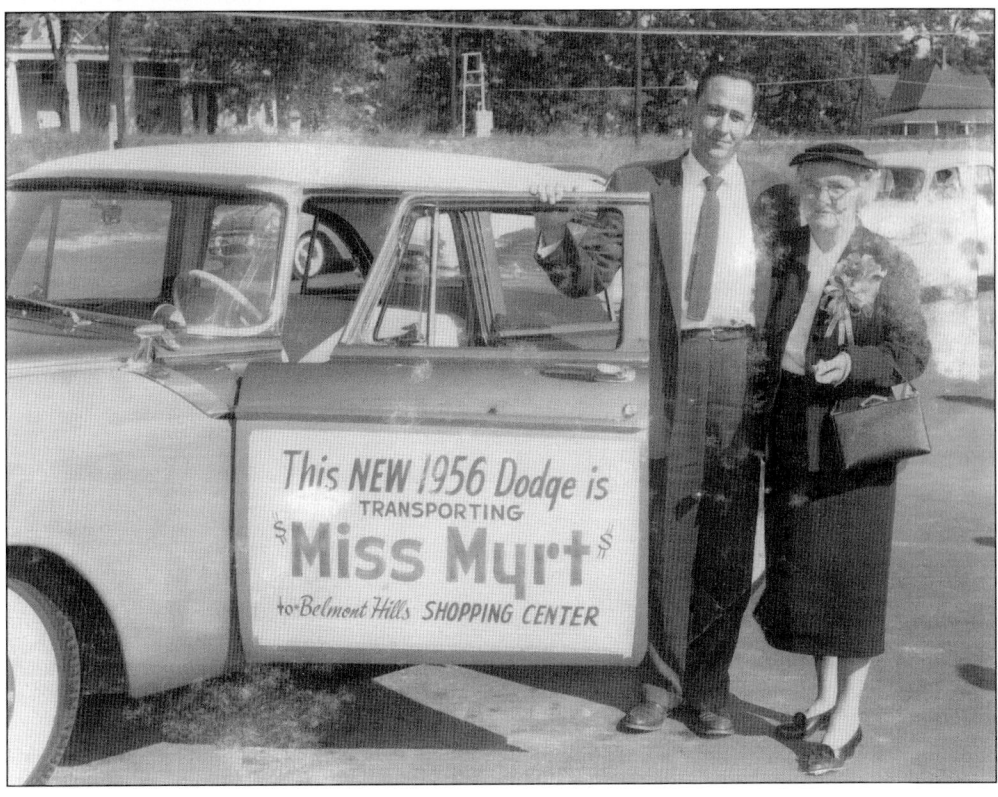

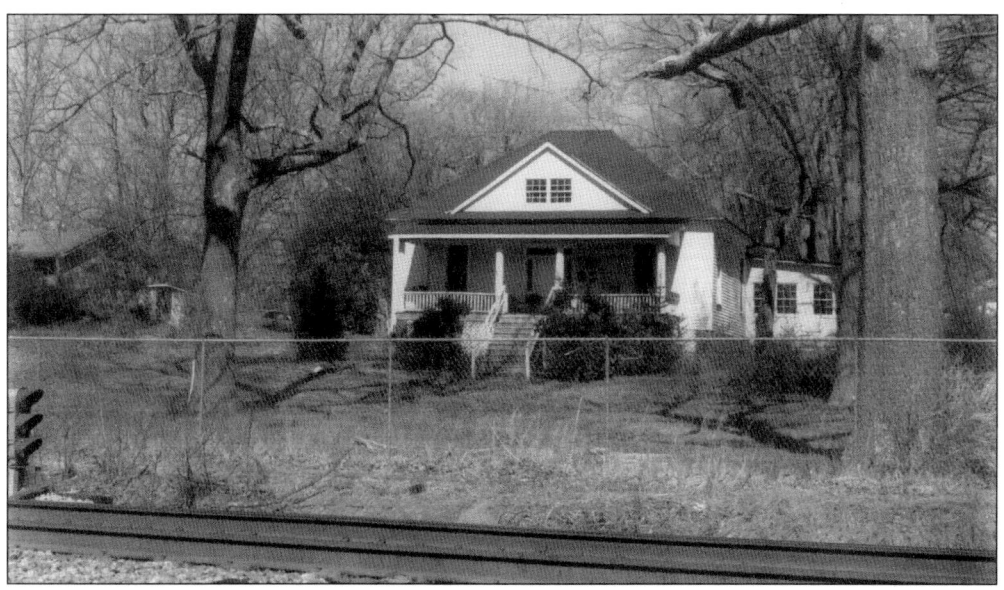

Mazie Whitfield Nelson was born in her home on Atlanta Road on January 1, 1890. She lived there until her death. She was Smyrna's library director from 1957 until December 1963. Her father, Thomas P. Whitfield, was a grocer for many years. Her grandfather, Thomas M. Whitfield, served on the city council. Mazie self-published her 42-page memoir, *Past, Present, and Future*, which was printed directly from her typed manuscript. She married Luther T. Nelson on June 1, 1922, but was widowed a few years later when her husband was killed in an automobile accident. Mazie Nelson sold insurance for the Macabees for more than 20 years. She was well known and loved by the citizens of Smyrna because of her work, both volunteer and paid, with the Smyrna Library. The historical marker in Smyrna Memorial tells her story.

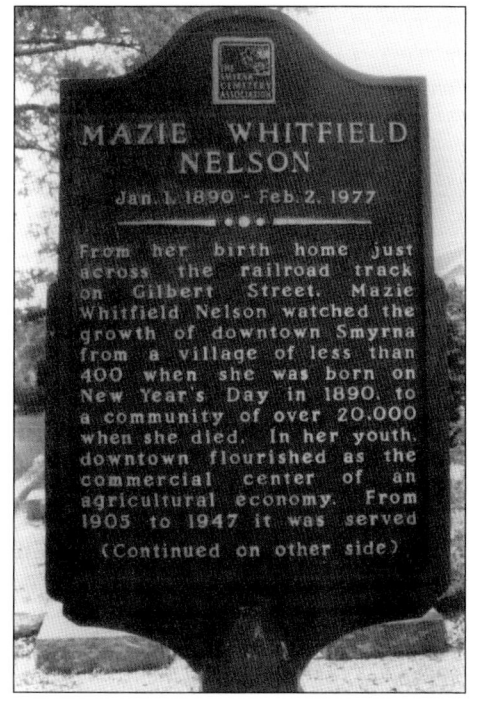

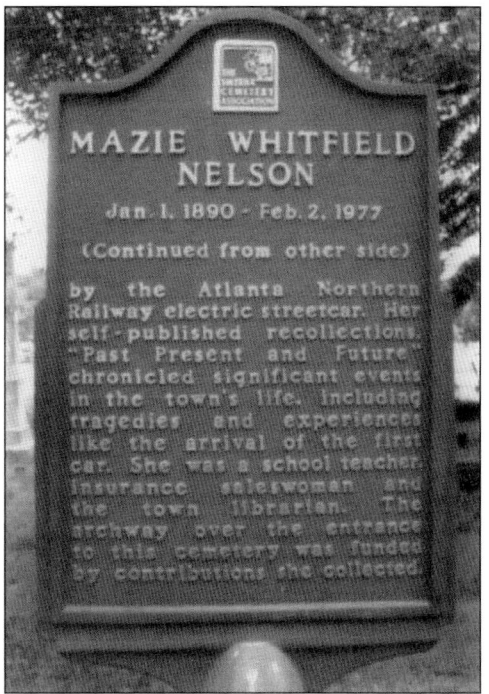

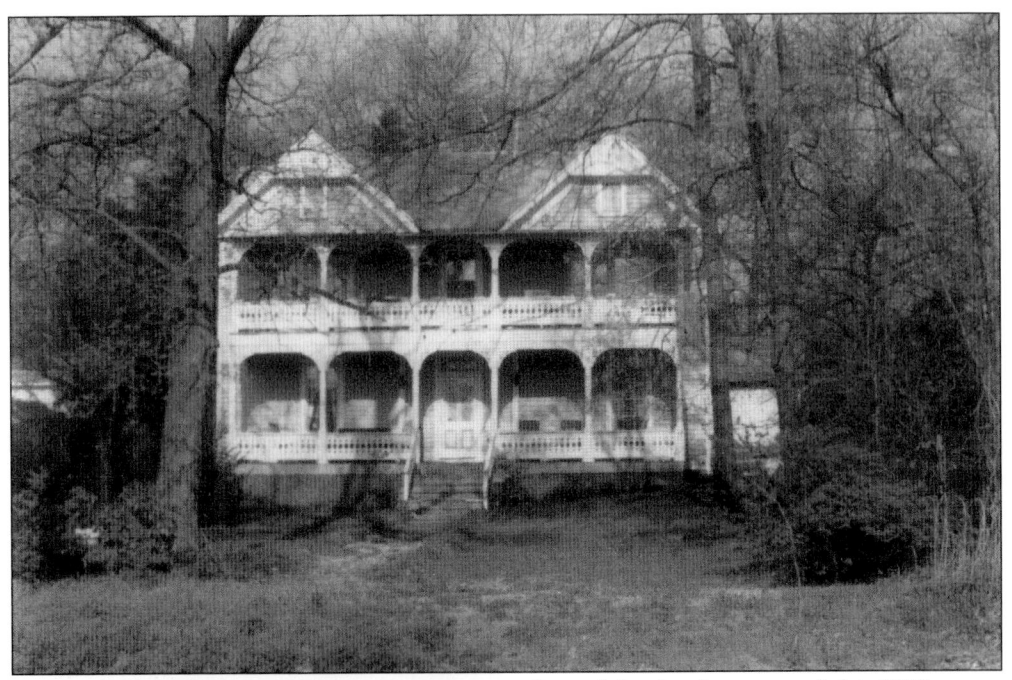

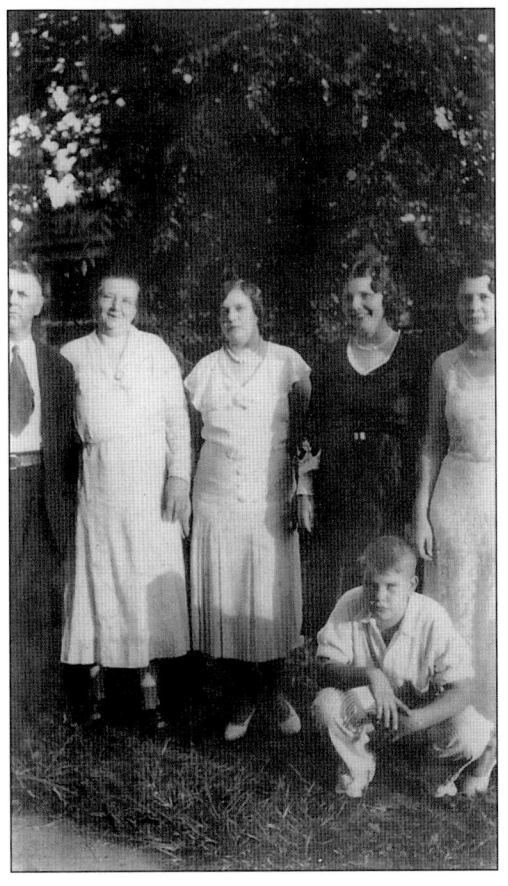

Several families have owned this 1880s home on the east side of Atlanta Road. It stands beyond the railroad tracks, almost directly across from the entrance to the Village Green. It is several hundred feet south of Mazie Whitfield Nelson's former home. The Reed family resided here for many years. (Courtesy Harold Smith.)

In this 1931 photograph are, from left to right, Benjamin Franklin and Palma Reed Sr. with their children, Gertrude, Vicki, Colene, and Bill. They are posing in front of the Reed House, which is shown in the photograph above. (Courtesy Mark Reed.)

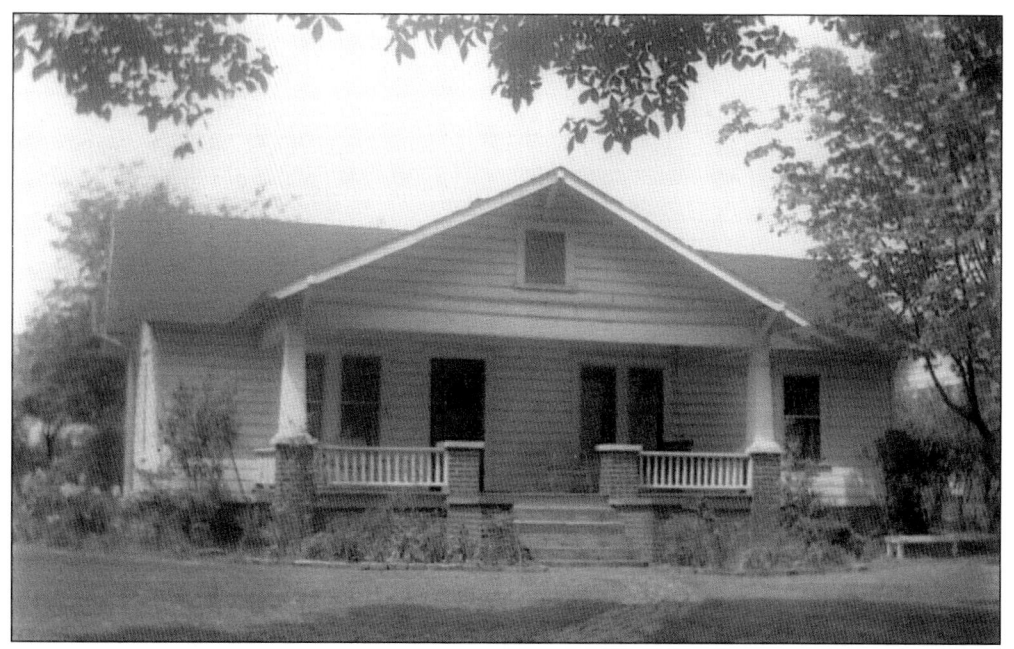

This 1928 photograph shows 377 North Atlanta Road, the home of Robert Lee and Zelma Motter. The house was typical of residences lining the main artery. Anyone sitting on the porch had a good view of the streetcars that passed through Smyrna. They could also see the Belmont stop, where passengers waited for arriving cars. The Motters had two children, Robert and Mary. (Courtesy Mary Motter Fowler.)

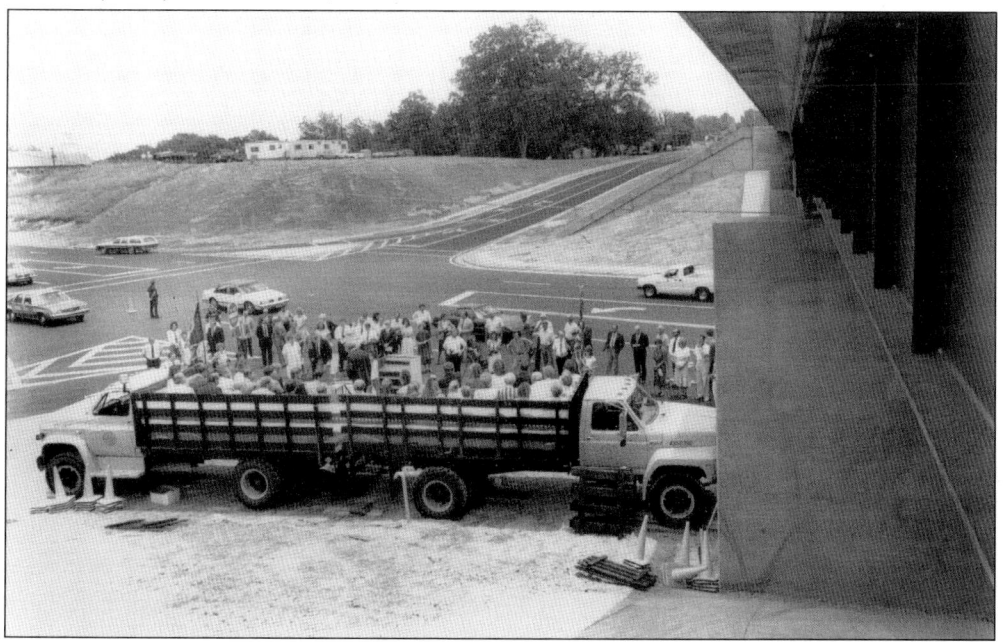

A major change in traffic occurred in 1987, when an underpass was installed where Cherokee Road had previously come to a dead end. The new route allowed a direct connection from Windy Hill to I-75. The underpass was later named the Arthur Bacon Underpass, in honor of Smyrna's former mayor and the father of the current mayor. He served two terms and died while still in office.

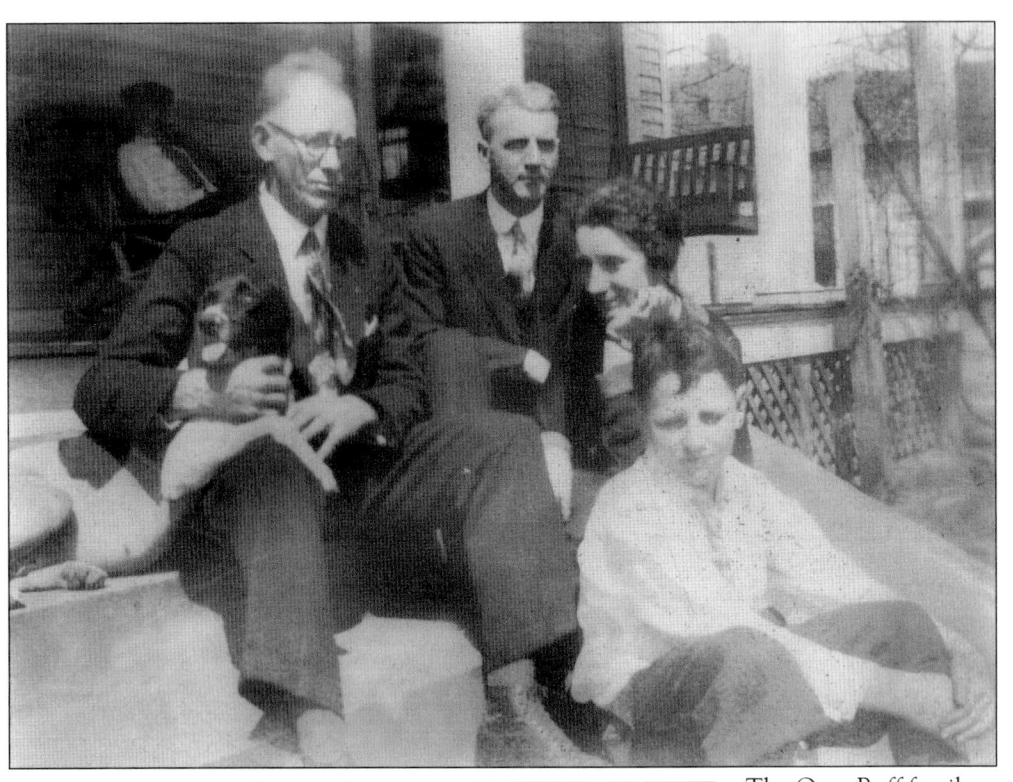

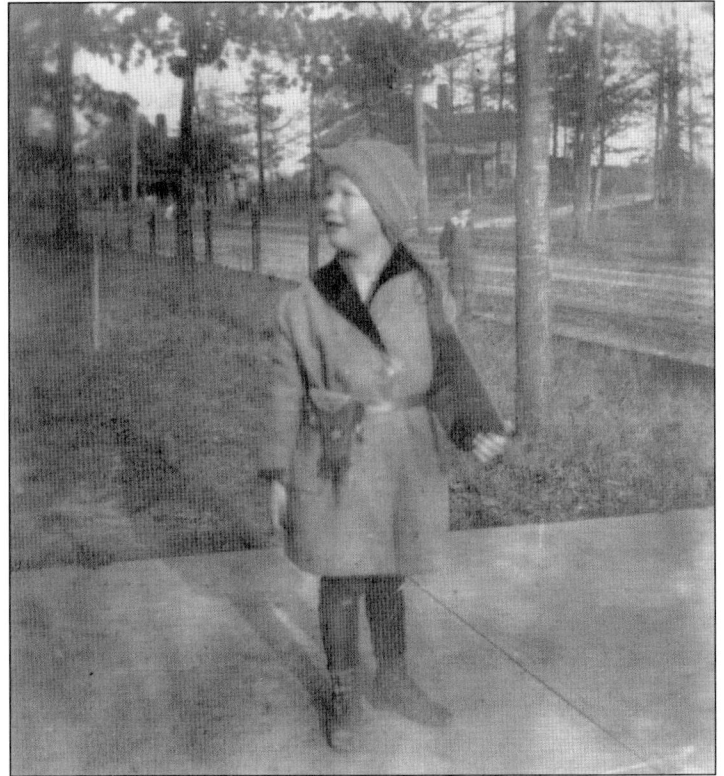

The Oren Ruff family posed together with a pet on the front porch of the Carl C. Terrell home on Roswell Street in 1927. (Courtesy Helen Terrell McGee.)

Bob McGee plays soldier in front of his Roswell Street home in 1919. The house is located in Smyrna's oldest neighborhood, now called Williams Park. The view is looking northeast toward the intersection of Whitfield Street. Note that Roswell Street is unpaved. (Courtesy Nancy McGee.)

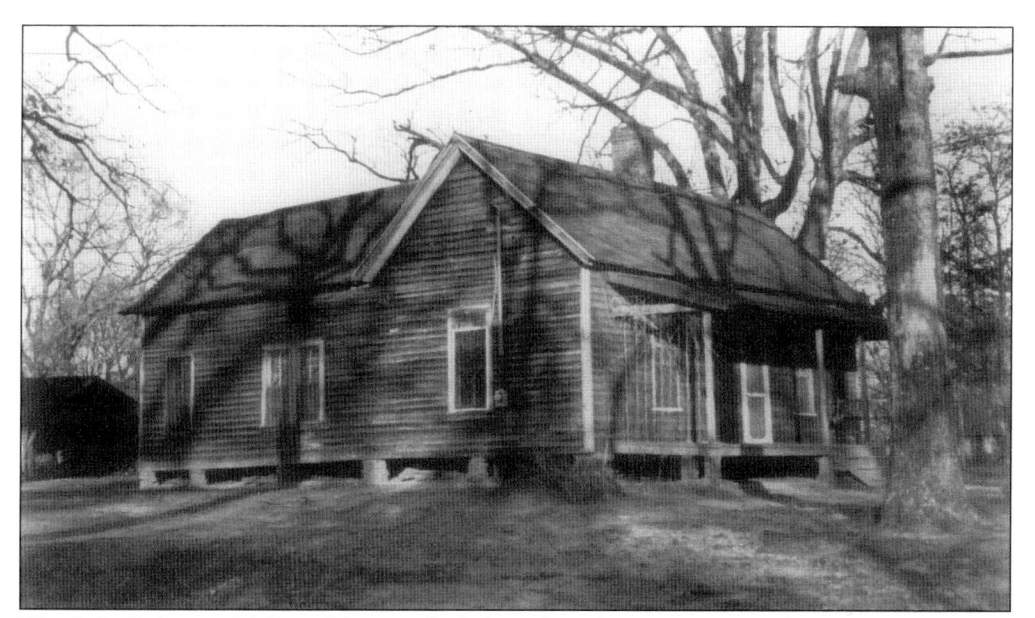

The Sadie Robinson McDowell home, which dates from the late 1800s, was located on East Spring Street near Mathews Street. The home remained in the Robinson family until it was demolished in the early 2000s. Joe and Sadie McDowell lived on Dixie Avenue with their children, Howard, Joann, and Shelba. Howard was pastor of Vinings First Baptist Church for many years. (Courtesy Joann McDowell.)

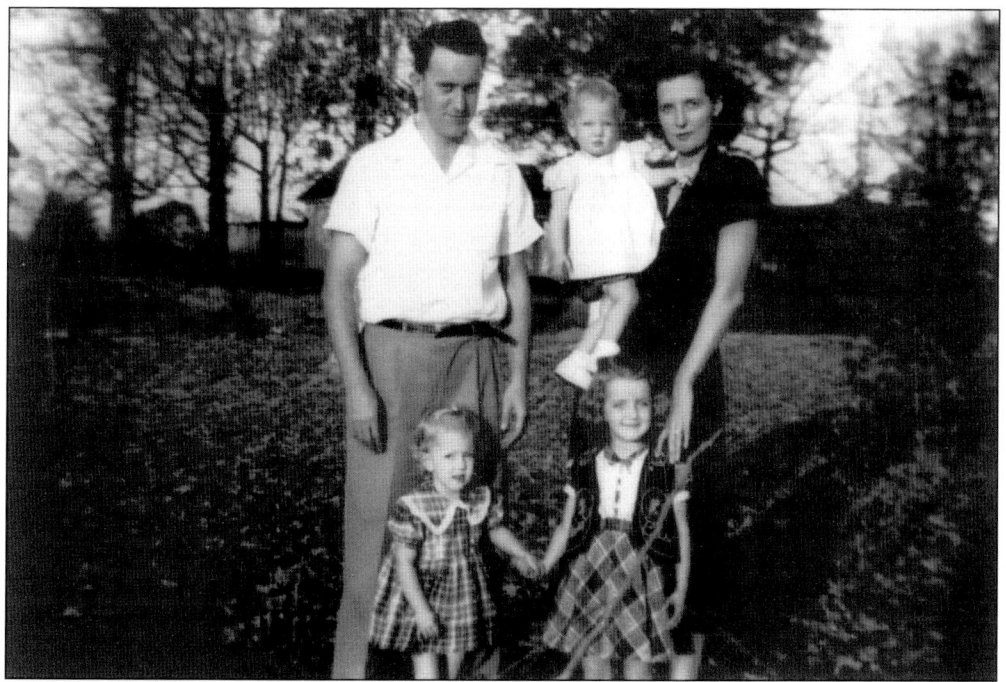

James Ira Moore and his wife, Martha, lived on Spring Street near the intersections of Anderson Circle and Matthews Street. The Moores lived across the street from the Robinson house, seen in the photograph above. Martha is holding Kathy. Janet (left) and Dianne are in front. (Courtesy Kathy Moore Graham.)

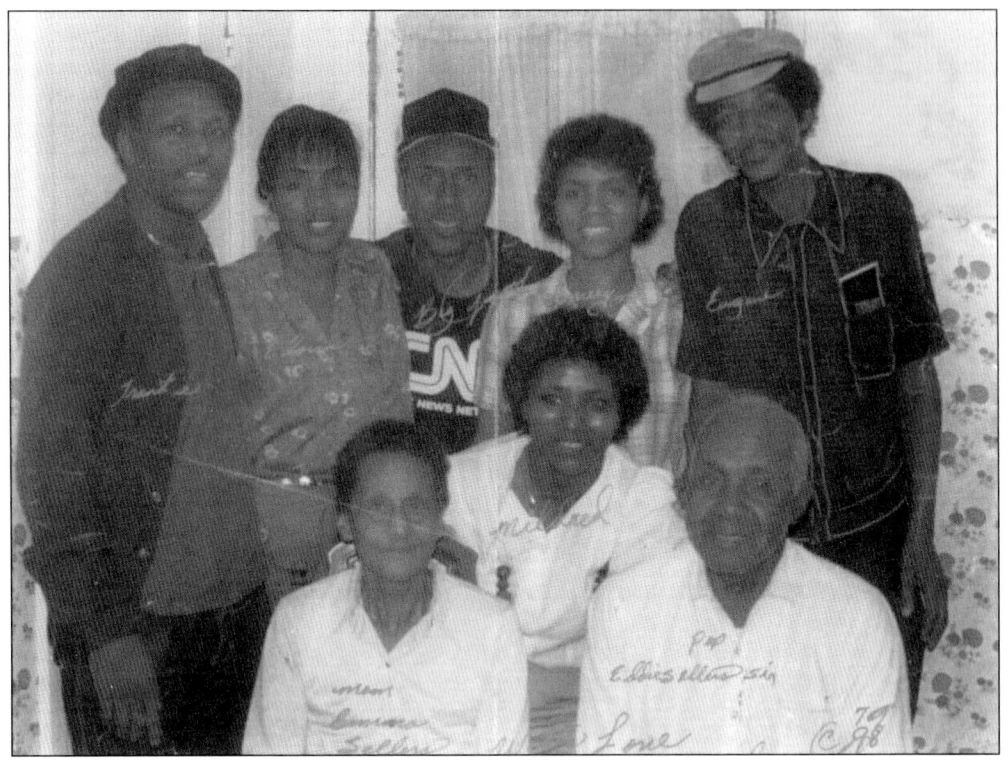

Davenport Town, on the eastern edge of Smyrna, was not annexed into the city until recent years. It was the first African American community in the area, dating to the late 1870s. The Sellers family, shown here, and their ancestors were early residents, and many still reside there. Shown here are, from left to right, (first row) "Mom" Emma, Mildred, and "Pop" Eddie; (second row) Frankie, Eloise, Jimmy, Emelyn, and Eugene. (Courtesy Jimmy Sellers.)

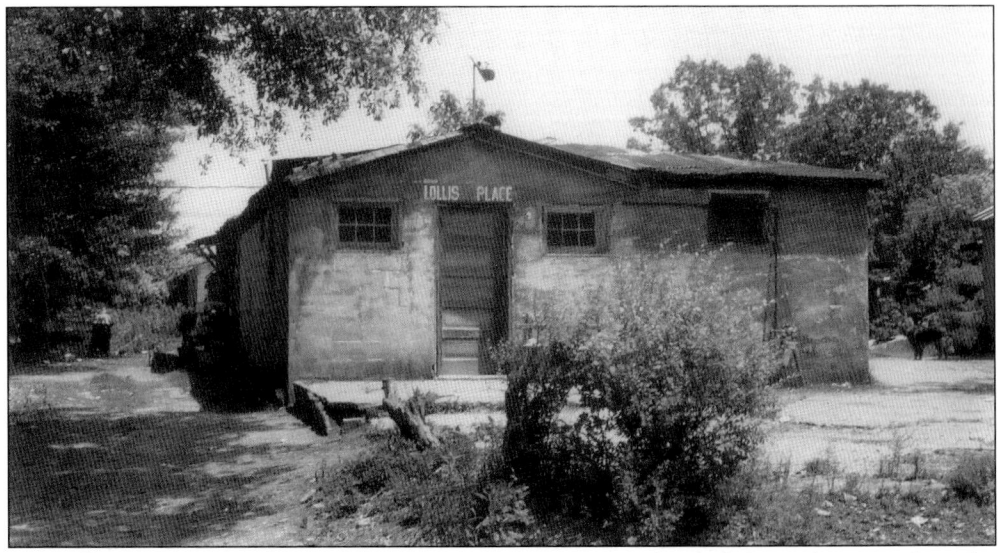

Lollis Place was a popular café at 151 Davenport Street. It was located across the street from the Mount Zion Baptist Church. This photograph was taken in June 1978 by Larry Blair. (Courtesy Larry Blair.)

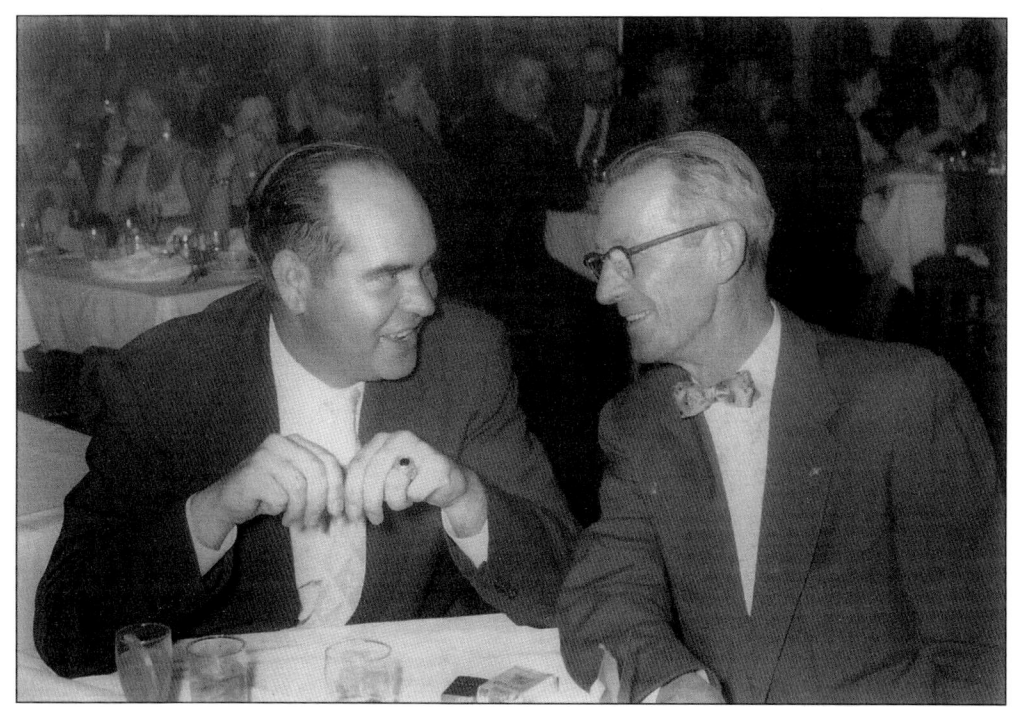

Having dinner at the American Legion Post are real estate developer Bill Reed (left) and Smyrna mayor J.M. "Hoot" Gibson. They were developers of one of the first middle-class African American suburban subdivisions in the state of Georgia. It was at the beginning of the tremendous growth that was brought about by the reopening of the old Bell Bomber Plant by the Lockheed Corporation. (Courtesy Mark Reed.)

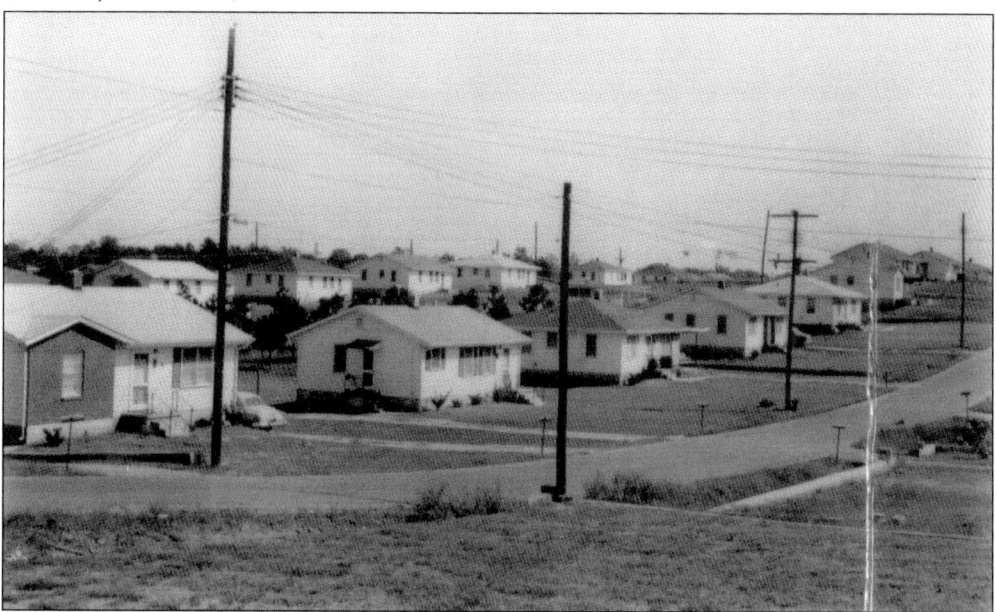

This Rose Garden Hills development was located in the area between Davenport Town on the west and Pasadena Boulevard (now Village Parkway) on the east. Prior to that time, the area had been farmland of the Chastain, Nash, and Crowe families. (Courtesy Keep Smyrna Beautiful.)

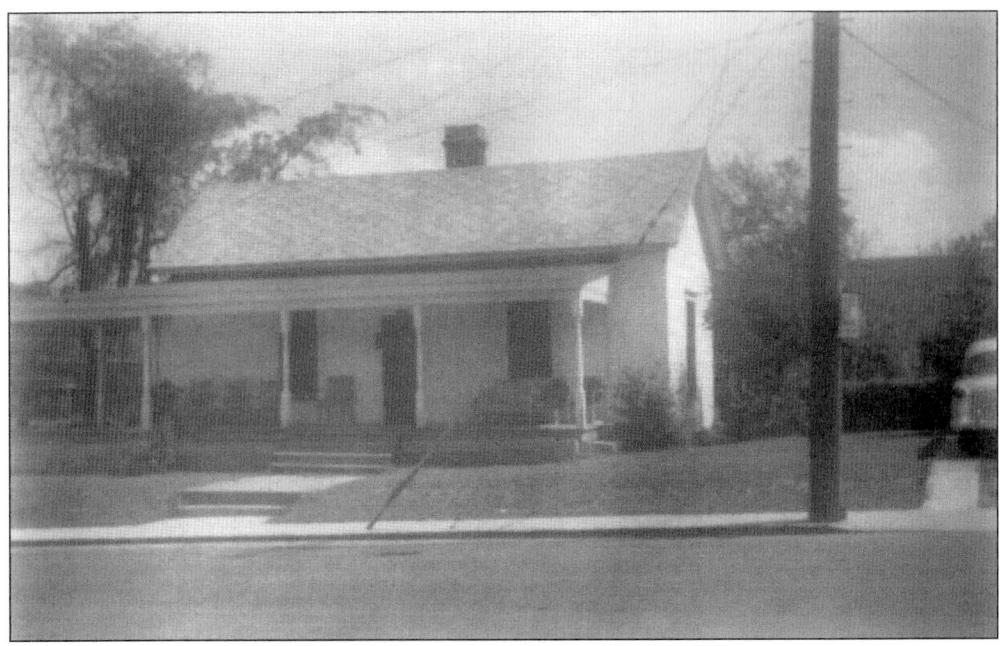

Construction of the Bank of Smyrna in 1910 brought about the name change from Ireland Street to Bank Street. The home seen here was the first residence constructed on Bank Street. When this photograph was taken, it was owned by Jennette Jackson. The first city hall was constructed in 1958 next door. The Jackson house was later purchased for additional city hall parking. (Courtesy Tommy Thatch.)

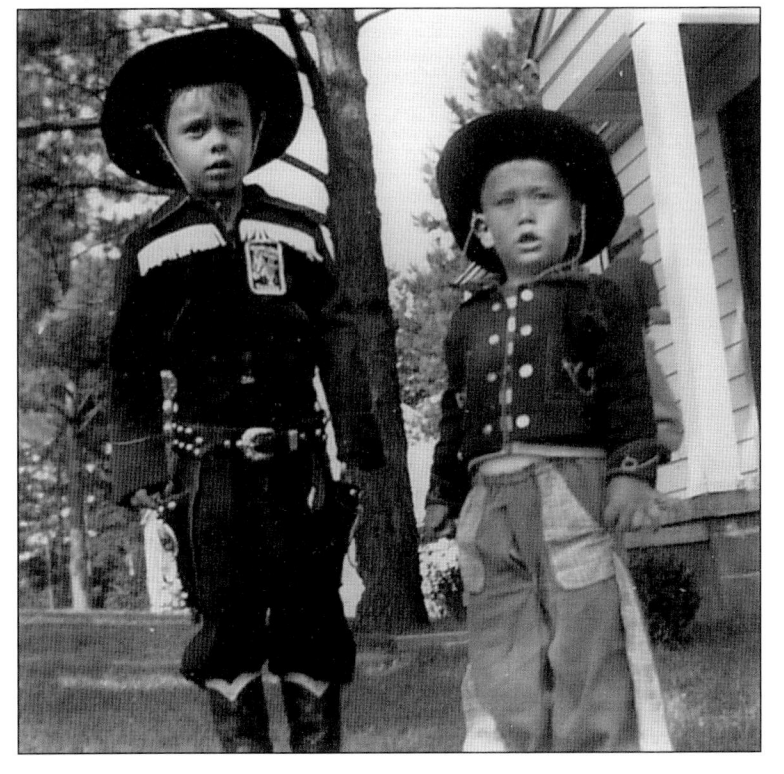

Mark Reed (left) was the son of real estate developer Bill Reed, a descendent of the Smyrna pioneer Reed family. The father of Wayne Colquitt (right), Hubert Colquitt, was instrumental in the development of downtown Smyrna in the early 1950s. The boys are playing cowboys and Indians on Bank Street.

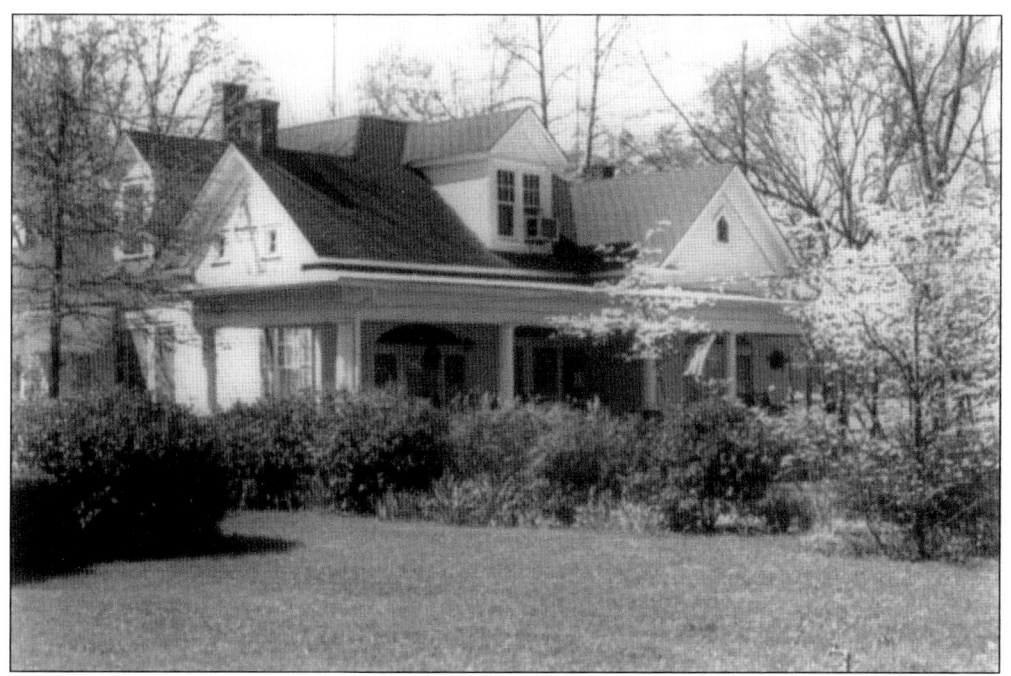

The yard at the home of Parker M. Rice, located at the intersection of Church and King Streets, was covered in bright yellow jonquils every spring. Bill and Juanita Sanders purchased the home and converted it to a funeral home. When it was damaged beyond repair by fire in 1980, it was replaced by the Carmichael Funeral Home.

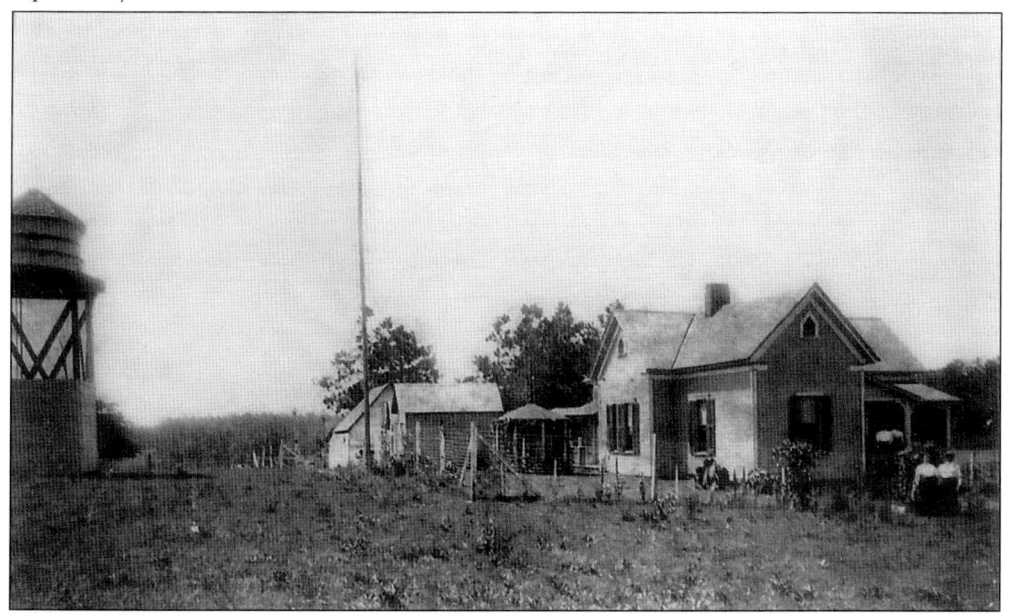

The Henry Gautchey residence, at Concord and King Springs Roads, was formerly the site of a distillery, which was closed after Prohibition was established. The home, later owned by J.J. Baldwin, Smyrna's first rural delivery postman, was one of the few houses in Smyrna that had its own water storage. The 15-acre farm included a barn, smokehouse, shed, and, of course, an outhouse. (Courtesy Robert Baldwin.)

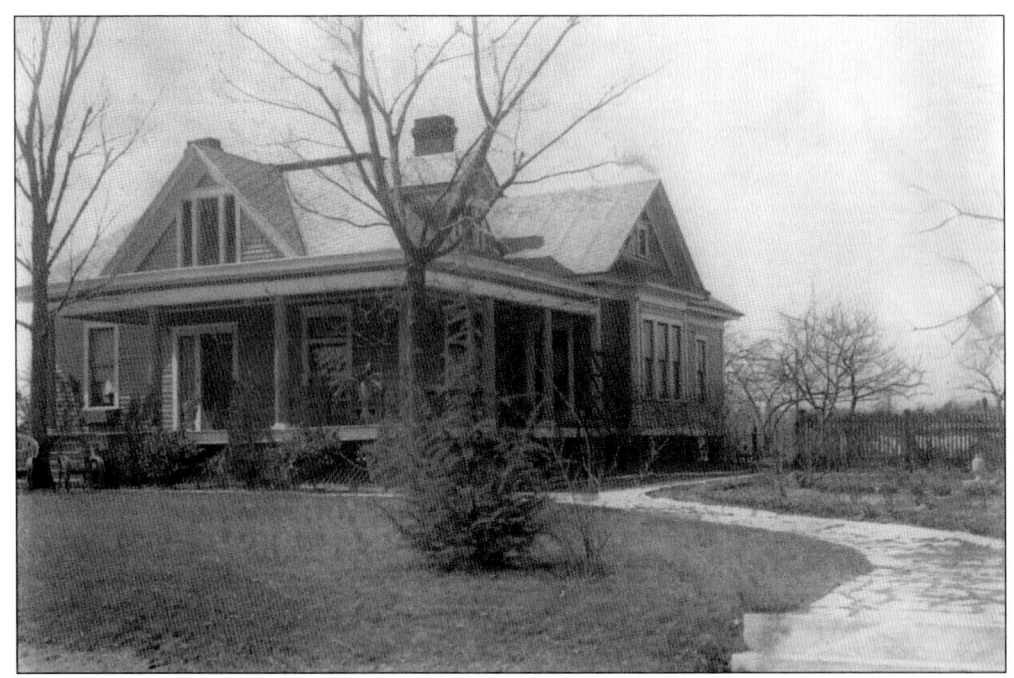

Joe and Jewell Camp lived on the north side of Concord Road along with their children, Mary Ellen, Mac, and Tom. Jewell was a teacher and also worked at the Bell Bomber Plant during World War II. (Courtesy Tom Camp.)

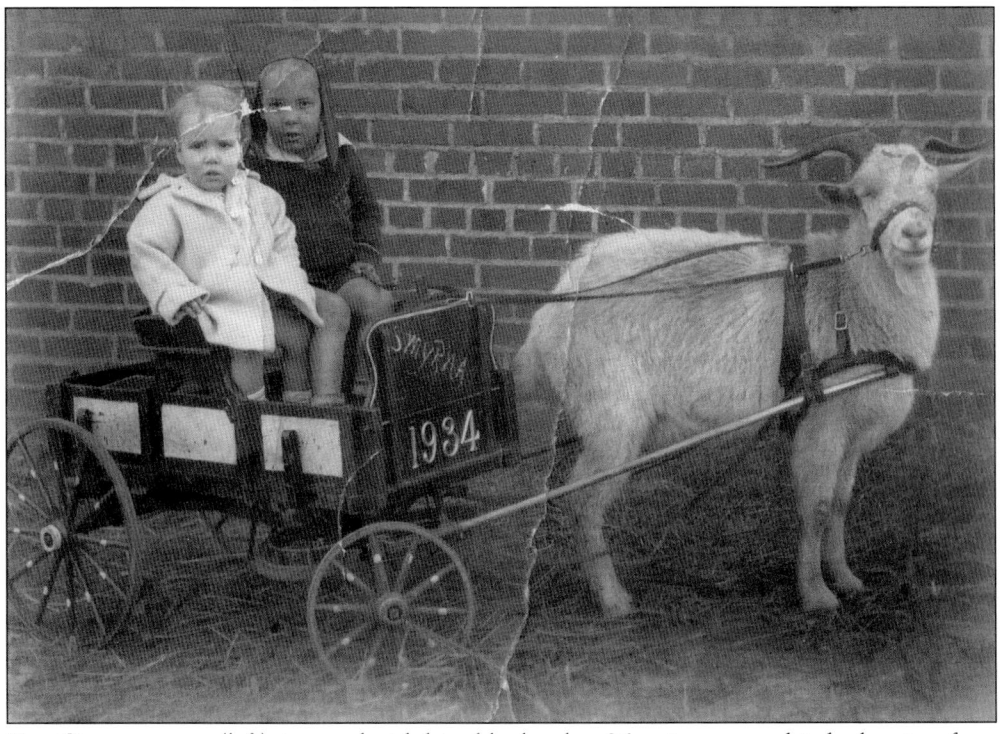

Tom Camp, age two (left), is seated with his older brother, Mac, in a wagon hitched up to a farm animal. (Courtesy Tom Camp.)

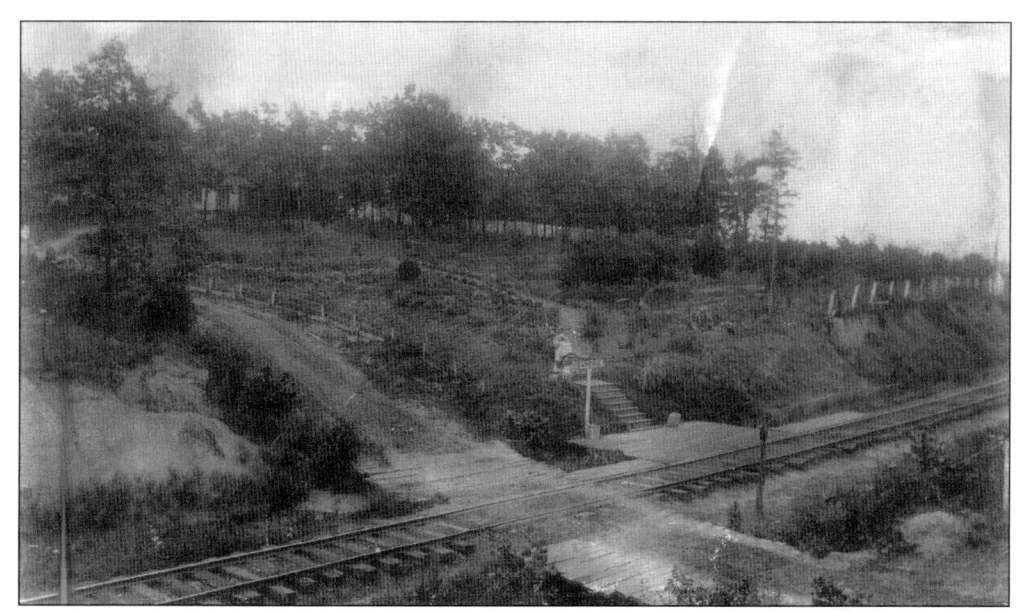

Argyle was named for the ancestral home of Richard Orme Campbell. Built in the late 1800s, it was originally a family summer home. Campbell's daughter, Isolene Campbell, later turned it into Aunt Fanny's Cabin Restaurant. Isolene is seen here in the arms of her mother at the landing near the Western & Atlantic Railroad tracks.

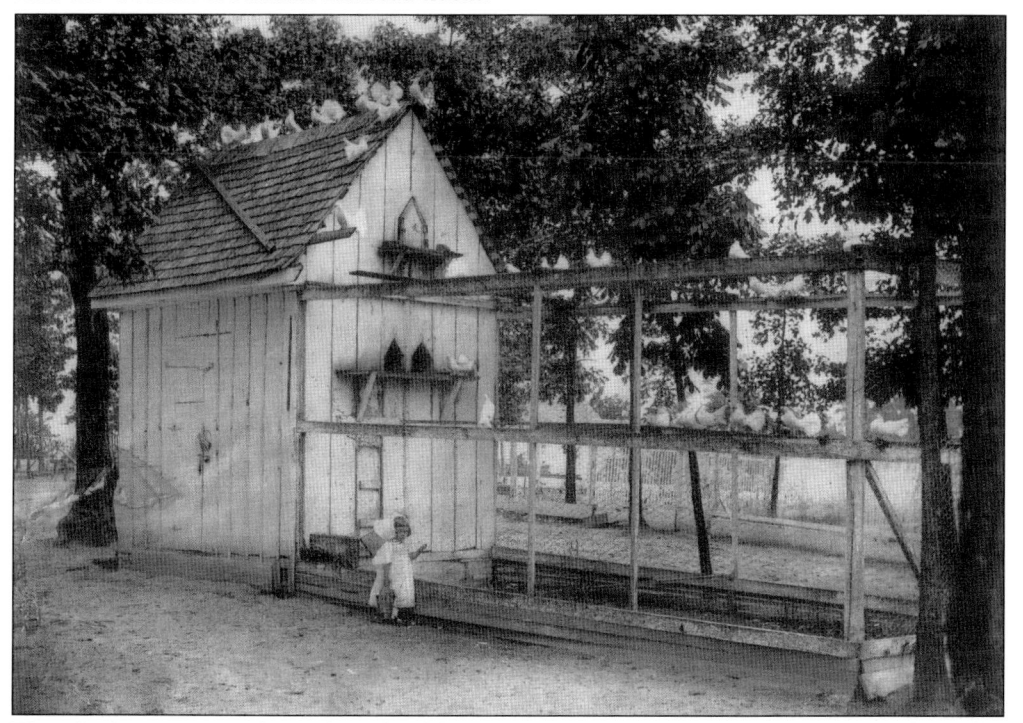

This chicken roost was located south of the Argyle house, in the area at the top of the hill seen in the photograph above. As a working farm, tenants raised vegetables that were then sold, along with eggs and other farm products. Isolene is standing near the bottom of the roost, near the chicken house.

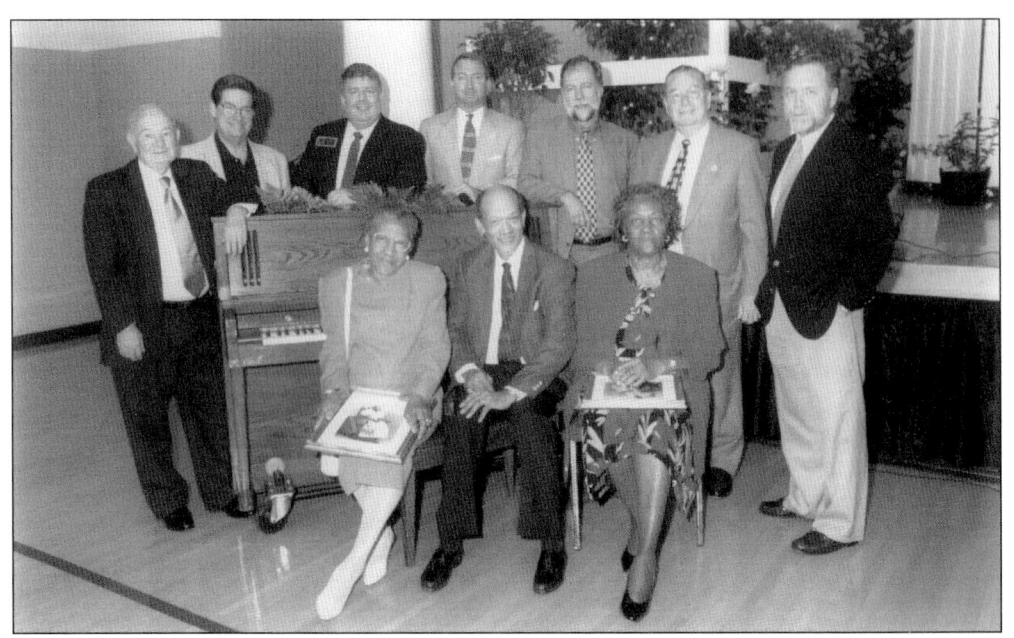

When the property on Campbell Road was sold for the construction of a subdivision, Frank Johnson purchased the historic Aunt Fanny's Cabin and donated it to the city. A relocation fundraiser was held on April 24, 1998. In attendance were, from left to right, (first row) an unidentified employee, the restaurant's former piano player, Bill Odum, and an unidentified employee; (second row) councilmen Pete Wood, Jim Hawkins, Wade Lnenicka, Jack Cramer, Ron Newcomb, and Mayor Max Bacon.

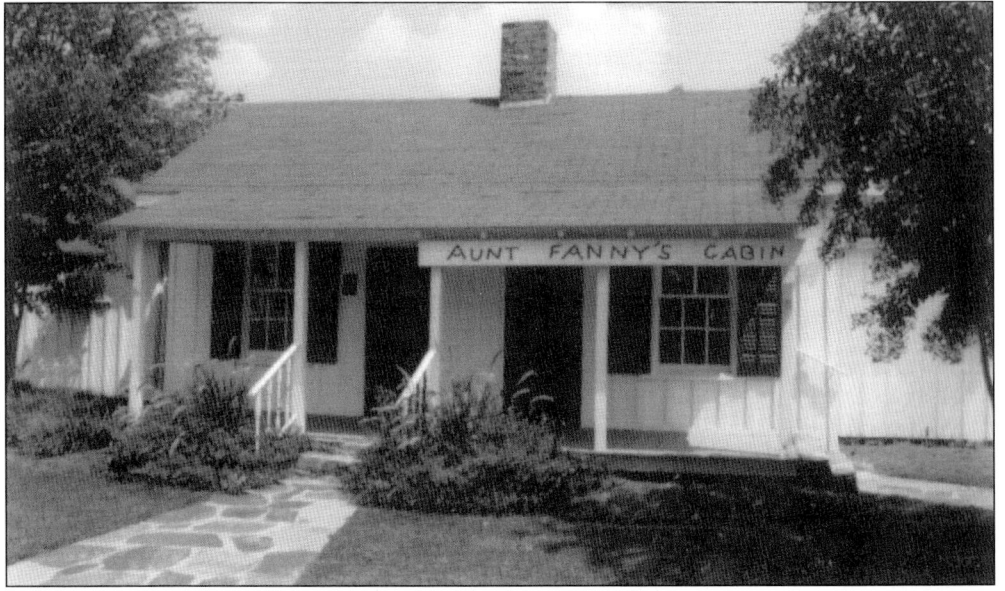

Aunt Fanny's Cabin opened in 1941 and was in operation until 1994. By 1945, it had become a place to see movie stars and other celebrities who were visiting the area. They would sign the guestbook, and many left autographed photographs. The 1890s cabin and terrace room, which was added in 1946, were moved downtown in 1999 and now serve as Smyrna's welcome center. Many of the old photographs are still on display.

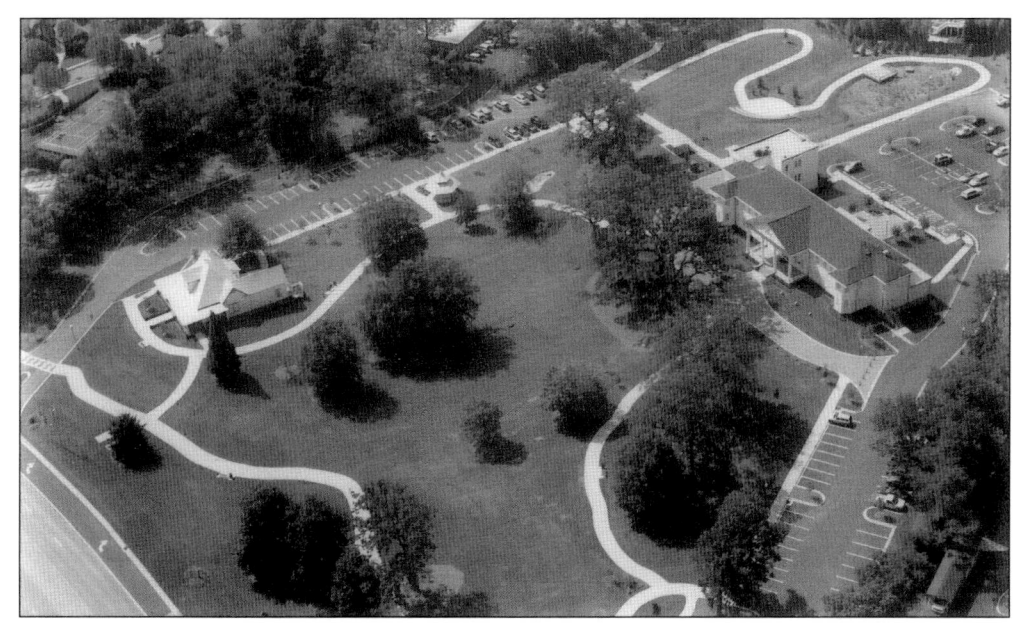

This aerial photograph by Jack Collings shows the 12-acre, 13-building complex known as Brawner Hospital. After the city purchased the complex, all of the structures were demolished except the hospital building and the Taylor-Brawner House. The two structures were restored by the nonprofit Taylor-Brawner House Preservation Foundation and are now listed in the National Register of Historic Places. They are the first registered structures in the city limits of Smyrna.

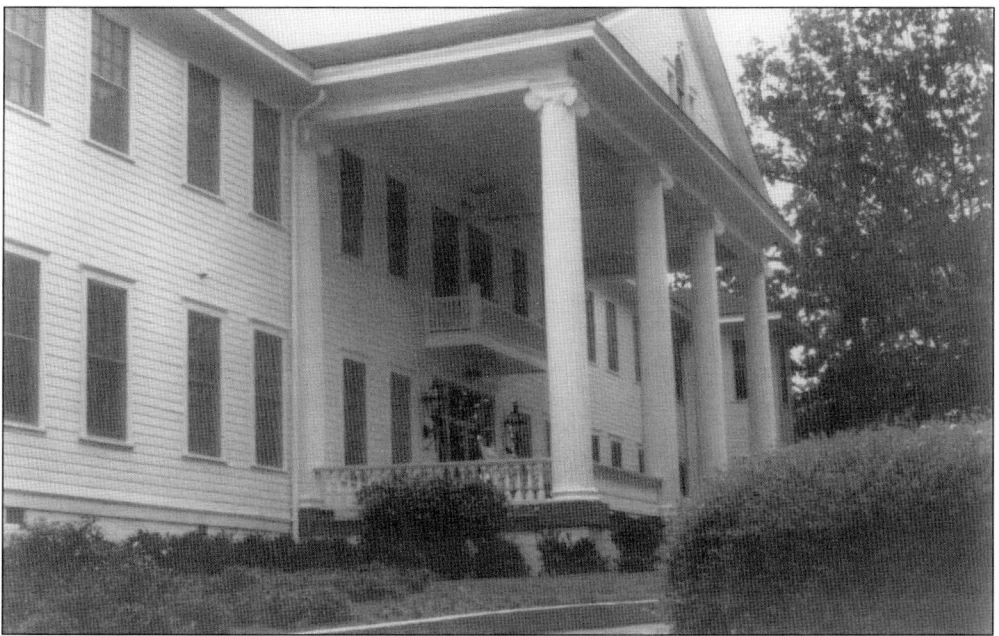

Dr. Albert Brawner, a mental health visionary, opened the Brawner Sanitarium, a world-class treatment facility for people with mental illnesses and addictions. His 13,000-square-foot hospital opened in 1910. Treatment regimens were modeled after successful hospital programs in Europe, where he had studied psychiatry. Dr. Brawner was instrumental in changing the public's perceptions of mental illness and setting higher expectations as to how it could be treated.

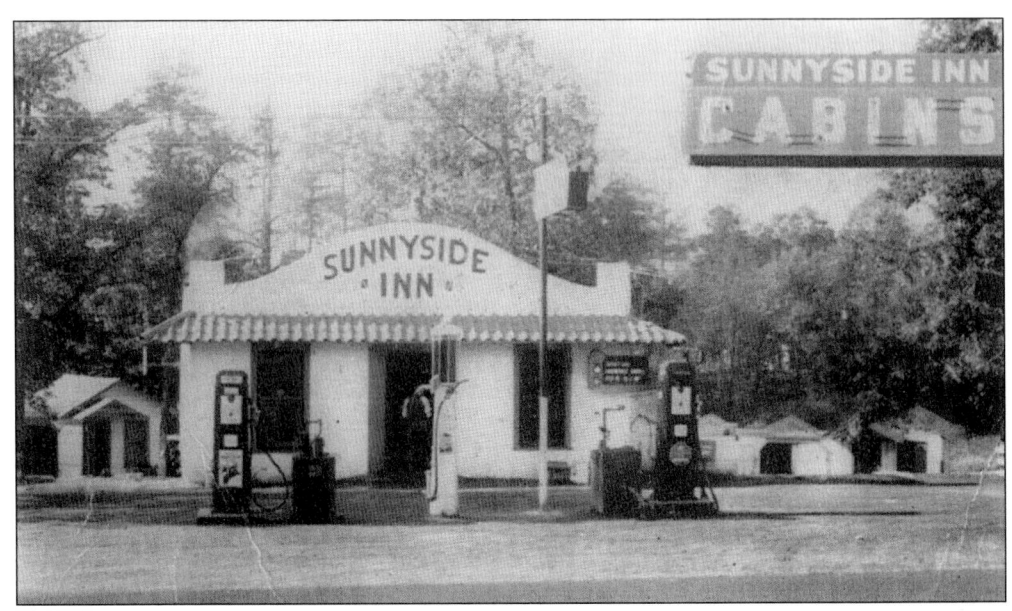

Sunnyside Inn and Tourist Court was located on US Highway 41 (The Dixie Highway), which stretched from Michigan to Florida. It was located across Atlanta Road from the intersection with Campbell Road. The business was owned and operated by the A.T. Parks family. (Courtesy Larry Osborne Blair.)

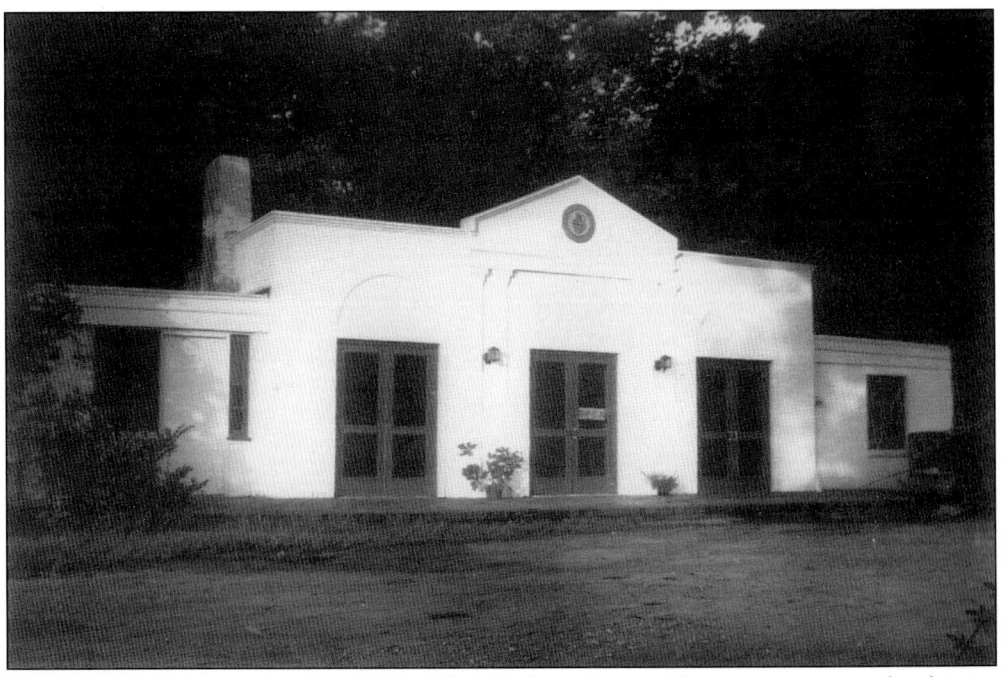

The Guernsey Jug was opened in 1931 by Edith Hudgins Crowe. The restaurant specialized in ice cream, milkshakes, sandwiches, hamburgers, and snacks. Crowe was the widow of Dr. Walter A. Crowe. The restaurant, located on Atlanta Road, was popular with the tourist trade. The "Jug" was billed as a roadside market of Creatwood Farm and Dairy, developed primarily for the sale of products from the dairy.

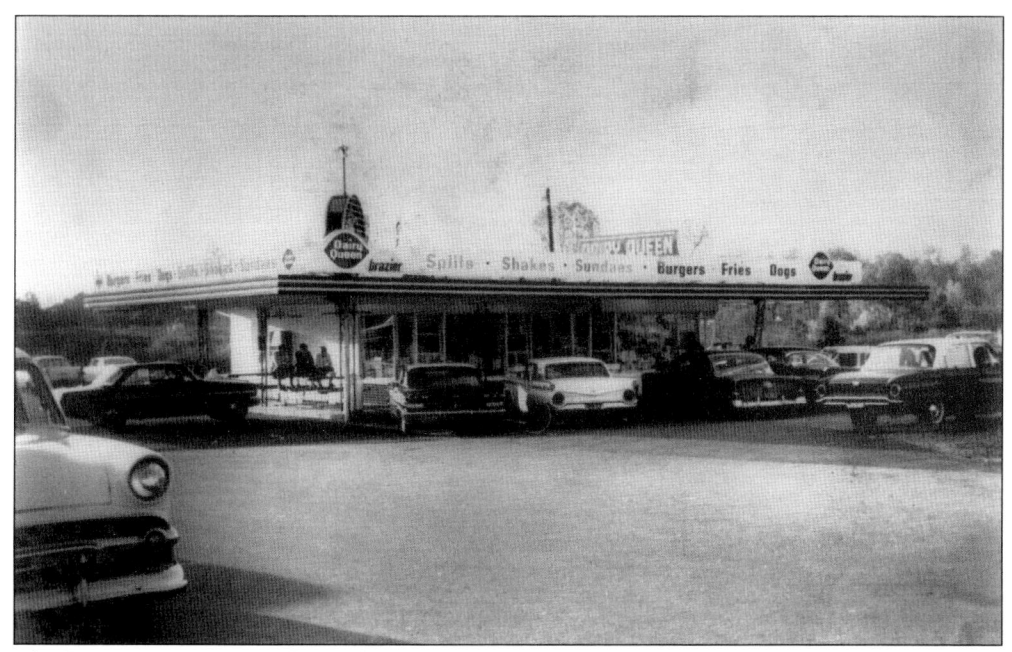

The Dairy Queen Brazier, located at 370 South Cobb Drive, was named No. 1 in the nation in total sales volume as of April 1, 1962. It was owned by Mr. and Mrs. John D. Sargent and, later, by Bogie and Dale Sargent Stoner and their son, Georgia state senator Doug Stoner. This photograph was taken in October 1962. (Courtesy *Smyrna Herald*.)

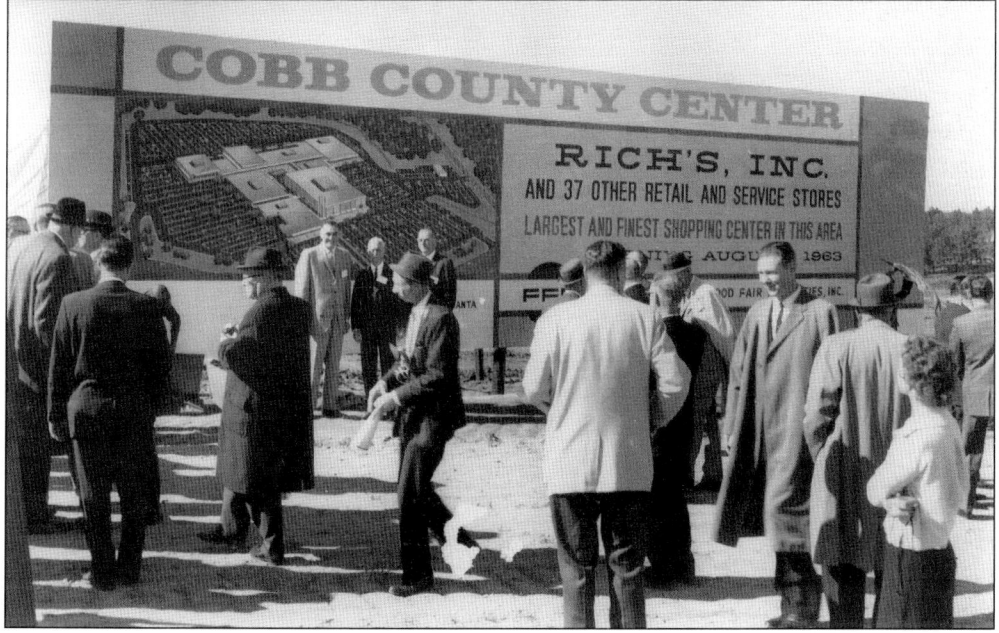

Opening in 1963, Cobb Center Mall on South Cobb Drive featured the first location for Rich's Department Store outside Atlanta. Cobb Center drew people away from Belmont Hills until Cumberland Mall opened in 1973 as the largest mall in the United States, with 1.2 million square feet. Cumberland Mall was the only mall in Georgia with Davison's, Rich's, J.C. Penney, and Sears. (Courtesy *Smyrna Herald*.)

85

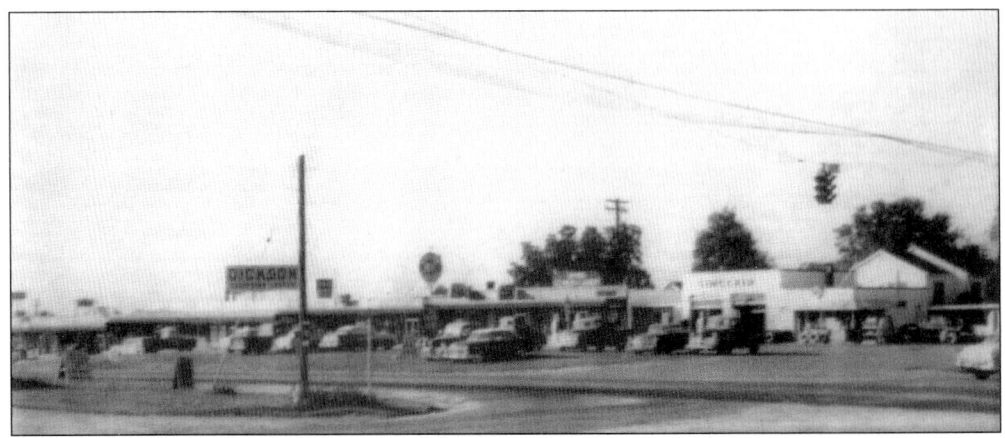

Dickson Shopping Center grew from one grocery store located on "Access Highway" (South Cobb Drive) to become one of the most enduring centers in the area. The highway was built after the beginning of World War II for easy access from Atlanta for employees of the Bell Bomber Plant. The shopping center was annexed into the Smyrna city limits in 1959 and is still owned and operated by T.L. Dickson's son, John, and his family.

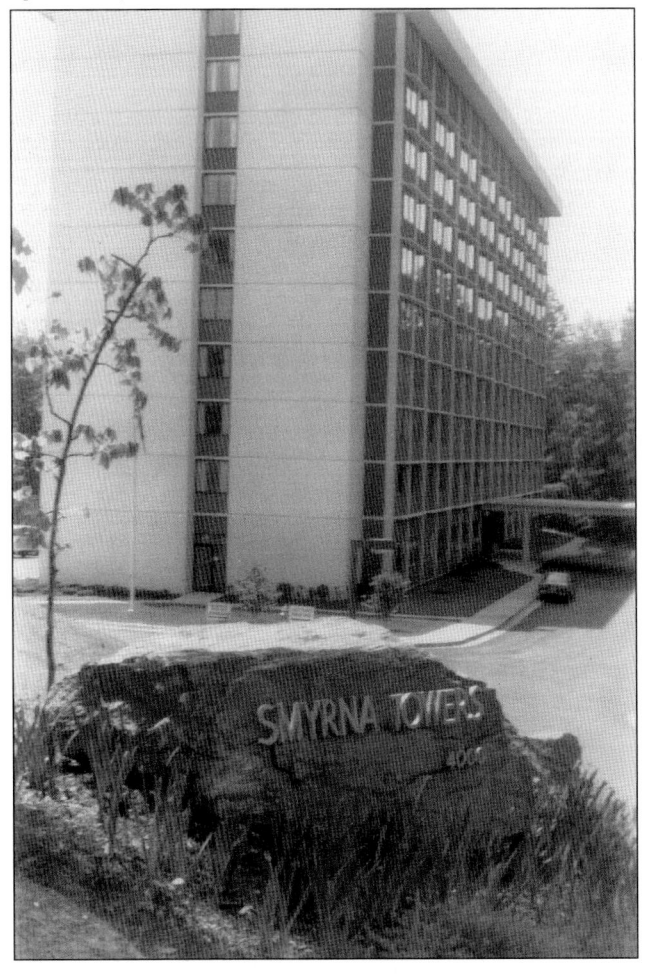

Smyrna Towers, located on South Cobb Drive, is the tallest building in Smyrna. Constructed in 1979, it houses a community of 160 independent-living residents, age 62 and older. The Towers was a joint project of Smyrna Hospital and the Georgia Conference Association of Seventh-day Adventists. The rent is based on the resident's income. The facility provides a variety of civic, church, and community involvement.

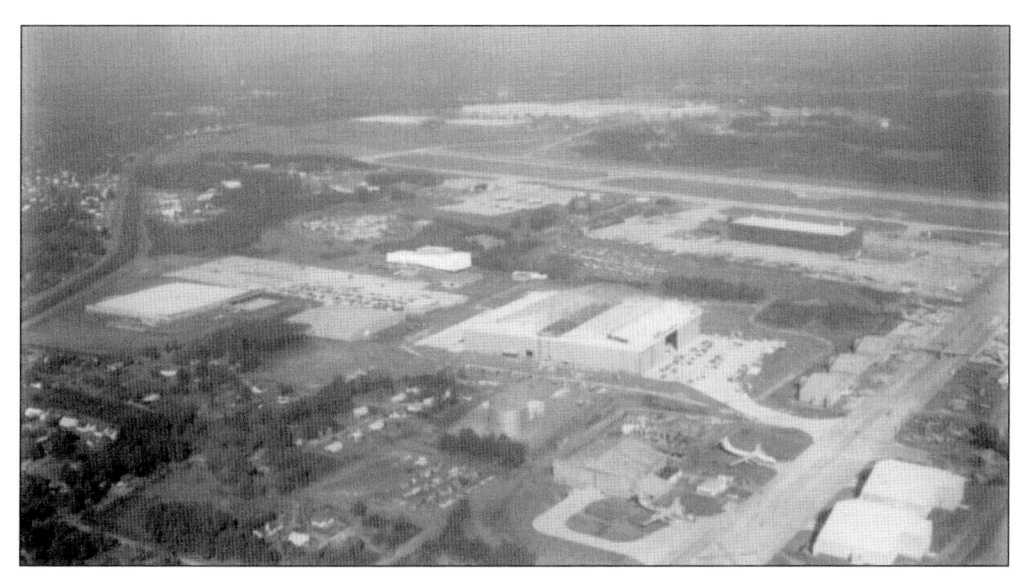

The population of Smyrna mushroomed, from 2,005 residents in 1950 to over 10,000 at the end of the decade. Lockheed Georgia had reopened the Bell Bomber Plant in 1951 (pictured here in 1968), creating thousands of jobs and a high demand for housing. A large housing development was built off Cherokee Road, with streets named after cities in California, the home state of Lockheed corporate headquarters. Smyrna's population nearly doubled, to 19,157 residents, by 1970.

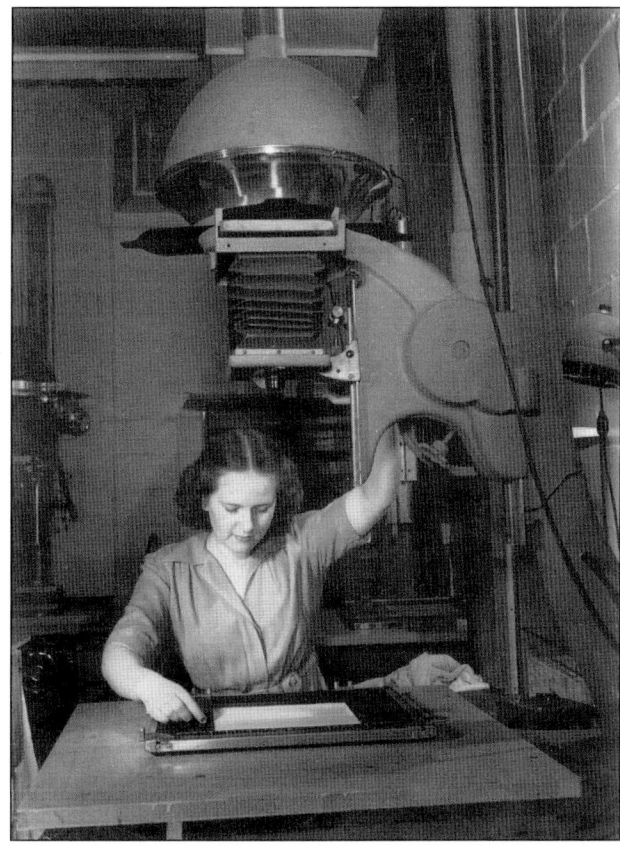

Louise Lindley Harper, a Smyrna native and an active member in many civic and service clubs, was a professional photographer. When the Bell Bomber Plant opened in the early 1940s, she worked in the photography lab at the new plant until the end of World War II.

87

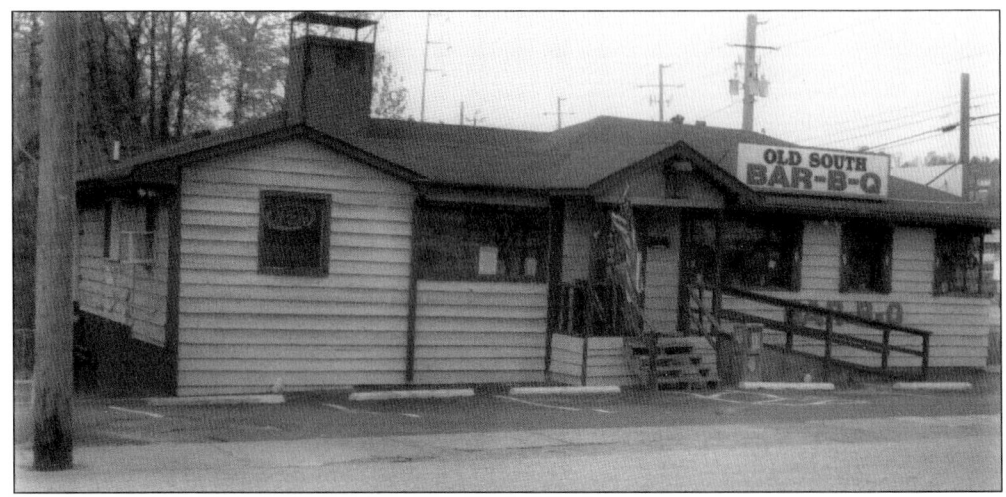

Old South Bar-B-Q is one of only 10 restaurants in Cobb County remaining since the 1960s. Still in the same location as when Jim and Helen Llwallyn opened it in 1968, the five-room house, built around 1950, has seen few changes. Hundreds of photographs of customers line the walls. People return for the best barbeque in Smyrna and a hug from the friendliest people, including members of the Llwallyn family, who still own and operate the restaurant.

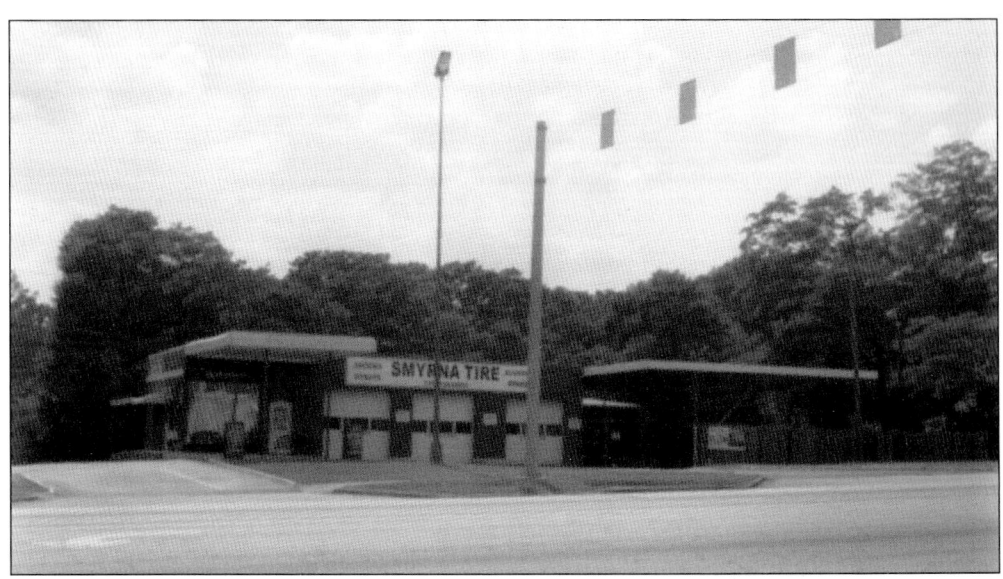

In 1973, Bobby Myers opened Smyrna Tire Company on the corner of Smyrna Powder Spring Road and South Cobb Drive. A previous occupant at the location was a Gulf service station, operated by James E. and Estelle Fortner, who lived just a few houses down from the station. Bobby Myers recently passed away; however, his family still runs Smyrna Tire.

Five

ORGANIZATIONS, CLUBS, AND SCHOOLS

As early as the 1880s, a number of organizations and clubs were contributing to the civic and social life of Smyrna. No official records have been found for most of these organizations, but newspaper accounts mention names of officers and activities of some in almost every edition. Early civic organizations included the International Order of Odd Fellows, International Order of Grand Templars, Shakespeare Reading Club, Brothers and Sisters of Love, Rook & Bridge, Canasta, Music Clubs, and various organizations of farmers.

The oldest continuous organization in Smyrna, other than some churches, is Nelms Mason Lodge 323. This organization includes Order of Eastern Star, Order of Rainbow, and Demolay. The Smyrna Social Club for young ladies formed in 1908, and the Smyrna Woman's Club was formed in 1925. The Smyrna Men's Club, organized in July 1933, helped the ladies finance the library. In the 1950s, it evolved into the Smyrna Chamber of Commerce, which later became a division of the Cobb Chamber of Commerce.

Of the garden clubs, the Jonquil Club has the longest history. Organized in October 1937, it has been in the forefront of helping the city look beautiful, and in social and civic life as well. As the town grew in the early 1960s, neighborhood garden clubs emerged: Argyle, Whispering Pines, Azalea, Green Ridge, Green Acres, Hoe & Hope, Log Cabin, Pretty Branch, and others. Of the older clubs, one of the few that survived is the Jonquil Garden Club. Another club that has remained active is the Bennett Woods Garden Club, founded in 1974. Its activities have promoted a variety of citywide projects to raise money for many good causes.

Among the service organizations was the Smyrna Lion's Club, organized in 1947. It was disbanded, along with its female auxiliary, shortly after its 50th anniversary. Also in 1947, the Smyrna American Legion Post 160 was organized. It annually co-sponsors Memorial Day activities with the 20th Century Veterans Association, which was organized to construct a memorial on Village Green to the veterans. The Smyrna Jaycees, chartered in 1959, conducted major projects, like constructing a new health clinic and administering the first polio vaccines. It disbanded several years ago. The Rotary Club, organized in December 1967, continues its weekly meeting as an active force among Smyrna businesspeople. The Smyrna-Oakdale Moose Lodge sponsors a variety of activities. The Smyrna Optimist Club, organized in April 1962, has weekly breakfast meetings. Its motto is "Friend of Youth."

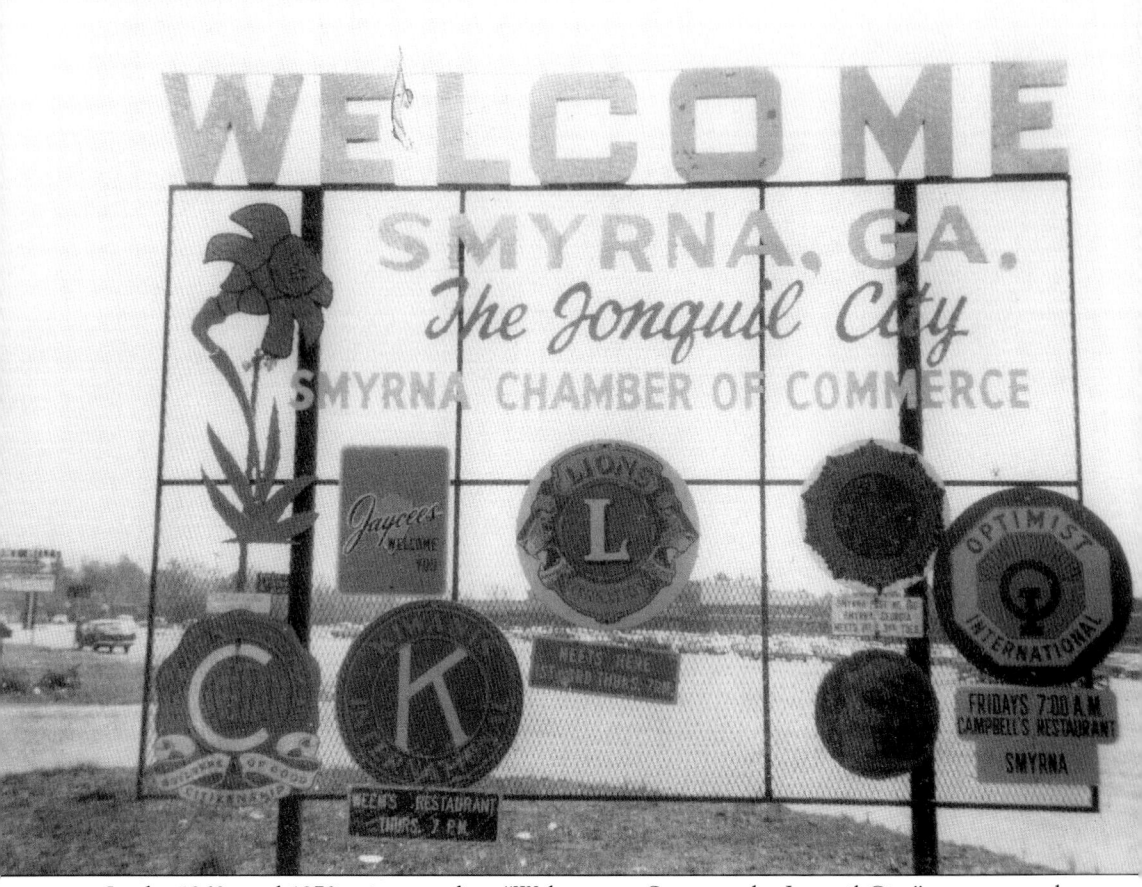

In the 1960s and 1970s, signs reading "Welcome to Smyrna, the Jonquil City" were erected on every major road leading into the city. They were a joint effort of many of the civic and service organizations that provided the leadership Smyrna needed for decades of growth, when hundreds of families were moving from the inner city to the suburbs.

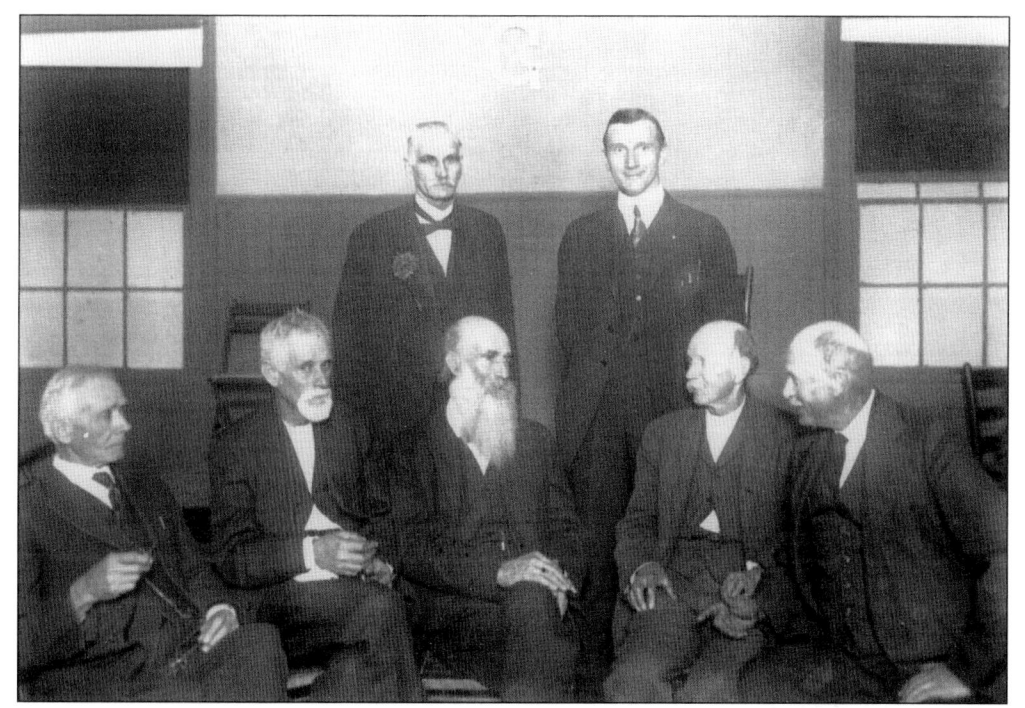

On November 12, 1886, Georgia Nelms Lodge No. 323 of Free and Accepted Masons was chartered. The founding members were John Stone, W.H. Baldwin, John Henry Cantrell, J.N. Dodge, Rufus A. Eaton, T.P. Whitfield, J.R. Kendley, Stephen Blair, John W. Irelan, A.T. Hill, John L. Reed, John H. Turner, Thomas M. Hooper, James R. Love, Benjamin F. Mackey, and John W. Nelms. Many members served as Smyrna mayors and councilmen. (Courtesy Nelms Lodge.)

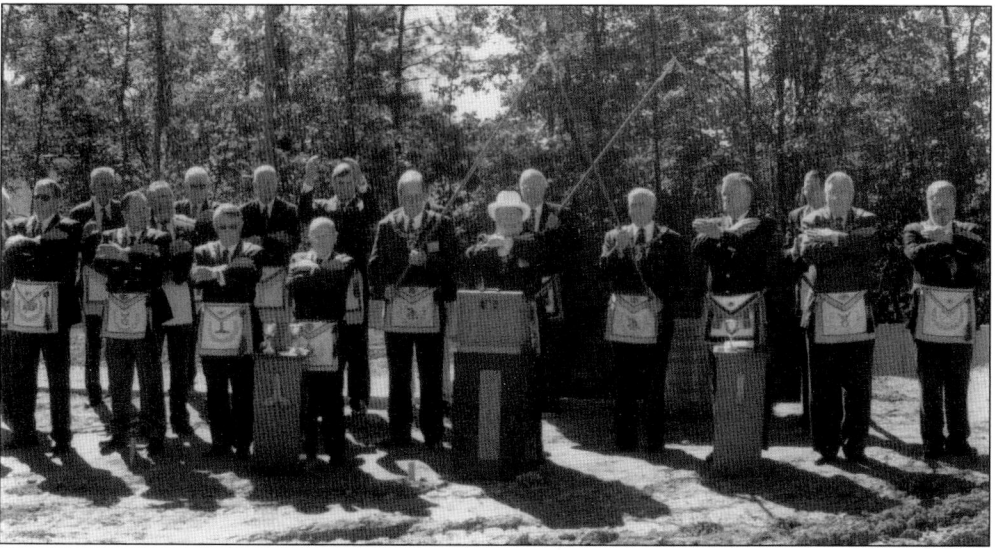

The relocated Nelms Lodge 323 had its cornerstone dedication ceremony at the new site, near the intersection of Concord and Hurt Roads, in 2001. State and local officers conducted ceremonies that included using instruments of the Mason's trade (square, level, plumb bob) to check proper installation of the cornerstone. Also, goblets of corn, wine, and oil were poured over the stone in accordance with ceremonial requirements. (Courtesy Harold Smith.)

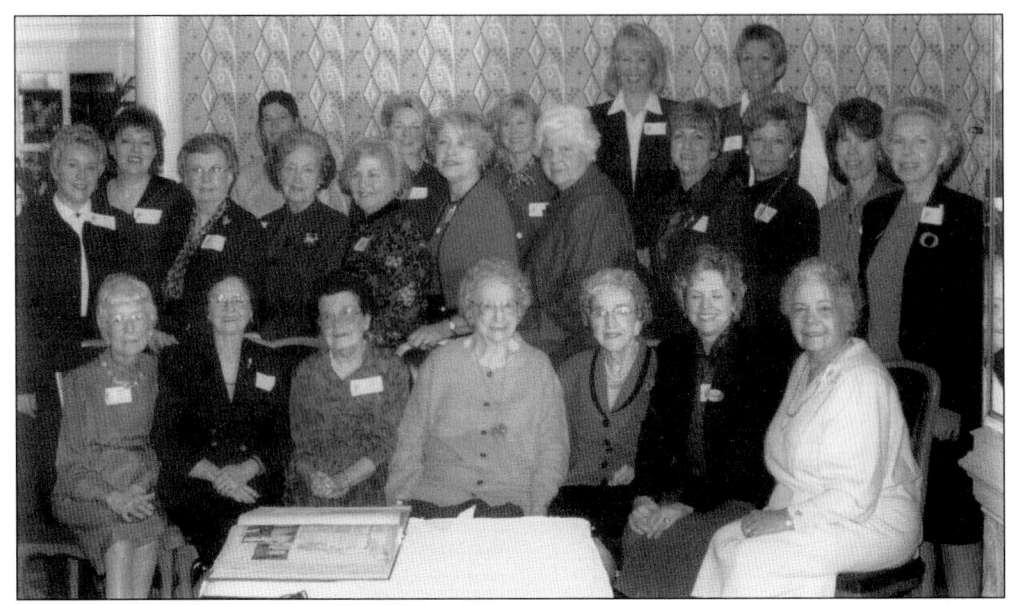

Smyrna Social Club was organized on November 8, 1908, in the home of Ida and Leila Gilbert. The club held its 90th anniversary at Marietta Country Club. Ladies between 17 and 24 years old who were present or former Smyrna residents were eligible for membership, but only if there was a vacancy. "The object of the club," according to Mary Carson, was, "bringing together ladies in a social way for self-improvement." (Courtesy Harold Smith.)

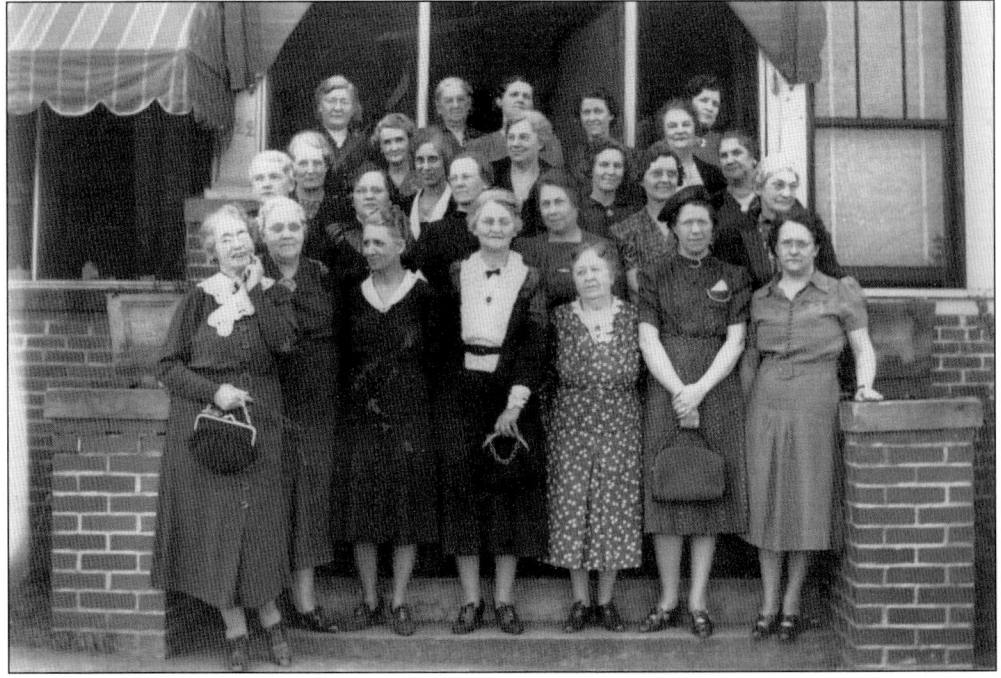

In 1937, eighteen local ladies established the Jonquil Garden Club, named after the flower that was adopted by Smyrna as its official logo. They adopted the Smyrna Memorial Cemetery as a beautification project and installed a stone marker there. The club continues to work with Keep Smyrna Beautiful and other organizations.

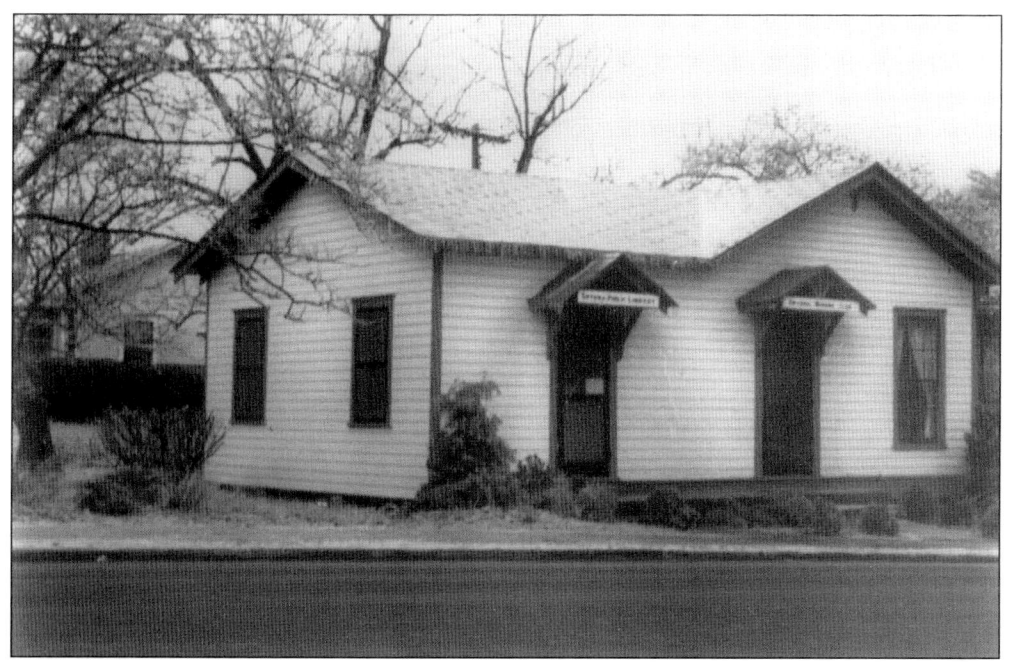

The Smyrna Woman's Club was chartered in 1925 and federated in 1926. It engaged in a variety of activities to raise funds for various civic improvements as well as for social purposes. In 1929, the club bought a residence on Atlanta Road (shown here) to use as its meeting place. It was becoming a major force in helping to influence activities of the city. (Courtesy Smyrna Woman's Club.)

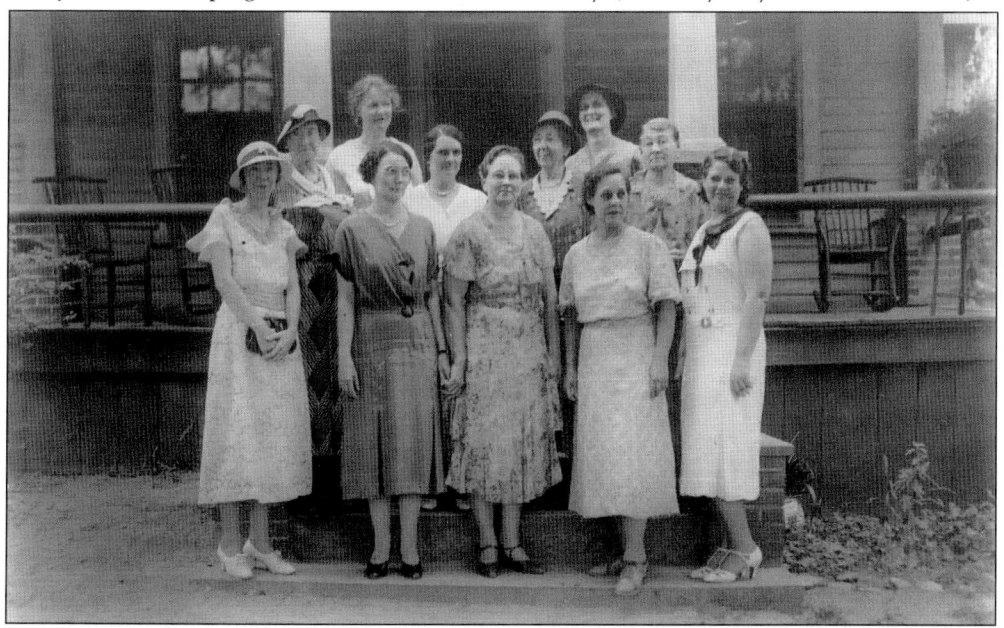

The Springhill Garden Club was organized May 1933 at the home of Mrs. Paul Lovejoy. The charter members were (in no particular order) Mrs. Lovejoy, Mrs. J.M. Byrd, Mrs. S.H. McGillis, Mrs. H.A. Hutchings, Mrs. C.J. Hohen Schutz, Mrs. H.O. Craven, Mrs. R.L. McIntyre, Mrs. Edgar Anderson, Mrs. W.A. Crowe, Mrs. Fannie McNabb, Mrs. W.A. Hoyt, Mrs. Pearce Matthews, Mrs. R.G. Flinch, and Mrs. G.C. Green. (Courtesy Kathy Hatcher.)

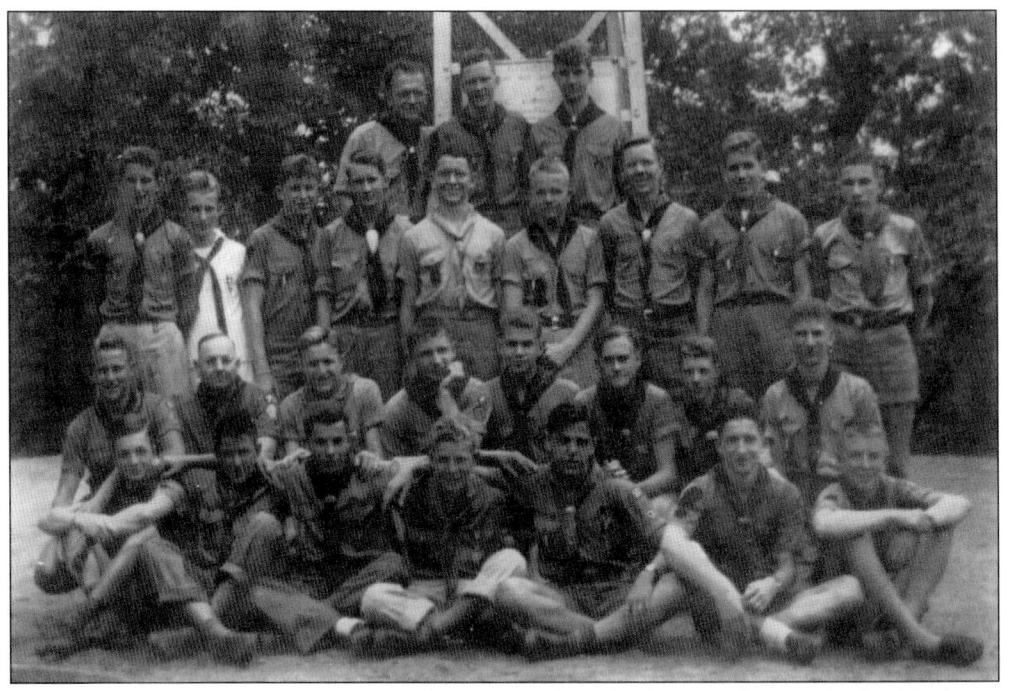

Bert Adams Boy Scout Camp (1926–1960) was located north of present-day Cumberland Parkway. The 1945–1946 summer staff, not all of whom are pictured, were James Hewell, Bob Ginsberg, Alan Kapland, Chief J.B. Humphries, John Outler, Frank Boykin, Bobby Karr, George Goldman, Harold Smith, George Broadnax, Robert "Red" Smith, Dewey Benefield, John Lewis, "Honey" Almand, Hugh Riddle, Jimmy Major, Bobby Pruitt, Dick Giblin, "Irish" Donoghue, Terrell Bradley, Walter Bradley, Terry McGowan, Robert Green, Bob Gordon, Dewey Benefield, Ham Stockton, Charles Wilson, O.L. DeLozier, Dan Austin, Merrill Grennor, Harry Hearn, Bubba Paget, Wiley McGriff, and Ross Goddard.

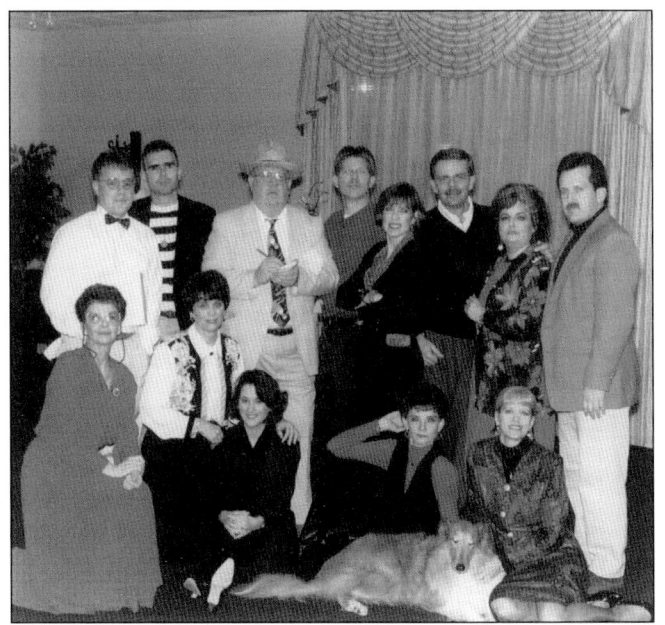

The Friends of the Smyrna Library started April 5, 1990, but was completely reorganized in October 1994 and grew into one of the largest "Friends" organizations in Georgia. Projects like *Murder Takes the Stage*, in February 1996, provided funds for unbudgeted items for the library. The cast for that play are pictured here from left to right (first row) Betty Wilson, JoAnn Cagle, Lisa Peterson, Melinda Wilson, and Lynda Peterson; (second row) Jimmy Flanagan, Joe Morris, Dana Freeman, Steve Olson, Jane Ferguson, Mark Howard, Gloria Sikes, and Kevin Jeffrey. (Courtesy Harold Smith.)

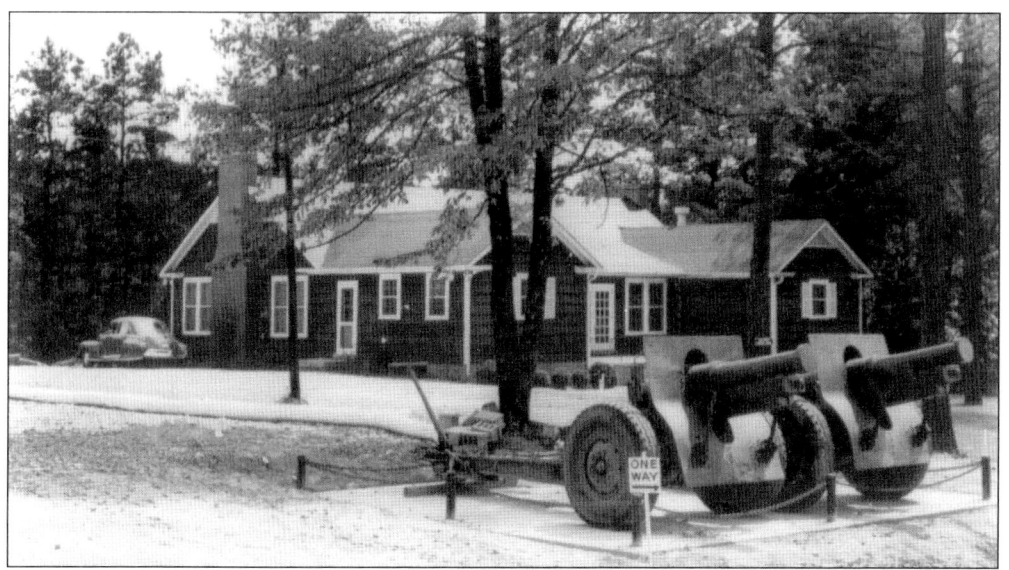

The July 5, 1948, grand opening of the American Legion Post 160 lodge on Pine Street was a big occasion. The festivities were attended by state commissioner Ben T. Huitt, Sen. Richard B. Russell Jr., Secretary of State Ben Forsten, Post 160 commander Henry Mitchell, state commander Earle Cocke Jr., and Smyrna mayor Lorena Pace Pruitt. (Courtesy Smyrna Museum.)

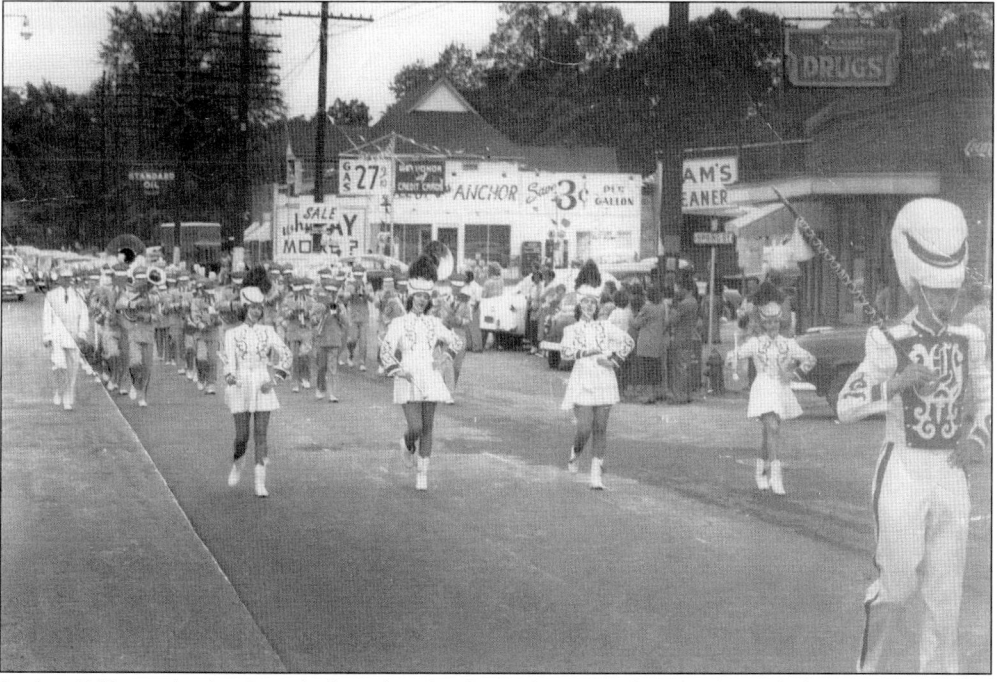

In this 1953 parade, the Campbell High School Marching Band passes through downtown Smyrna. American Legion Post 160 contributed to the purchase of the first band uniforms for the newly opened high school. The drum majorettes are, from left to right, Sylvia Barnes, Dorothy Besack, Laura Helen Jones, and Peggy Driver. The drum major, at far right, is Fowler Martin. The band director, not pictured, was Ken Stanton. The location of this photograph is the current site of the Market Village entrance. (Courtesy Ray and Janet Brown.)

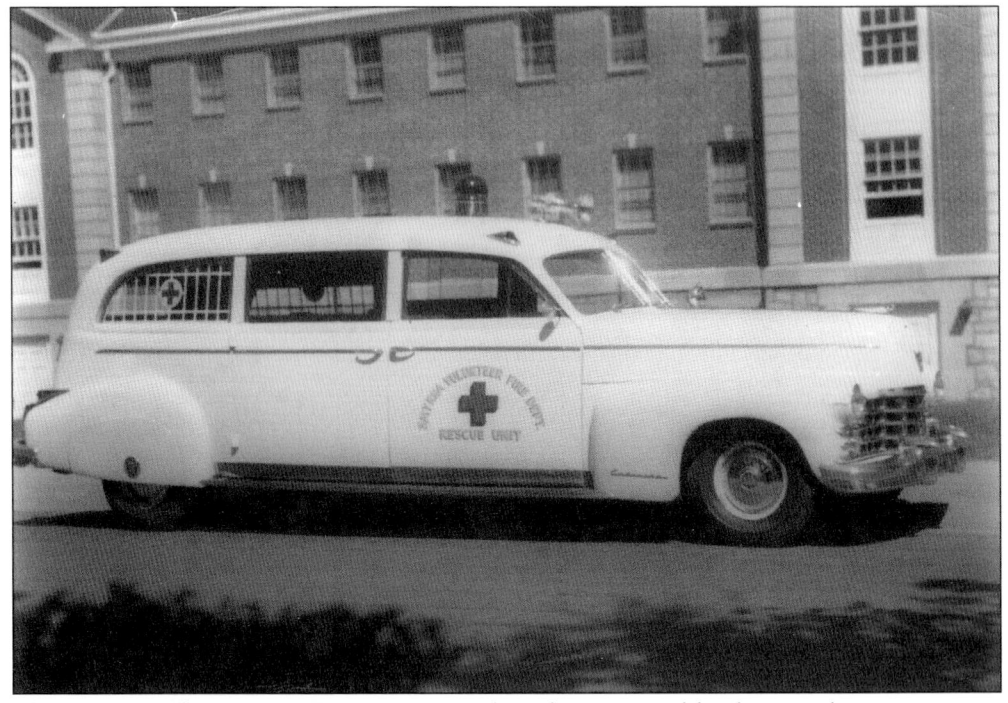

The Smyrna Volunteer Fire Department conducted a variety of fundraisers, dances, concerts, barbeques, and plays, and sold burgers and hot dogs at the North Georgia State Fair in the mid-1950s to finance the purchase of rescue units. It also signed notes to borrow money from the bank guaranteeing the loan. (Courtesy Smyrna Volunteer Fire Department.)

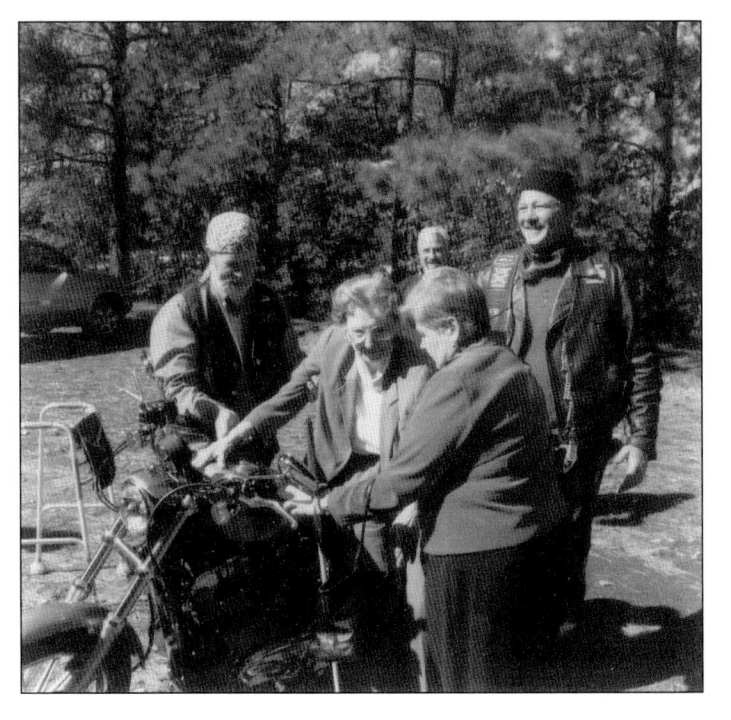

The Smyrna Oakdale Moose Lodge and Women of the Moose conducted an annual Citizens Award Banquet in January every year. They presented Mr. and Ms. Smyrna, Mr. and Ms. Cobb County, Humanitarian and Statesman of the Year, and a variety of other awards. Here, the Moose motorcycle riders are showing Blind and Low Vision Services of North Georgia founder, Sarah Sentell Scott, how to ride a motorcycle before they begin their Ride for Sight fundraiser. (Courtesy of Harold Smith.)

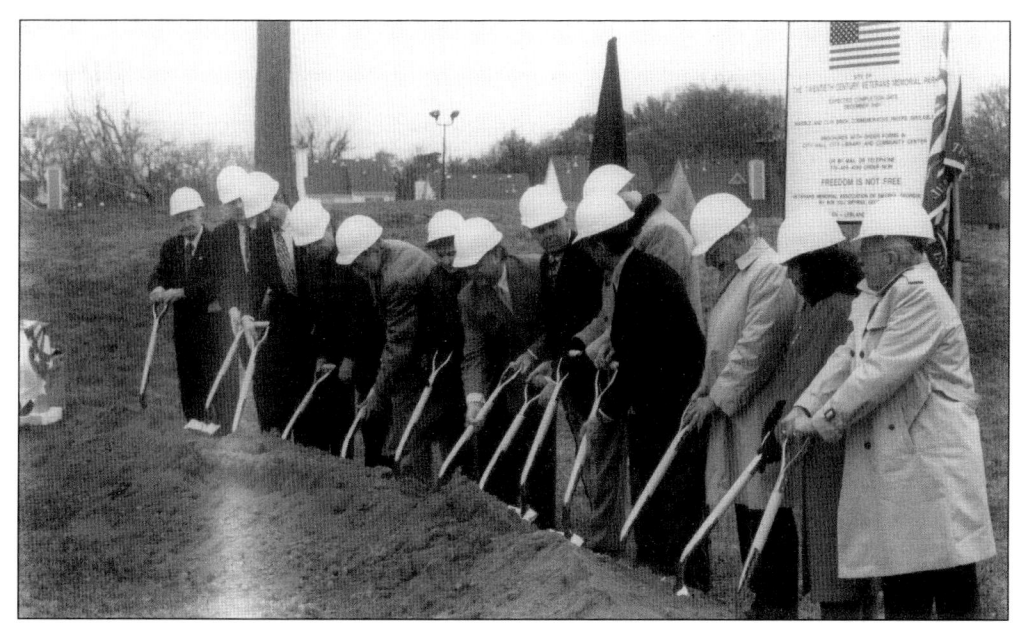

Ground-breaking ceremonies for the 20th Century Veterans Memorial took place on January 12, 2002. Veterans Memorial Association president Bill Lnenicka gave a history of the project. Shown here are, from left to right, city council members Pete Wood, Councilman Wade Lnenicka, Jack Cramer, Jim Hawkins, Ron Newcomb, and Melleny Pritchett; Mayor Max Bacon; US representative Johnny Isakson, keynote speaker for the event; President Bill Lnenicka; Ron Davis, master of ceremonies; Arthur Crowe, finance committee chairman; Mary Richardson; and Bill Brown.

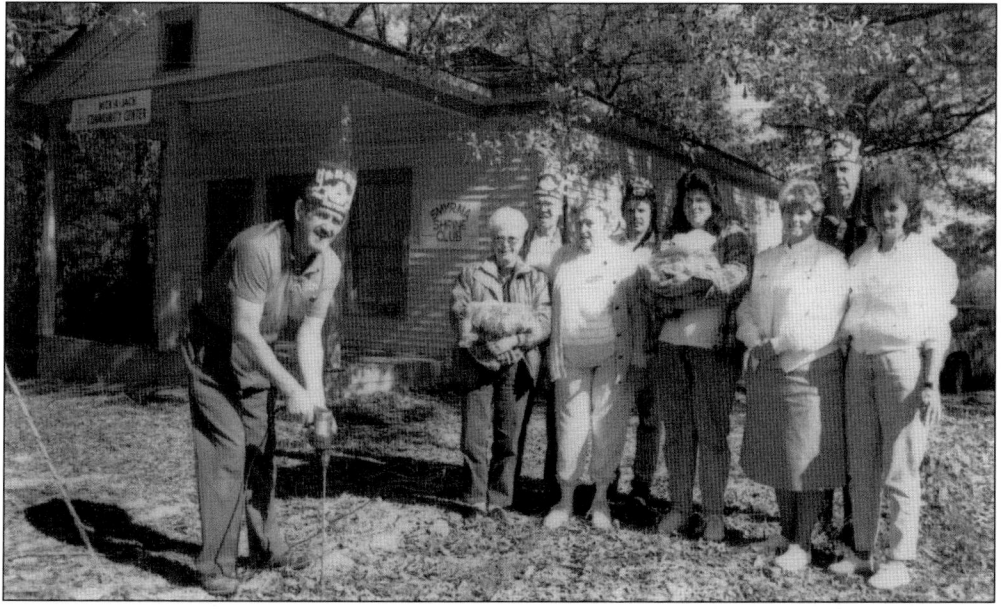

The Nickajack Shrine Lodge was originally a privately owned residence. The group acquired ownership of the building for $1 from the owner. Several years later, the club surrendered its charter, and members joined either the Smyrna or Oakdale groups. A community homeowners association later used the building, and then it was acquired by Cobb County for traffic improvement of the intersection, where an automobile accident had resulted in fatalities.

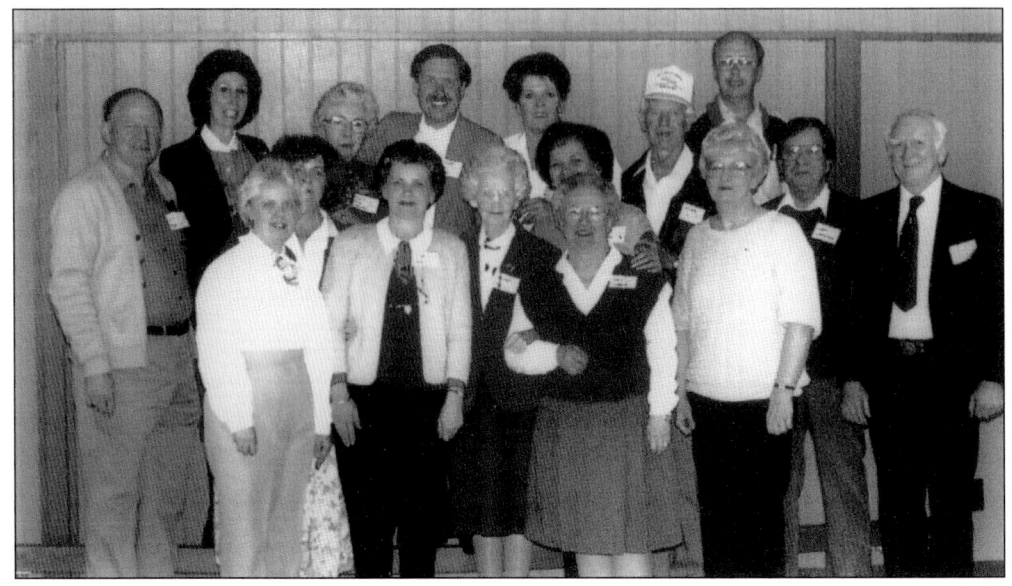

The first membership meeting of the Smyrna Historical and Genealogical Society Inc. was held on March 27, 1986, at King Springs Park (now Tolleson Park). Those in attendance were, from left to right, (first row) Carolyn Amburn, Jeane Travis, Corrine Hosch, Doris Morris, and Betty Smith; (second row) Emmett Yancey, Jean Bennett, Bobbie Shirley, George Carreker, and Harold Smith; (third row) Jane Yancey, Judith Lowry, Mayor Max Bacon, Joan Bennett, Tarver Shirley, and Bill Hamilton.

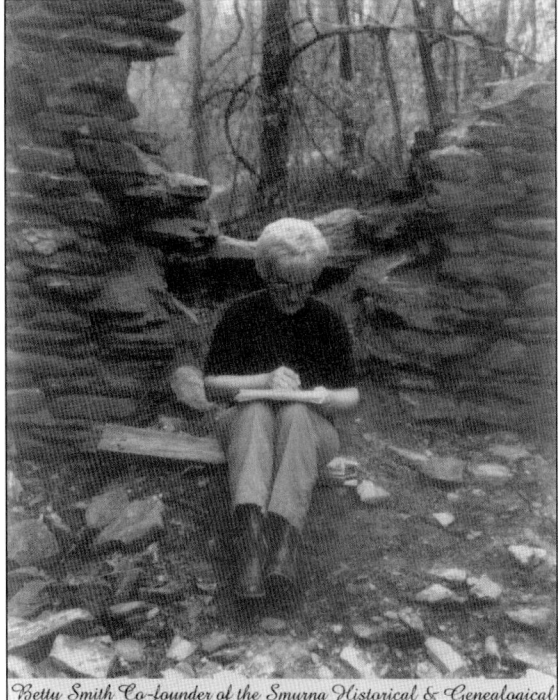

Betty Smith (September 10, 1931–September 20, 1993), a native Georgian and a Smyrna resident from 1955, was a cofounder of the Smyrna Historical and Genealogical Society Inc. and the Smyrna History Museum. She is seen here sketching the Concord Woolen Mill ruins in February 1983. (Courtesy Harold Smith.)

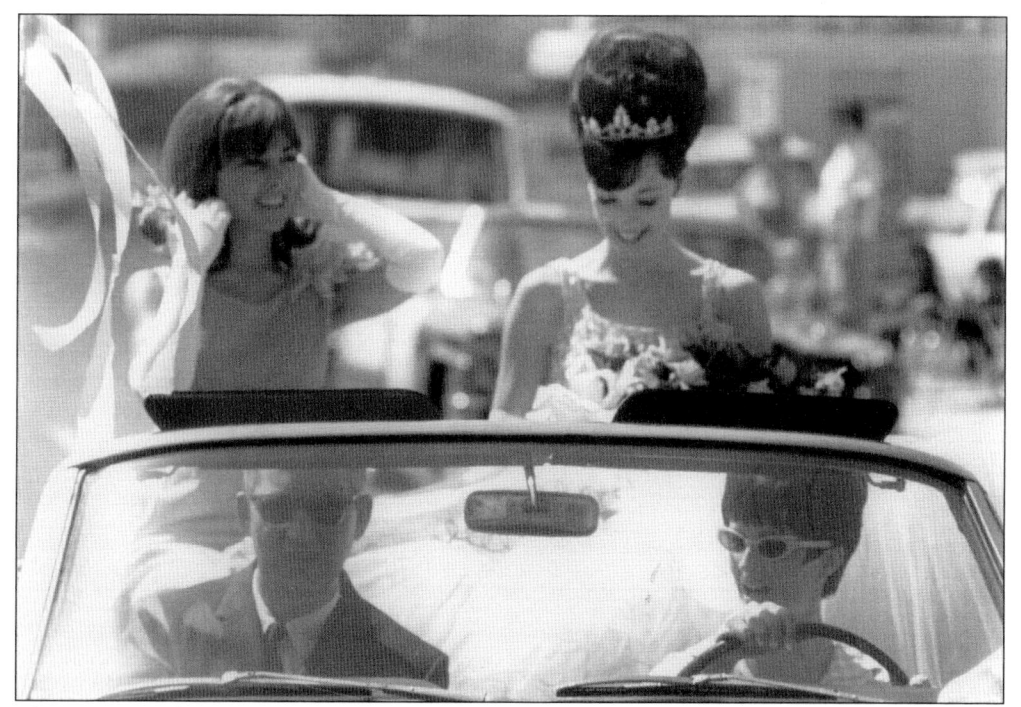

The Smyrna Chamber of Commerce's second annual Jonquil Festival lasted almost a month, unlike today's weekend celebration, which is sponsored by Smyrna Parks and Recreation. Other sponsors include Whispering Pines Garden Club, Junior Woman's Club, Opti-Mrs. Business and Professional Women, Kiwanis, Optimist, Lions, Rotary, Civitan, and Jaycees. Pricilla "Prissy" Durham, the 1967 Jonquil Queen, is shown here in the back wearing her tiara.

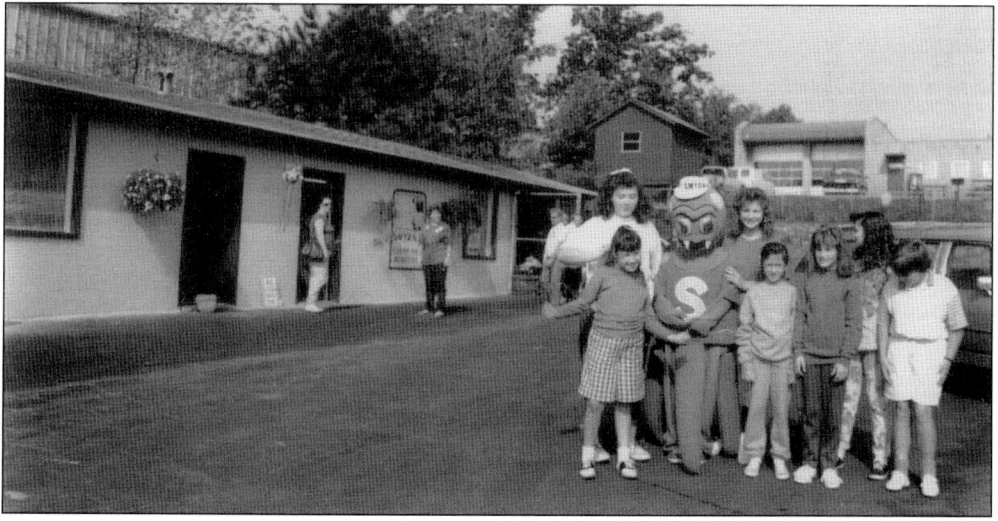

Pictured here are Adopt-a-Mile volunteers with the Keep Smyrna Beautiful mascot at Smyrna's recycling center on Smyrna Hill Road. Smyrna Clean and Beautiful started around 1987. It later became Keep Smyrna Beautiful. It is a city-sponsored, nonprofit organization. The governing board is made up of one mayoral appointee and one appointee from each ward. Ann Kirk is the current director. From September to December, the organization encourages residents to plant the jonquil bulbs that the organization sells.

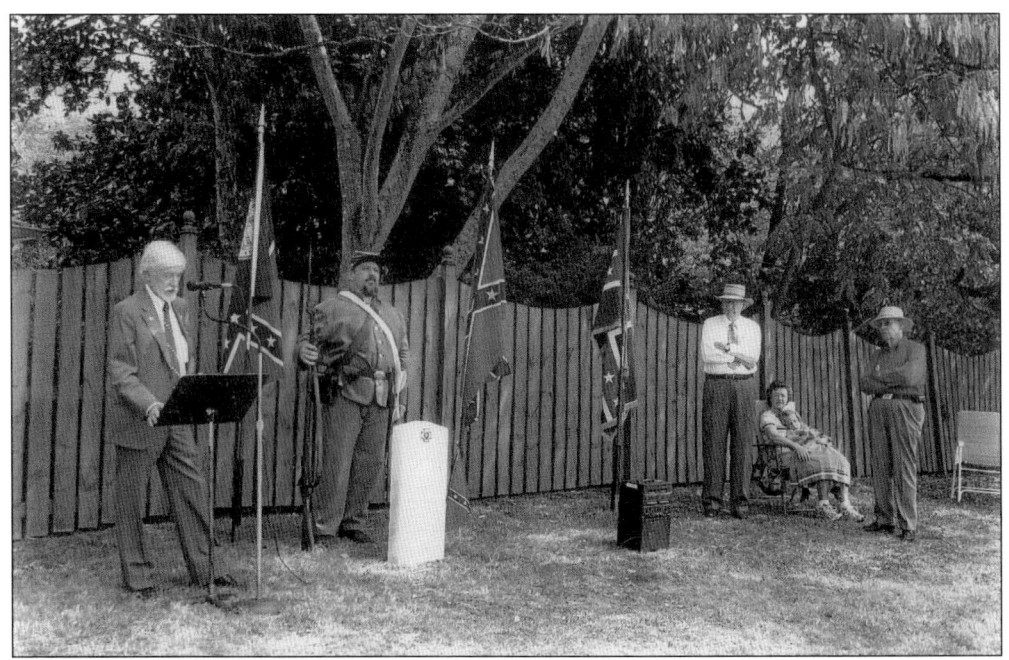

Shown here are members of the Smyrna Leonidas Polk Camp of the Sons of Confederate Veterans, from left to right, Garry Daniel, Tim Pilgrim, Emmett Yancey, and Charlie Cole. They are placing a grave marker in a special ceremony, with the inscription "Pvt. Giles B. Eidson, Co. A, 9BN GA ARTY, CSA, 1825 – June 29, 1905." Howard's Restaurant owners provided space adjacent to their parking lot, under which lies the Eidson family cemetery. (Courtesy Harold Smith.)

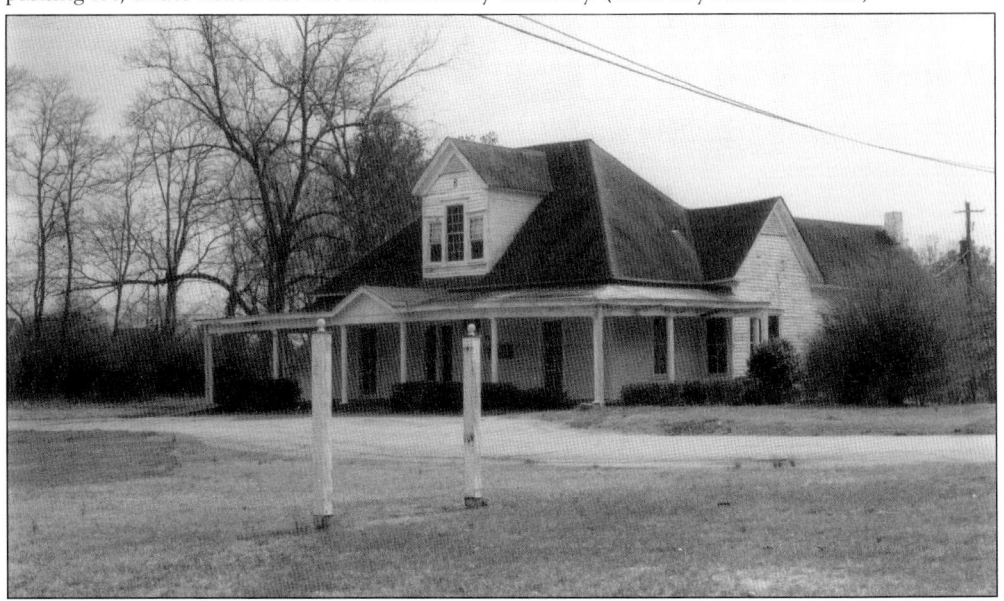

The Taylor-Brawner House Foundation Inc. raised almost a half-million dollars to save and restore one of Smyrna's oldest houses, built around 1890. Slated for demolition when purchased, the Taylor-Brawner House and Brawner Hall were saved through cooperation between the foundation and the city. On March 27, 2012, these become the first two structures inside the city limits to be listed in the National Register of Historic Places. (Courtesy Harold Smith.)

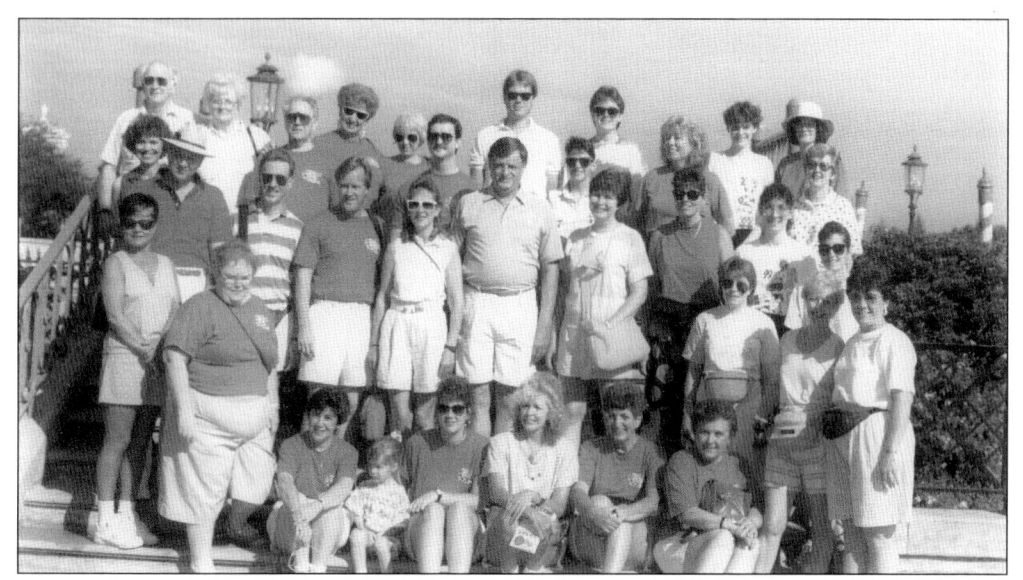

Smyrna Community Chorus, organized in 1975, presented its first performance in May 1976. It is the longest-performing nonprofessional community singing group in Cobb County. Its largest audience was at opening day for the Atlanta Braves in 1976. The chorus has performed in Disney World, Opryland, the Georgia governor's mansion, the Yellow Daisy Festival, Rich's Christmas tree lighting, and other community events. (Courtesy Smyrna Community Chorus.)

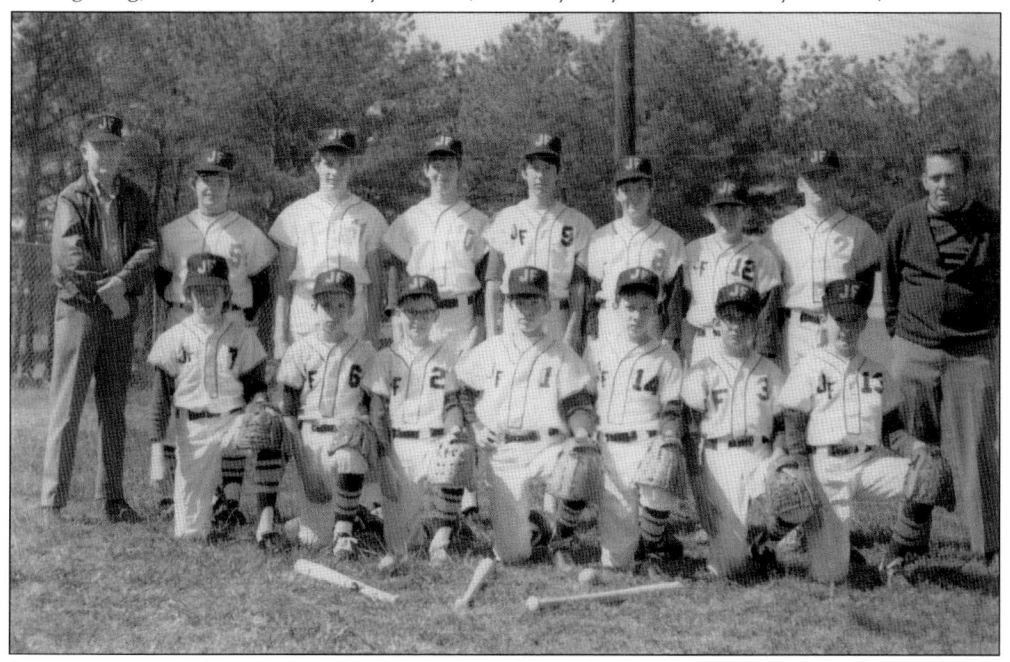

Smyrna Pony League was one of many sports programs developed between 1950 and 1970, when new families began to move into Smyrna. This 1971 team was sponsored by the Jarvis & Futrelle Carpet Company. Shown here are, from left to right, (first row) Joe Dudley, unidentified, Tony Wilkie, unidentified, Brad Verser, unidentified, and Bill Warren; (second row) unidentified coach, Gene Gray, David Tull, Keith Hendrix, Doug Hammett, Phil Bronson, unidentified, Lamar Tillerson, and unidentified coach. (Courtesy Phil and Nancy Futrelle.)

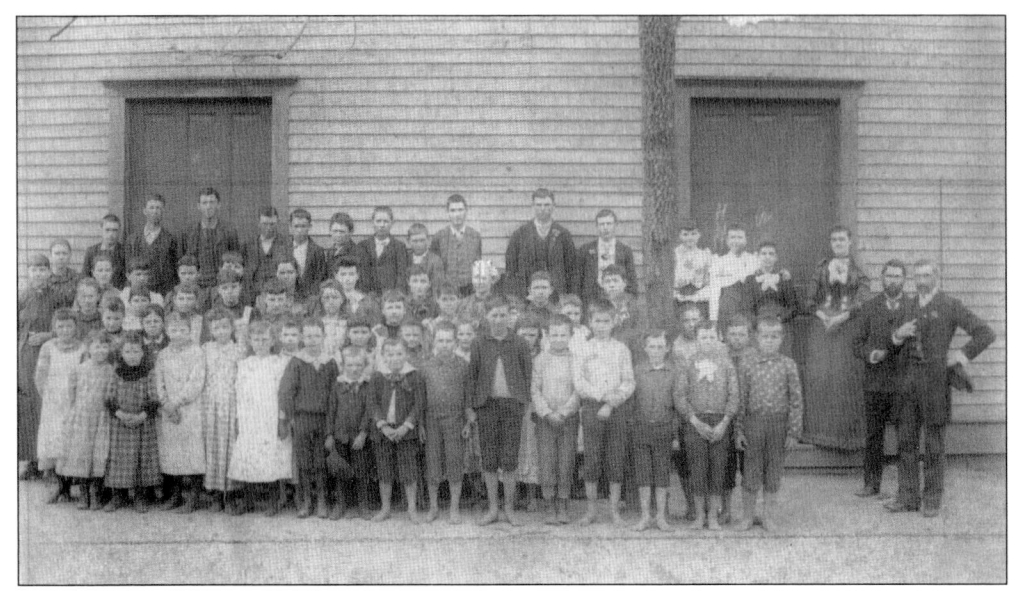

Mr. Mizell's School, seen in this 1895 photograph, was in the first floor of the old Nelms Masonic lodge building on Atlanta Road next to Smyrna First Baptist Church. This is the approximate location of the present-day Second Baptist Church. This building was destroyed by fire in 1924, along with the church and several other buildings in the area. (Courtesy Becky Nash Paden.)

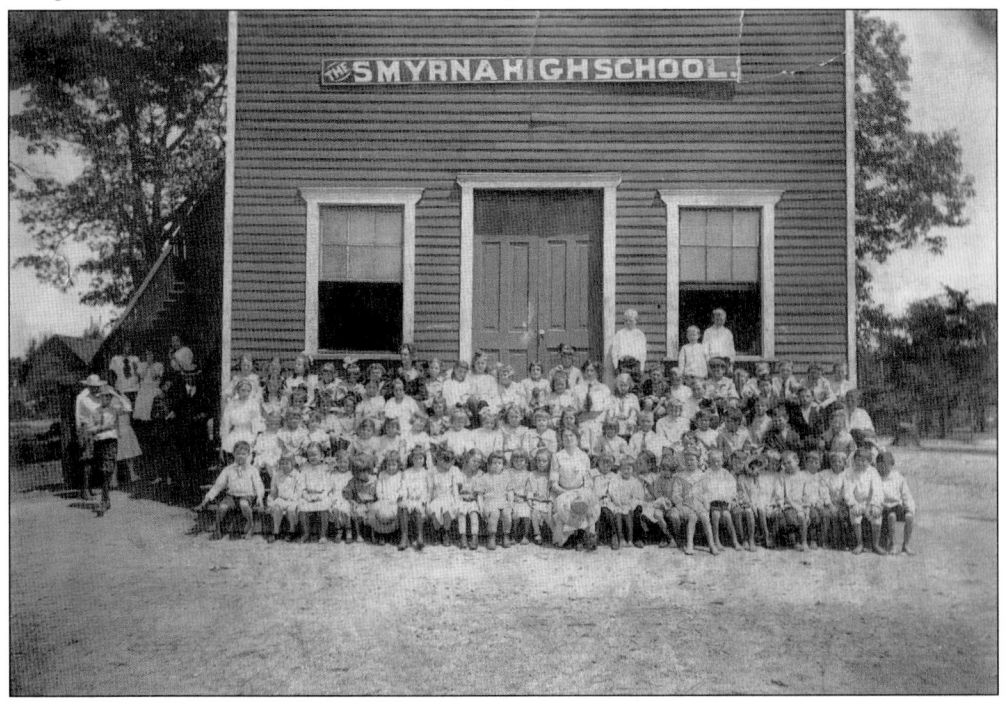

Smyrna Boys Academy, constructed around 1840, was originally all brick. It is believed to have been the only building left standing in Smyrna after the Civil War. It was later acquired by the Presbyterian Church. Around 1905, the Smyrna Board of Education purchased it and added the wooden front to provide more space for classrooms. The Masonic lodge bought the building in 1924. (Courtesy Mary Baldwin Terry.)

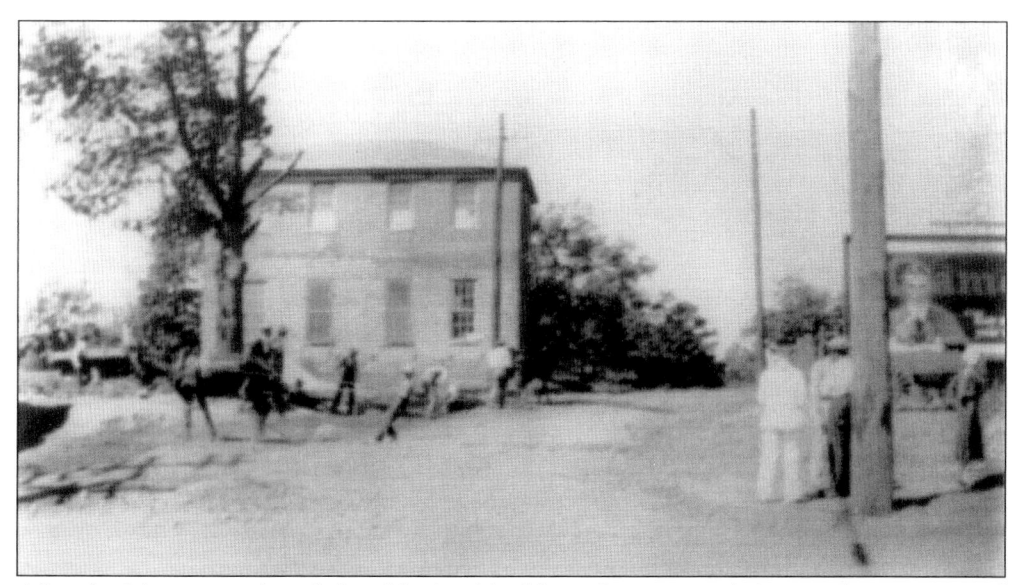

After the Masons purchased the old school building, they removed the wooden portion and extended what became West Spring Street. They also made a new entrance to the building. In 1954, the Masons demolished the historic Boys Academy and replaced it with one that looked almost identical. It remained there until the demolition program of the late 1990s for the construction of Market Village.

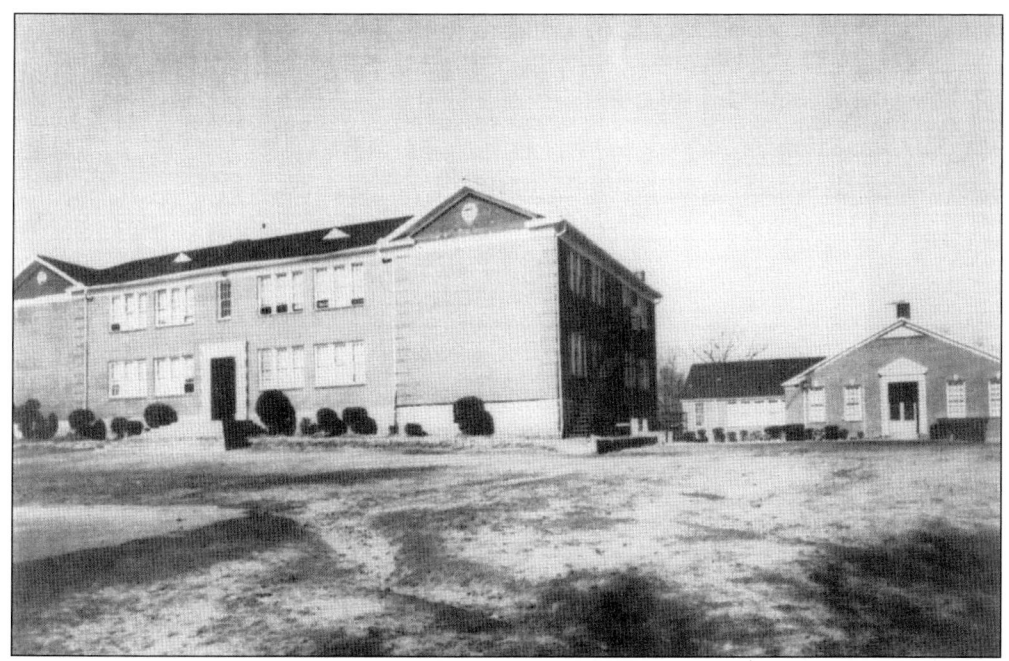

This Smyrna school building, at Church and King Streets, replaced a school that burned down in September 1924 after having been constructed at a cost of $30,000 in 1919. An all-grades school until 1938, it became the elementary school when the first high school was constructed on the same property. The Smyrna and Cobb County school systems consolidated at that time. Both buildings were sold to the First Baptist Church in 1972.

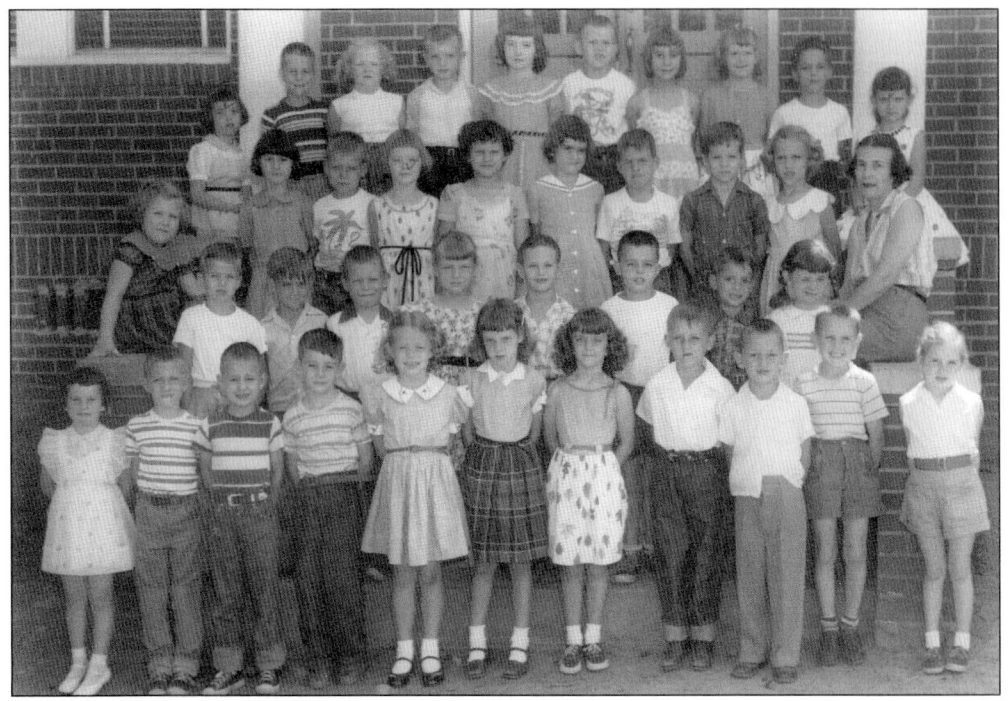

Shown here is Marion Mitchell's 1955 first-grade class at Smyrna Elementary School, where Paul Crump was the principal. Mitchell, a teacher in Smyrna for many years, had at one time been a school principal. She was considered sweet and was well liked by her students. Her daughter Genie Mitchell Brown is a resident of Smyrna and is married to Emory Brown.

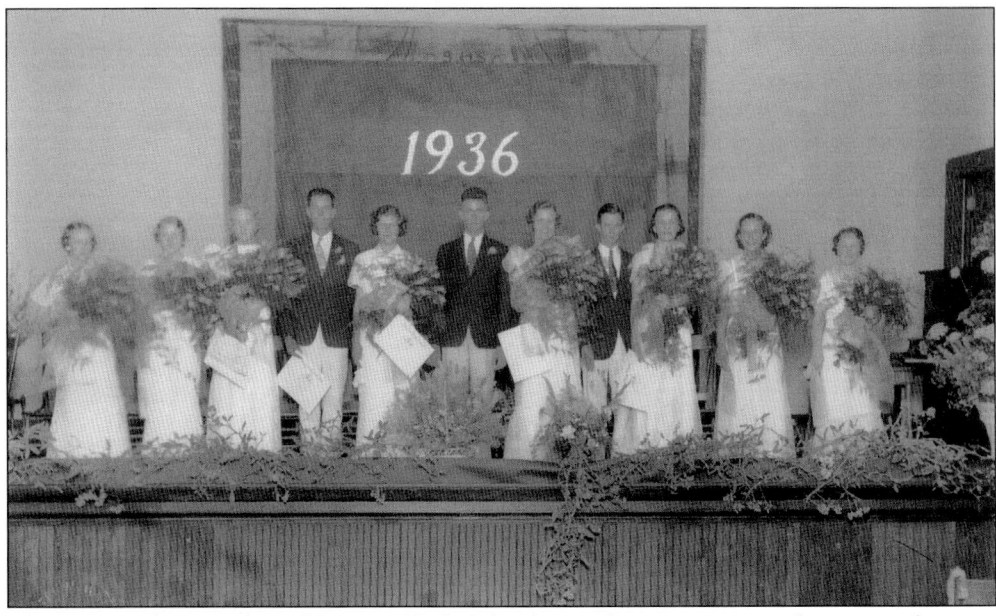

The 1936 graduating class of Smyrna High School attends a ceremony in the gym-auditorium building, constructed after the fire. Seen here are, from left to right, Miss Bacon, Miss Skelton, Miss Durham, Mr. Caldwell, Miss Dowda, Mr. Spratlin, Miss Motter, Miss Sanders, Miss Leathers, Miss Nabors, and Miss Lindley. (Courtesy Louise Lindley Haper.)

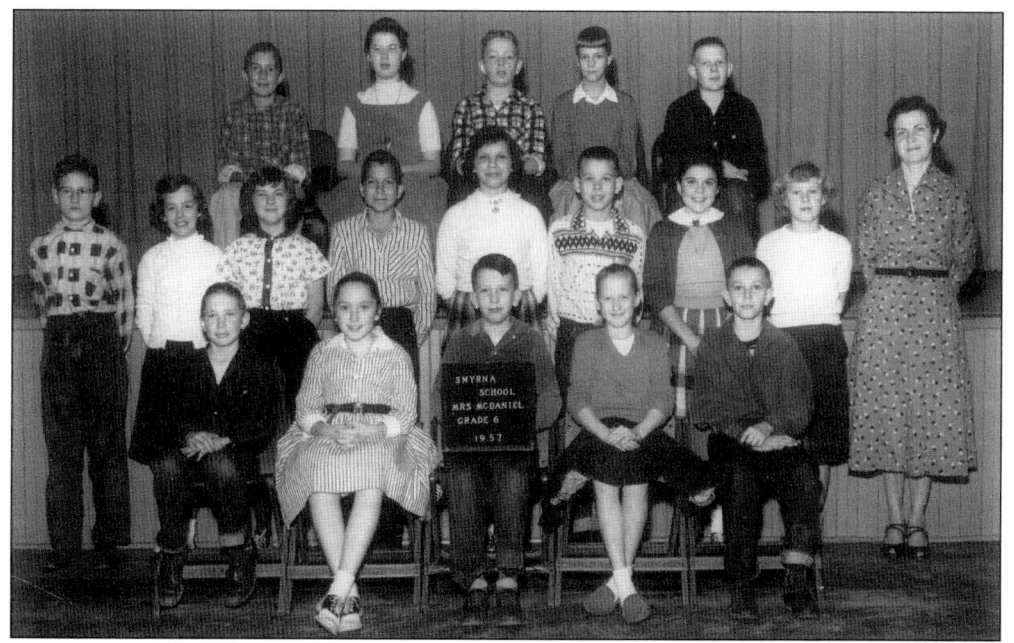

Mrs. McDaniel's Smyrna Elementary School class of 1957 gathers for a photograph. Seen here are, from left to right, (first row) Jackie Brown, Lynn Becker, Mike Monroe, Carolyn Gunn, and Johnny Nash; (second row) Wesley McGuire, Judy Womack, Lucy Jones, Roger Pryor, Sandra Waldron, Steve McRay, Nancy Konigsmark, Glenda ?, and Mrs. McDaniel; (third row) Bobby Ibill, Kathleen Reynold, John Powers, Kathy Hardage, and Eddie Jarrod. (Courtesy Melvin Holleman.)

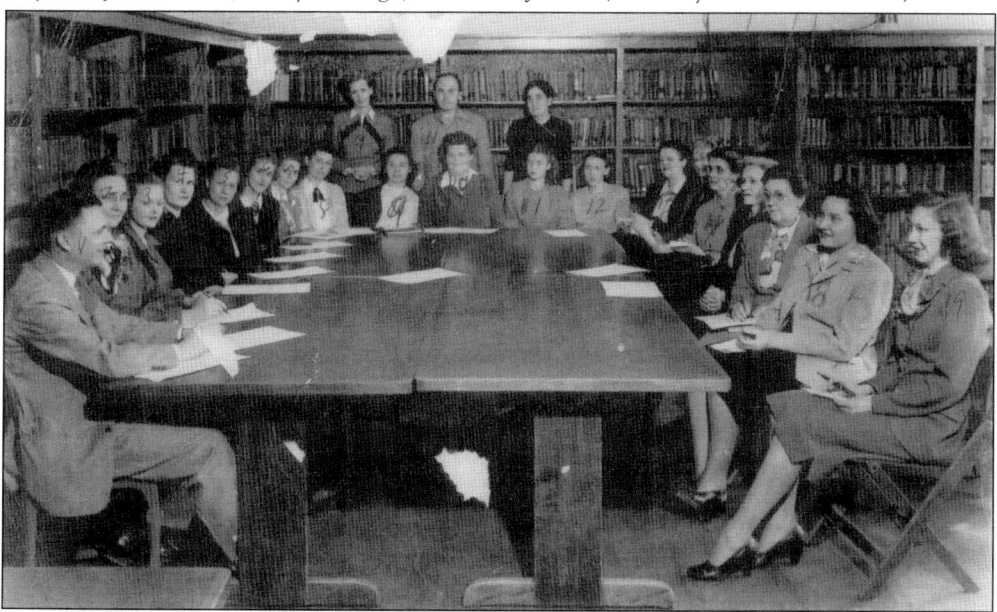

Shown here is the faculty for the first graduating class (1952–1953) of Campbell High School. Jasper Griffin (far left) was the principal at Smyrna High for a number of years. Others pictured in no particular order are Leslie Camp, Martha Crooks, Mrs. G.C. Green, Mrs. George Hylton, Callie Jay, H.B. McClure, Betty Jane Evans, Mrs. J.M. Fleming, Margaret Muse, Eunice Padgett, O.L. Parker, Merrill Stewart, Annie Vaughn, Mrs. R.P. Hosch, Alfred Koger, and Mr. and Mrs. Claude Walker.

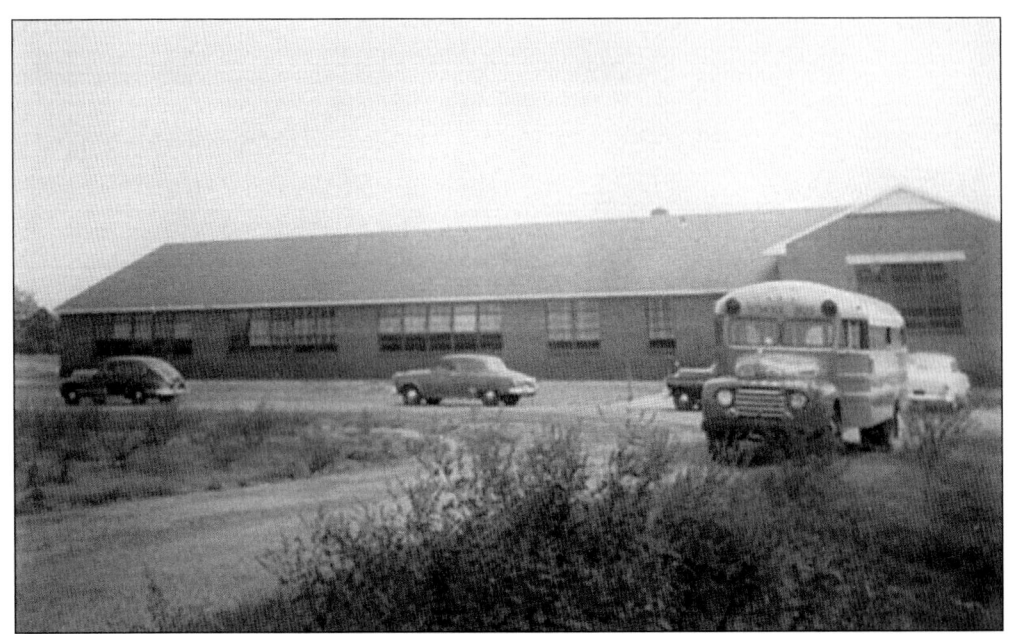

According to a Georgia Tech study commissioned by the city in July 1952, "a new brick school is being constructed near the old site and will be used by the colored elementary students from both Smyrna and Fitzhugh Lee." Rose Garden Hills School is the school referred to. When completed, it had six classrooms, a lunchroom, and indoor plumbing.

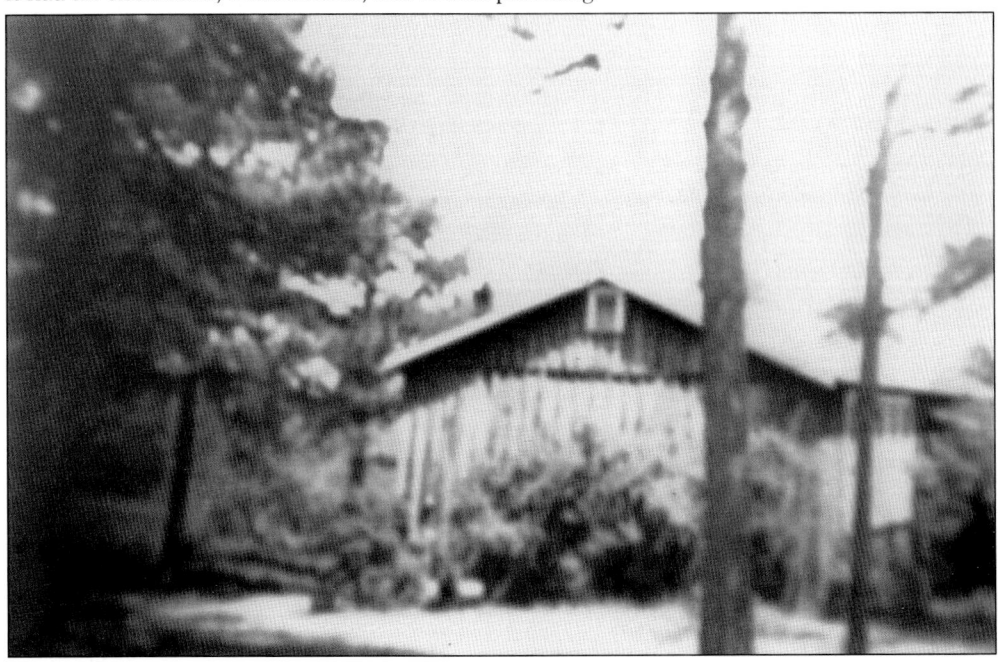

The building that Rose Garden replaced was described in the Georgia Tech study: "The Smyrna Colored School is housed in a wooden frame building and has an enrollment of ninety-five students. It was originally constructed with two classrooms separated by a large hall. The hall has been closed off and is now being used as a classroom making a total of three classroom staffed by three teachers."

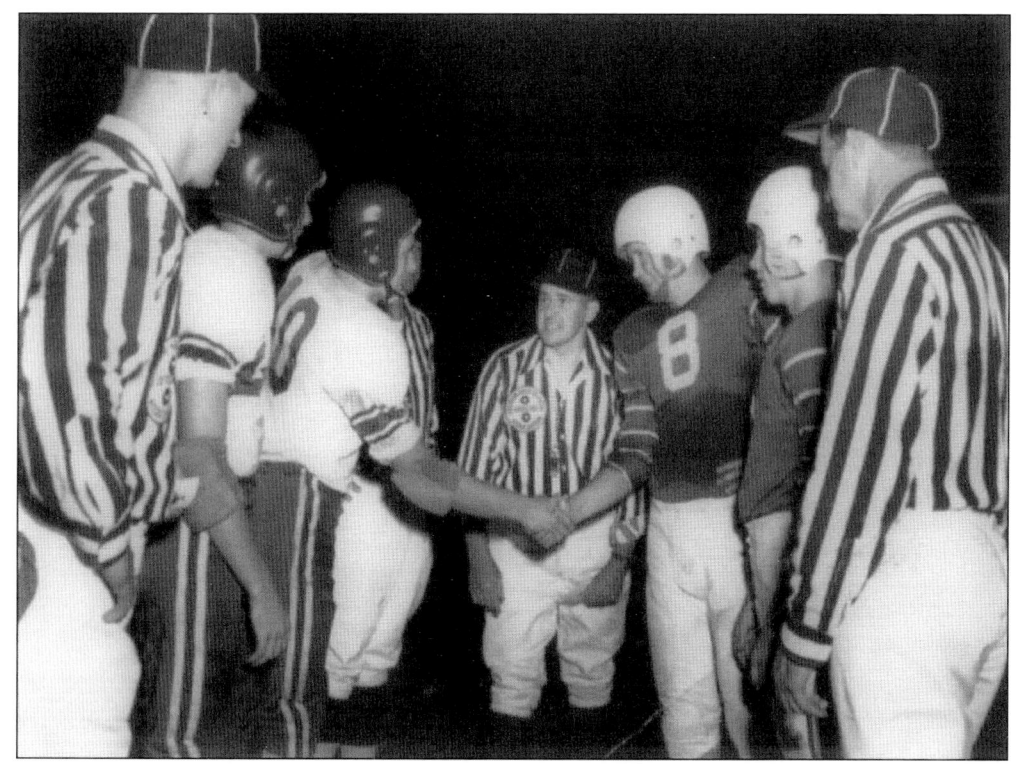

Orme Campbell High School, home of the Panthers, opened in 1952 with the merger of Smyrna High School and Fitzhugh Lee High School. It had a total of 425 students in grades eight through eleven. Shown here is the coin toss at a Campbell High School football game on Campbell Field, later renamed Joe Lantanzi Field for the former coach and assistant principal. (Courtesy Mark Reed.)

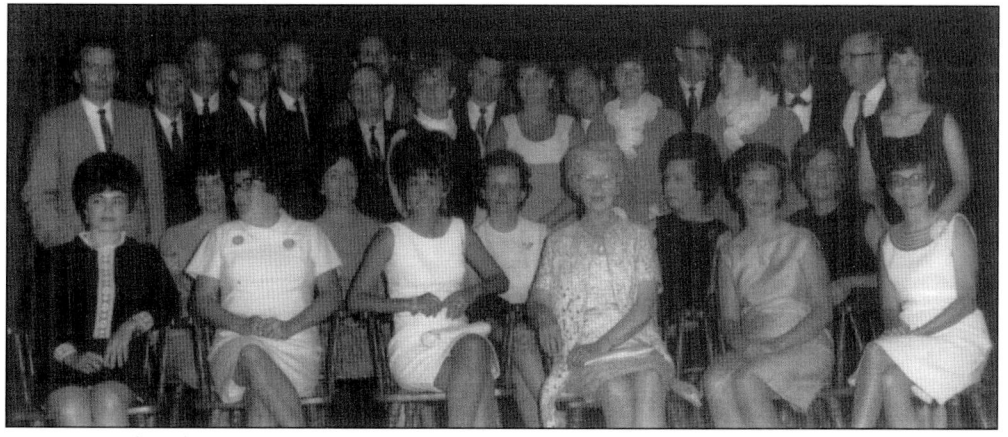

Smyrna High School's class of 1951 was the last class. It held its first reunion on June 1, 1968. Shown here are, from left to right, (seated) Peggy Lutz, Barbara Bryant Emmett, Joycelyn Wallace Fain, Bennie Lou O'Bryant Tacket, Peggy Duncan Dickson, Dodo Christian, Corrine Hosch (teacher), Mary Butler, Emma Jean Faucett Barden, Mildred Clayton Broyles, and Mary Motter Fowler; (standing) Lamar Akins, Grady Swafford, Lamar Tedder, Hoyt Dorris, Miller Davis, Pete Wood, Philip Walker, Joann McDowell, Fred Anderson, Milton White, Joan Bennett, Hugh Durham, Jean Bennett, Bob Fortner, Jasper Griffin (principal), and Doris Bailey Fowler. (Courtesy Jean and Joan Bennett.)

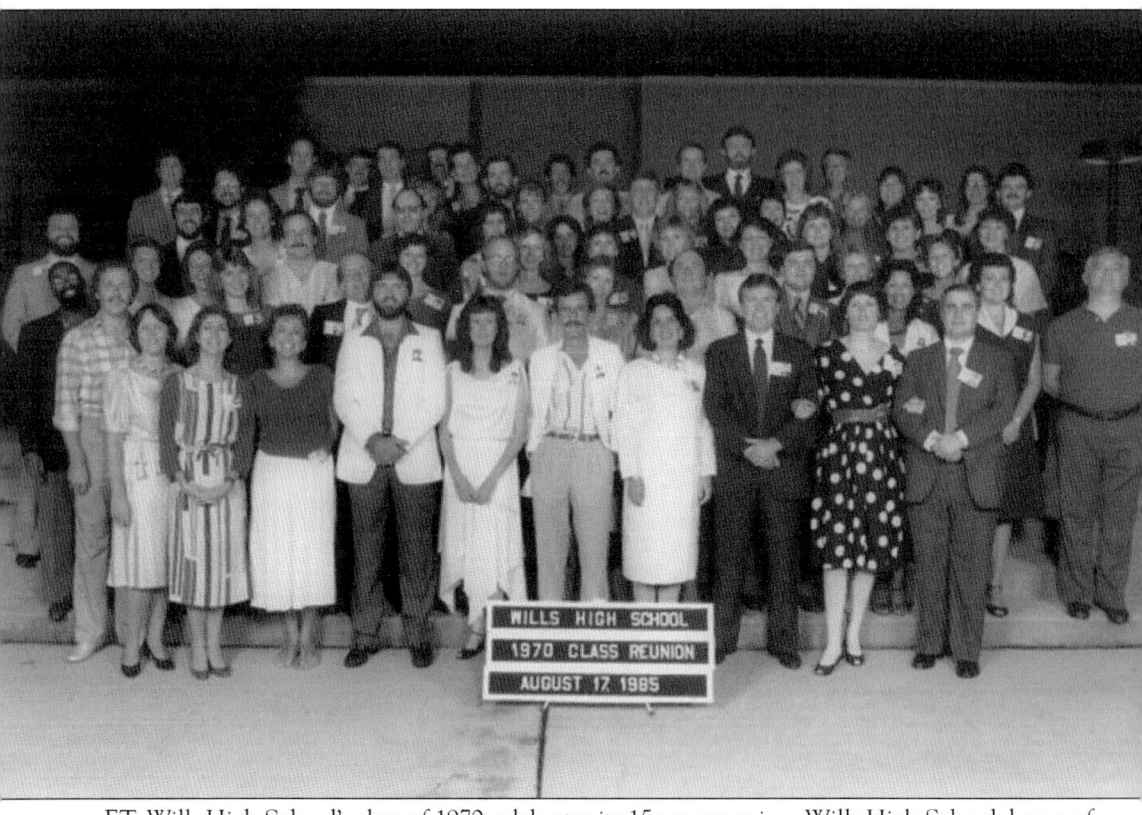

F.T. Wills High School's class of 1970 celebrates its 15-year reunion. Wills High School, home of the Tigers, opened in 1965. It was not uncommon for 5,000 people to attend the annual crosstown football classic between rival schools Wills and Campbell every fall. In 1989, Campbell and Wills were slated to merge and would revert to the Smyrna High name, which had been discontinued in 1951. Eliminating the Campbell name brought a suit from the Campbell family, and the name was restored. When the two schools merged, Wills had 790 students and Campbell had 1,076.

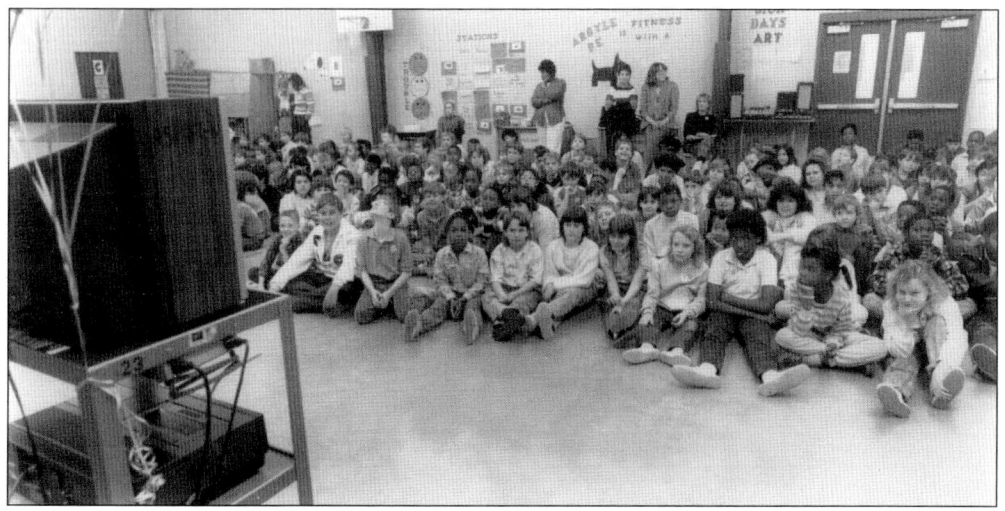

Argyle was chosen for the name of the new elementary school, because of its proximity to the Argyle Estates subdivision on Campbell Road. Nearby Cumberland Mall, the Cobb Galleria, and multifamily housing brought tremendous growth in the 1970s. Here, the students enjoy a presentation in the school's media center.

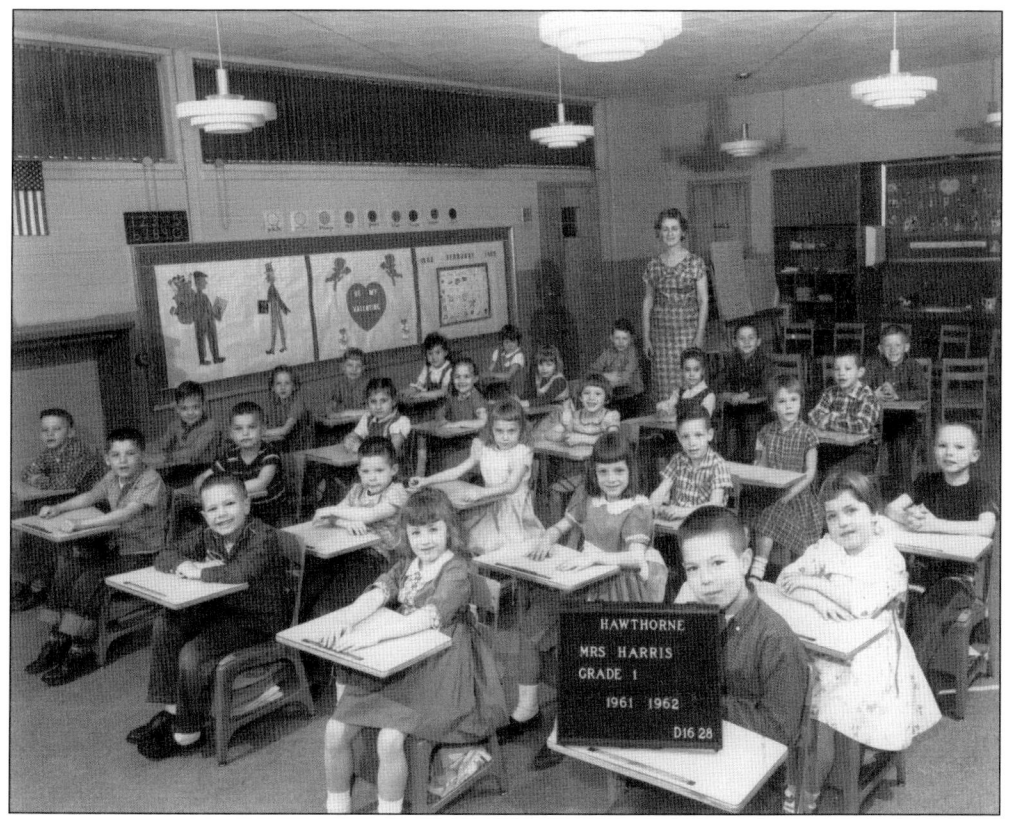

Hawthorne Elementary currently serves as one of Cobb County's Haven Academies, a special needs center. Located on the east side, it was an elementary school until changing demographics in Smyrna's oldest neighborhood reduced enrollment.

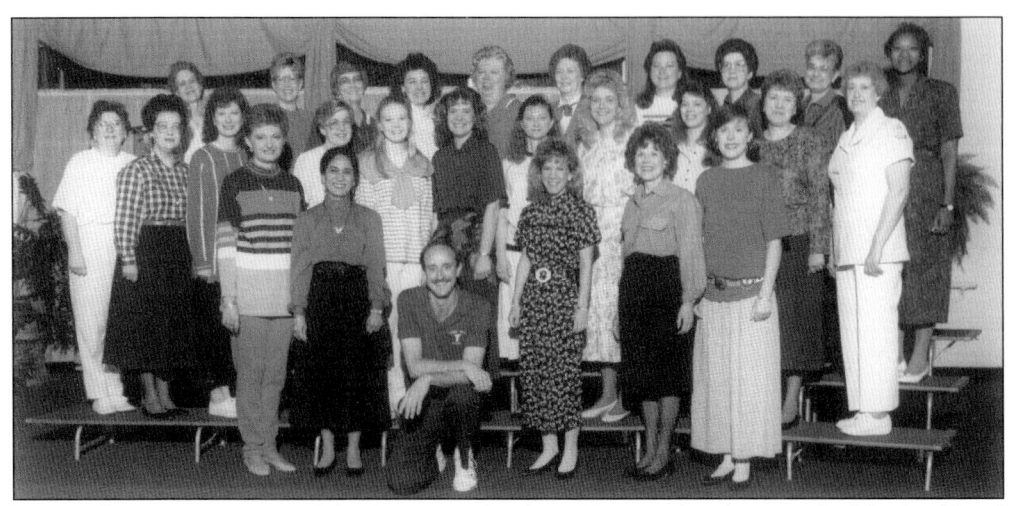

Brown Elementary was one of the first new schools in Smyrna after the arrival of the Lockheed Corporation in 1951 and the Belmont Hills Shopping Center in 1954. Its first class was 1955. In 2013, it closed its doors and combined with Belmont Hills and Argyle Elementary to provide the students with the new Smyrna Elementary. The faculty and staff for the 1990–1991 school year are shown here.

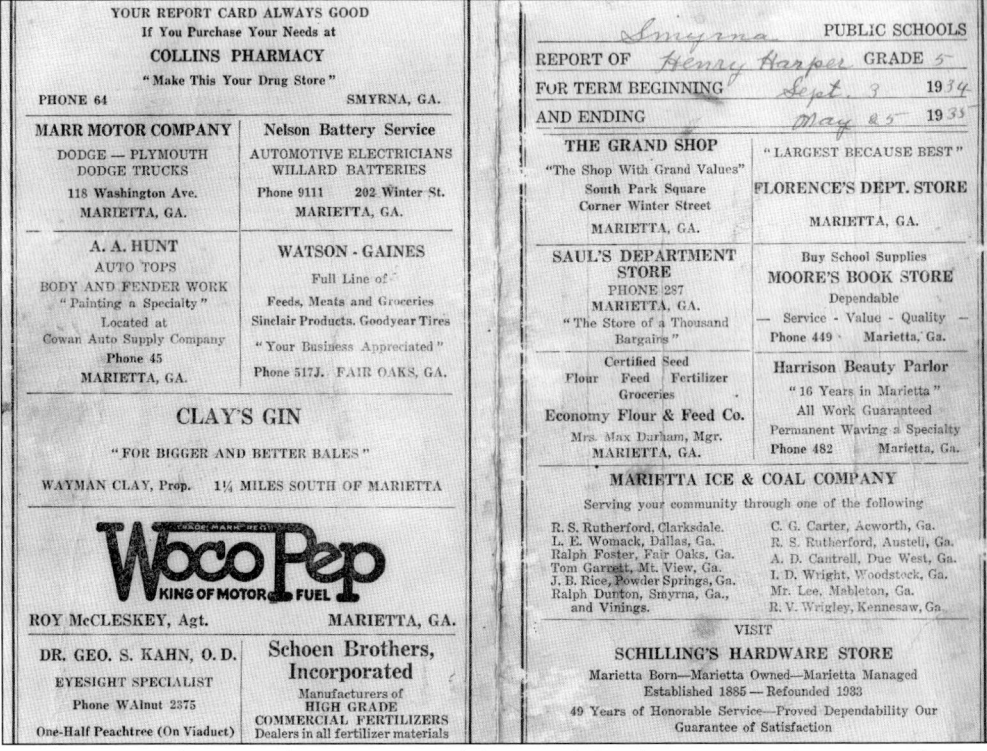

Before Smyrna Elementary became a part of the consolidated county school system in the late 1930s, students were required to pay a tuition fee. During the Depression, the Smyrna School Board sold advertisements on the student report cards. Henry Harper's 1934–1935 report cards reflect those hard times. The reverse side also has two advertisements under the grades. (Courtesy Louise Lindley Harper.)

Six

UNINCORPORATED SMYRNA

Smyrna's strategic location, midway between Marietta and Atlanta, was solidified with the completion of the Western & Atlantic Railroad in 1842. Its route had followed the Hightower Trail, constructed in 1822, linking Georgia with the Cherokees and Creeks. Around the turn of the 20th century, the road was called the Marietta and Atlanta Wagon Road, later US Highway 41—the Dixie Highway. It was paved in 1924, but in 1934 a new US Highway 41 was constructed three miles east and bypassed Smyrna completely.

The 1832 Gold and Land Lottery was another factor that determined the future development of the area. With the establishment of the Smyrna Camp Ground by the Methodists in 1833, the area became the center of religious and social life. The Atlanta Northern Railway, better known as the streetcar route, was established in 1905.

The communities in unincorporated Cobb County started developing with the arrival of the Powers, Pace, Maner, Collins, Hooper, Turner, Brown, Gann, Daniel, and Barber families, among others. They established homes and farms in the areas that are known as Vinings, Oakdale, Concord, Collins Spring, Carmichaels, Mableton, and Fair Oaks.

Early businesses included J.H. Carmichael & Sons, Woco Pep Gas Station, Mrs. Brooks' Gulf Station, Hattie Crow's Beauty Shop, B&H Skating Rink, Glovers, Robert Maner, George Anderson, Earl and J.D. Daniel grocery stores, Jake Smith, Pat Maddox, James Crowder Service Station, McMullan/Godwin Oakdale Pharmacy, and Drs. Parnell, Maner & Tanner. Later companies were Oakdale Ace Hardware and Long's Pac-A-Sac in Alverson's shopping strip.

One of the major factors that contributed to Smyrna's growth into unincorporated Cobb County in the decades of the 1950s, 1960s, and 1970s was the establishment of a water and sewer system in the 1920s. When developers started building subdivisions in the 1950s for people who came to work at the newly opened Lockheed plant, they found that the City of Smyrna was able to offer those services, but they had to annex the property into the city. The developers were willing to do it.

The unincorporated Smyrna area now includes Vinings and Cumberland, with a 30339 Atlanta zip code; the Oakdale area (30080); The Highland Office and Industrial Park, Smyrna (30082); and Vinings Estates, Mableton (30126), which is inside the Smyrna city limits. Smyrna shares some of its northern and western boundaries with the city of Marietta and its 30060 zip code. Smyrna is known as one of the best places in metropolitan Atlanta to live, work, and play.

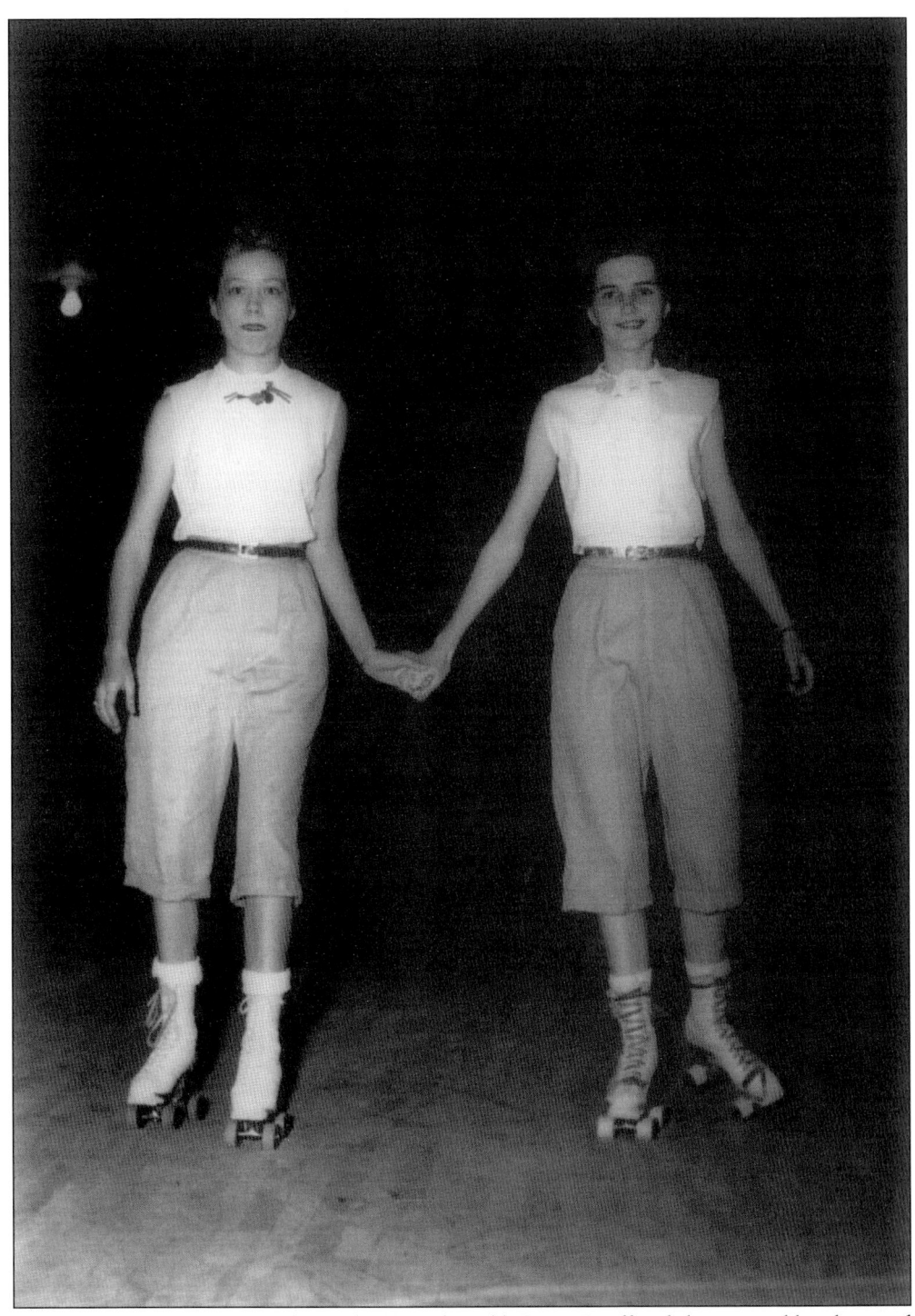

B&H Recreation Center was located on South Cobb Drive. It offered skating and bowling and was open every night except Sunday. It was owned by Glen and Mattie Lee Brown and Virlyn and Elizabeth Herren. Pictured here in 1951 at the skating rink are Peggy Jo Addison Walker (left) and Dorothy McDaniel Jeffares. (Courtesy B&H Recreation Center.)

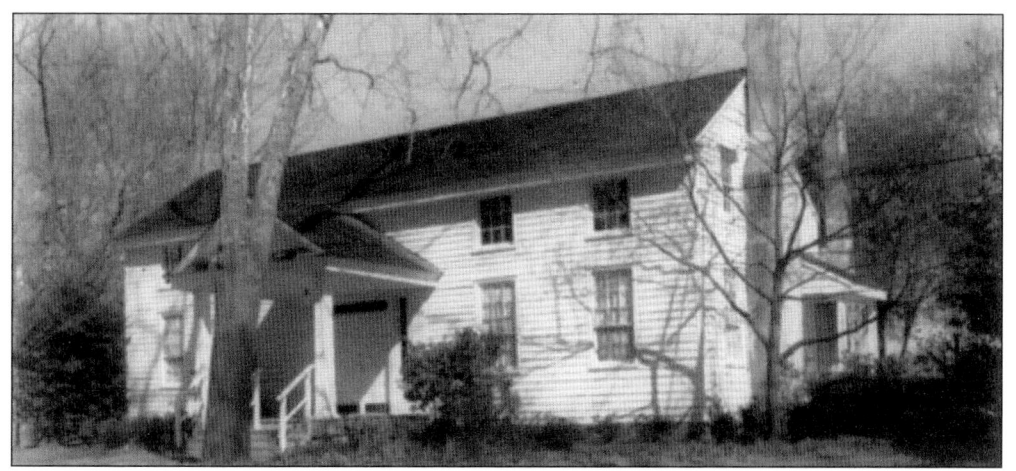

The Mable House, located at 5239 Floyd Road, was built in 1843 by Robert Mable, who came to Cobb County with his wife seeking land to mine for gold. He leased property and constructed this house, which is listed in the National Register of Historic Places. In July 1864, Union general John Blair led two divisions south from the Mable House, pursuing two Confederate cavalry brigades. Blair's troops continued until they came upon a line of earthworks on a ridge just west of Nickajack Creek occupied by Georgia militia. (Courtesy The Mable House.)

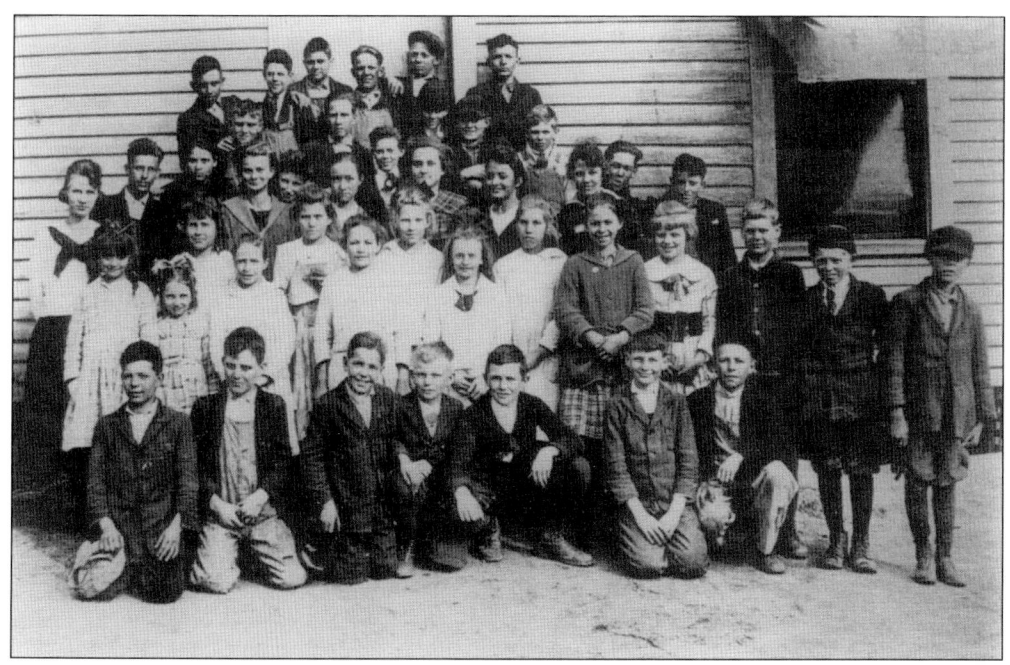

Among those shown here at Mableton Grammar School are Doris Daniell (second row, second from left), Earl Daniell (second row, second from right), Stella Daniell, teacher (third row, far left), and Cecil Daniell (fifth row, third from left in stocking cap). (Courtesy Daniell family.)

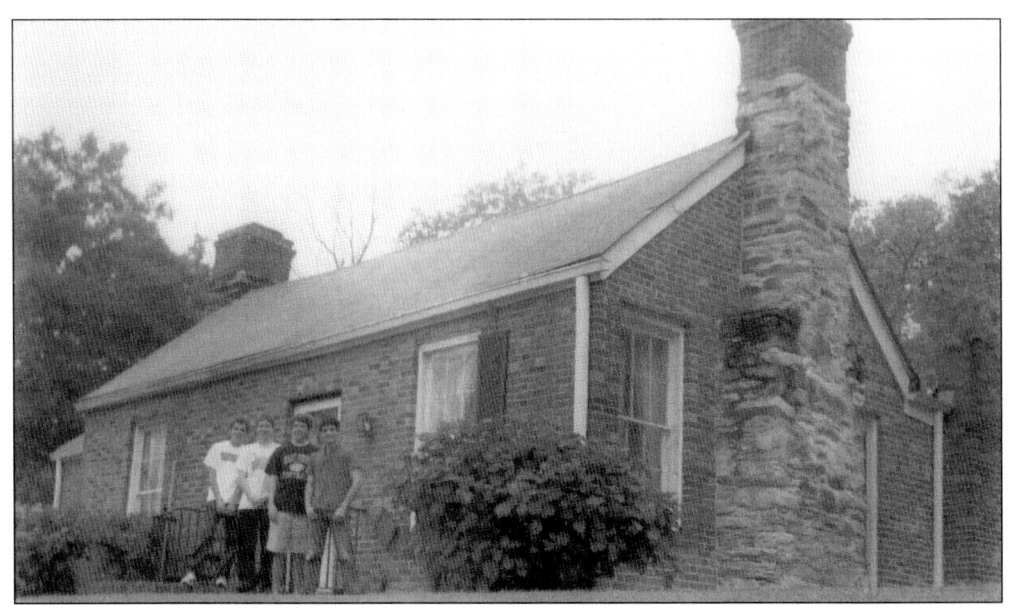

The Hooper-Turner House, located at 5811 Oakdale Road, is a mid-1800s, Civil War–era house purchased by the City of Smyrna in an effort to preserve the area's historic features. The Johnston River Line, a series of fortifications called shoupades, after Francis Shoup, the architect, were constructed as the final defense for Atlanta during the Civil War. (Courtesy Roberta Cook.)

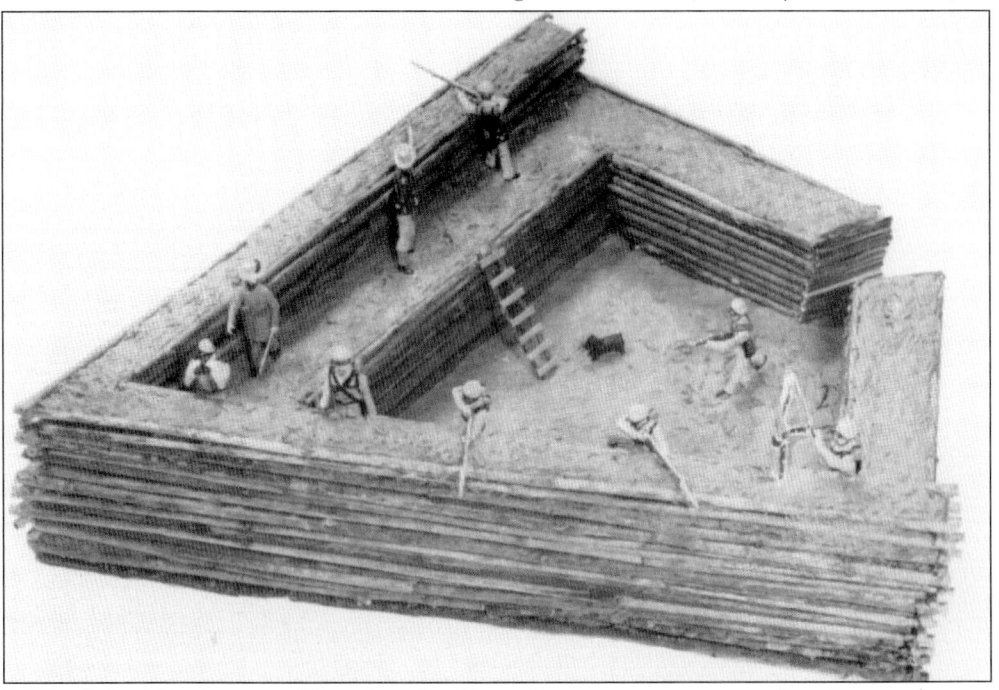

During July 1864, the main Chattahoochee River Line, a unique system of earthen works, was prepared by Confederate engineer Gen. Francis Asbury Shoup. The defensive formations, referred to as shoupades, were located about 225 meters east of the Hooper-Turner House. In his memoirs, Gen. William T. Sherman stated they were the most impressive fortifications he had ever seen. (Courtesy Jack Melton Jr.)

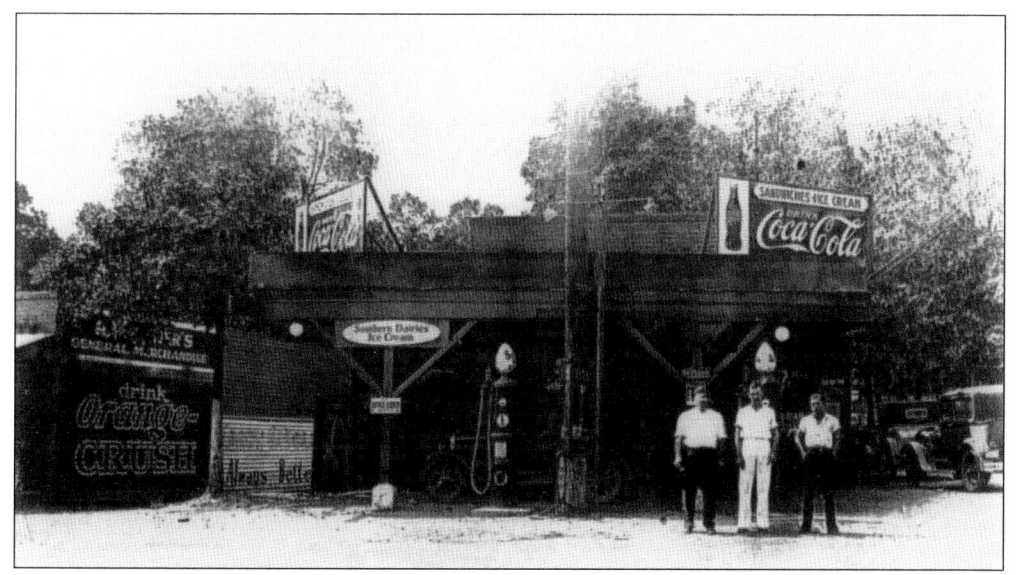

Mr. and Mrs. Glover's store, located in Oakdale on Atlanta Road at Camp Highland Road, was a grocery store that had a billiard parlor in the back. This photograph was taken in front of the store in 1930. Shown are Horace Wood (left), Bob Maner (center), and Rudolph Sentell. On the left can be seen Robert Maner's General Merchandise store. (Courtesy Shirley Sentell Parsons.)

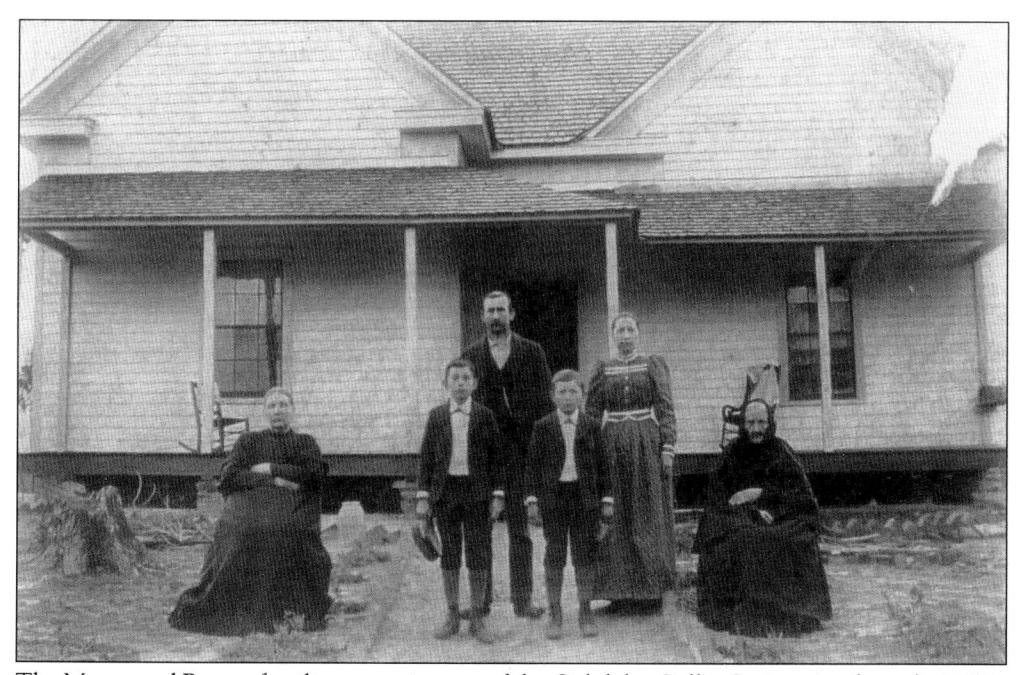

The Maner and Brown families were pioneers of the Oakdale–Collin Spring area from the 1850s. Pictured here are, from left to right, Sarah E. Maner, Floyd Lee Brown, James Warner Brown, William Earl Brown, Dellar Maner, and Sarah Mary Land Maner, wife of Hosea Maner. (Courtesy Gary Maner.)

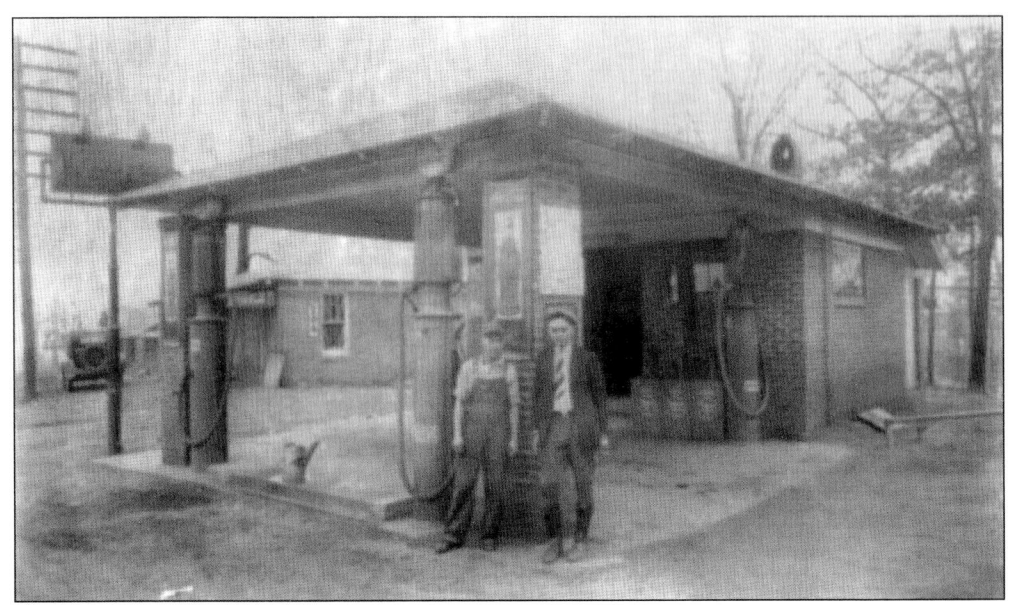

The Woco Pep Station was located at the corner of Atlanta and Oakdale Roads. Jack Wright and Cliff Wehunt served as managers of the store. Shown in this c. 1931 photograph are Earl Rice (left), father of Virginia Rice Sargent, and an unidentified companion. The Jottie and Lois Brown home can be seen on the left. (Courtesy Virginia Rice Sargent.)

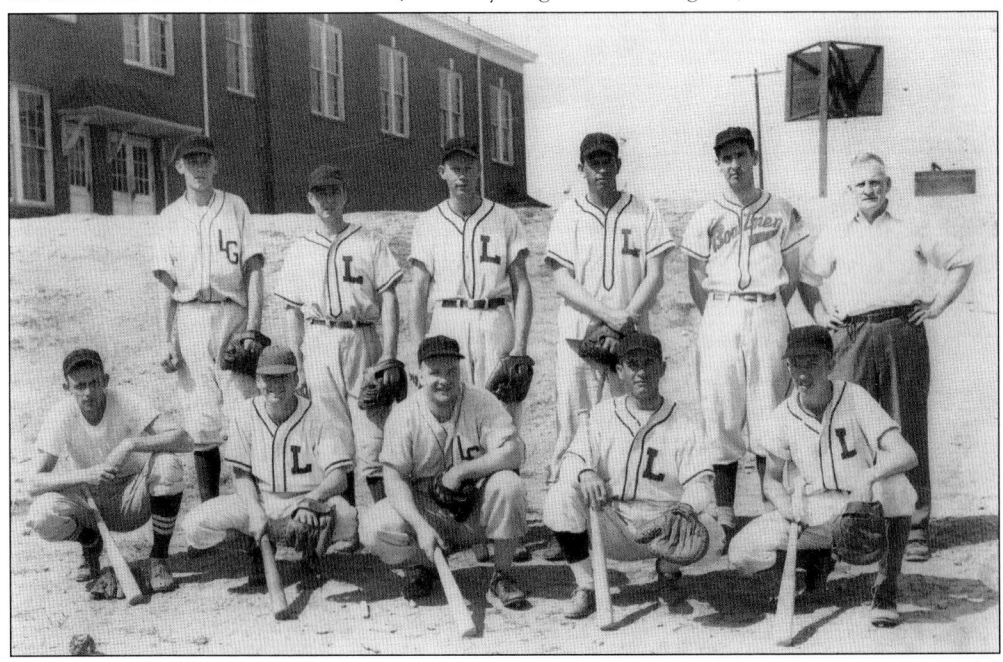

The Lemon's District Civic Club baseball team played games on the Fitzhugh Lee School field. The team was sponsored by Robert Earl Daniell's grocery. Daniell was a prominent resident of Oakdale-Smyrna. This 1948 team photograph shows, from left to right, (first row) Jimmy Bolling, Frank "Spankey" McDaniel, unidentified, Mac McCollum, and Wallace Gaines; (second row) Bill Cranford, Luther "Blue" Wood, Raymond Wright, J. Allen Couch, Hank Jordan, and Lloyd "Pop" Adair.

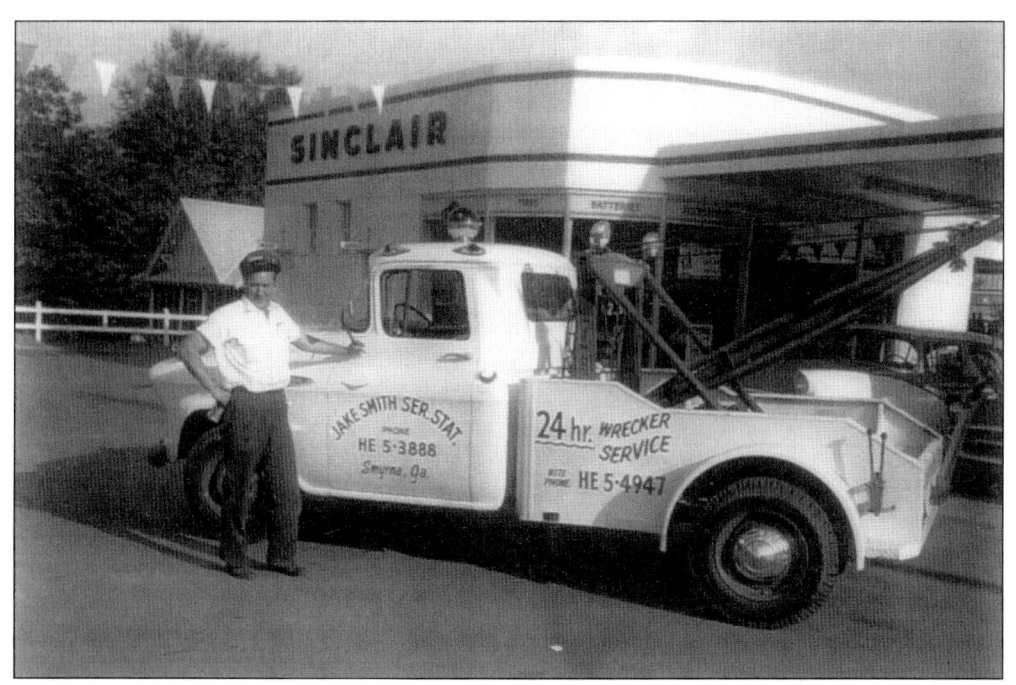

The Jake Smith service station was located in the Oakdale community, on South Atlanta Road at the corner of Young Street. (Courtesy the Smith family.)

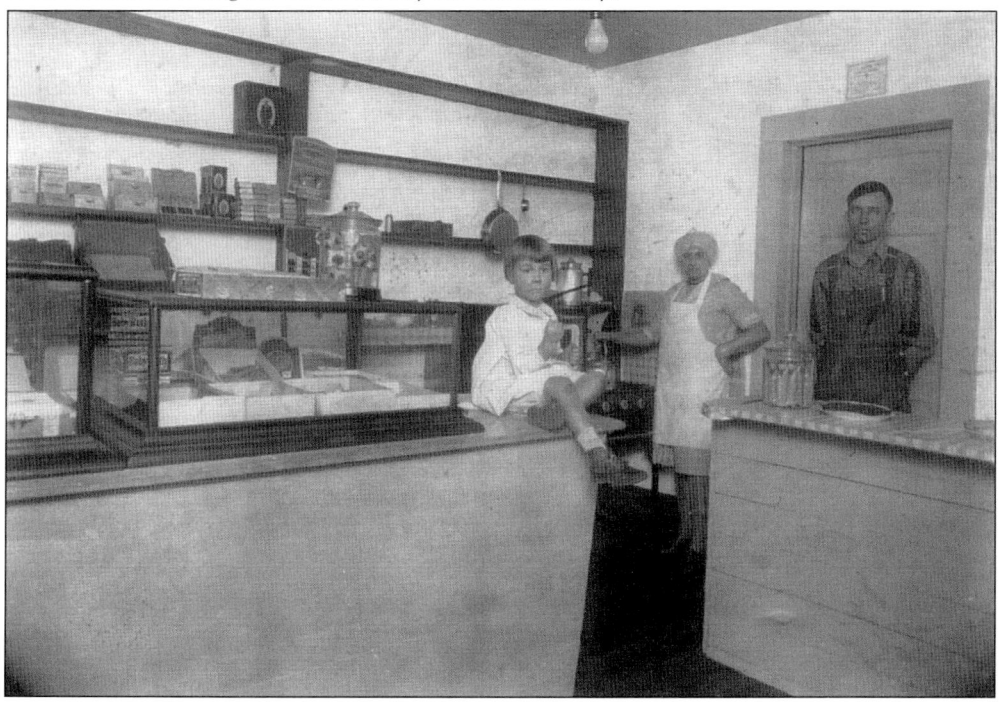

The Oakdale Hot Dog Stand, seen here in 1932, was located on Atlanta Road across from Oakdale Road. The young girl is Virginia Rice, who later married John Sargent of Smyrna. At center is her mother, Lillie Martin Rice. Standing at right is Halton Spinks, the son of Lillie's sister Maude Martin Spinks. (Courtesy Virginia Rice Sargent.)

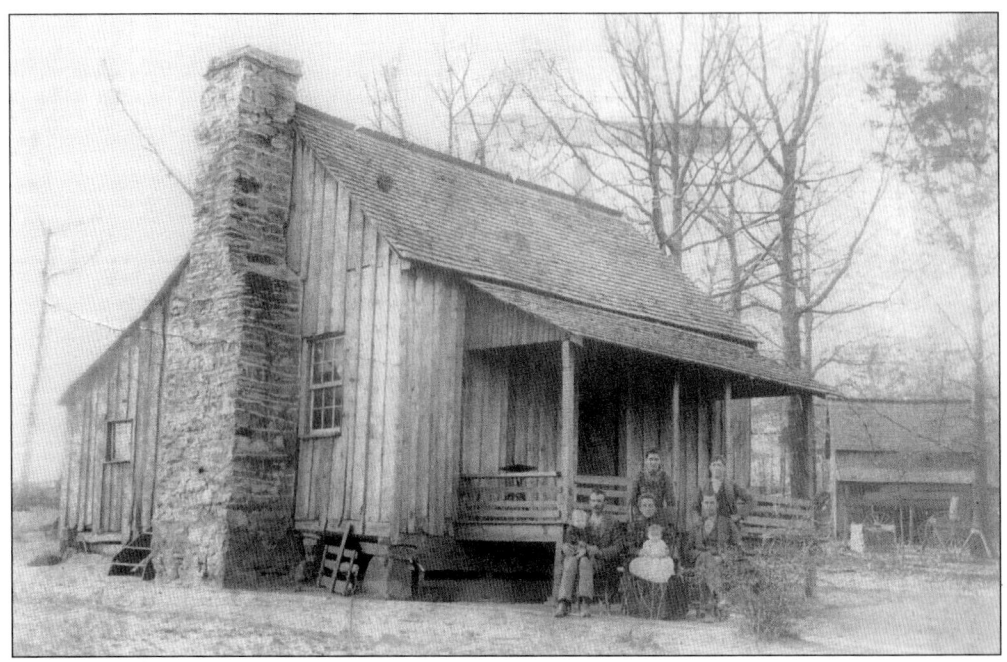

The home of the Brown family was located in the Oakdale community. Jennie Brown is seen here as a baby. (Courtesy Edie Argo.)

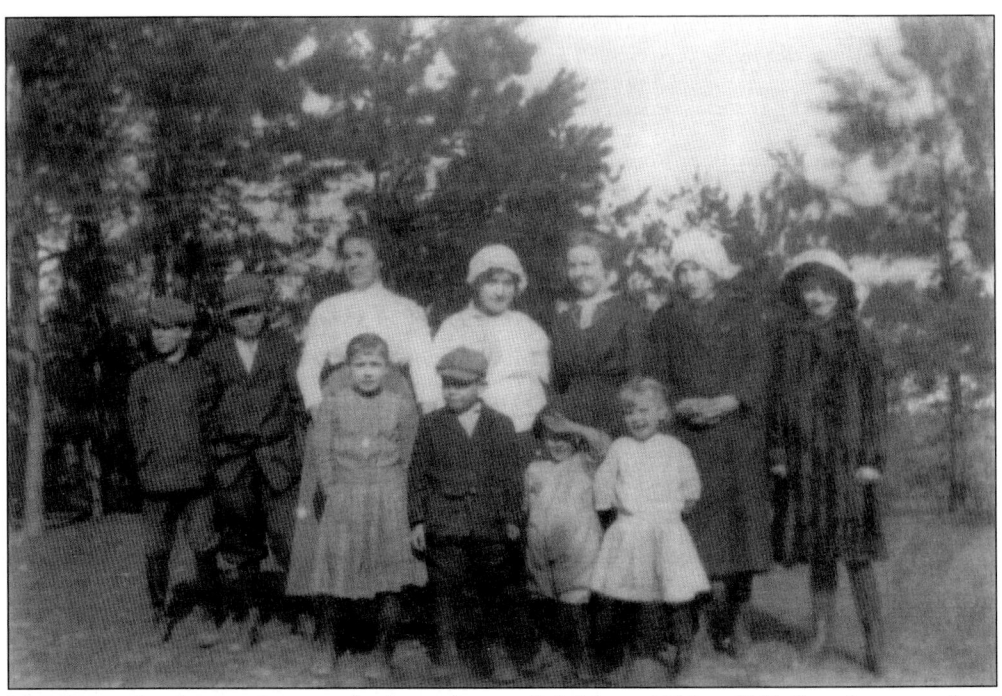

The Brown family was photographed together in Oakdale in 1916 or 1917. Seen here are, from left to right, (first row) Jessie Lee Brown, Jottie Brown, Molane Brown, and Lillie Mae Brown; (second row) Glen Brown, Ray Argo, Nell Ashendorf, Jennie Brown, Eula Argo, Lillian Maner, and Bessie Wilkie. (Courtesy the Brown family.)

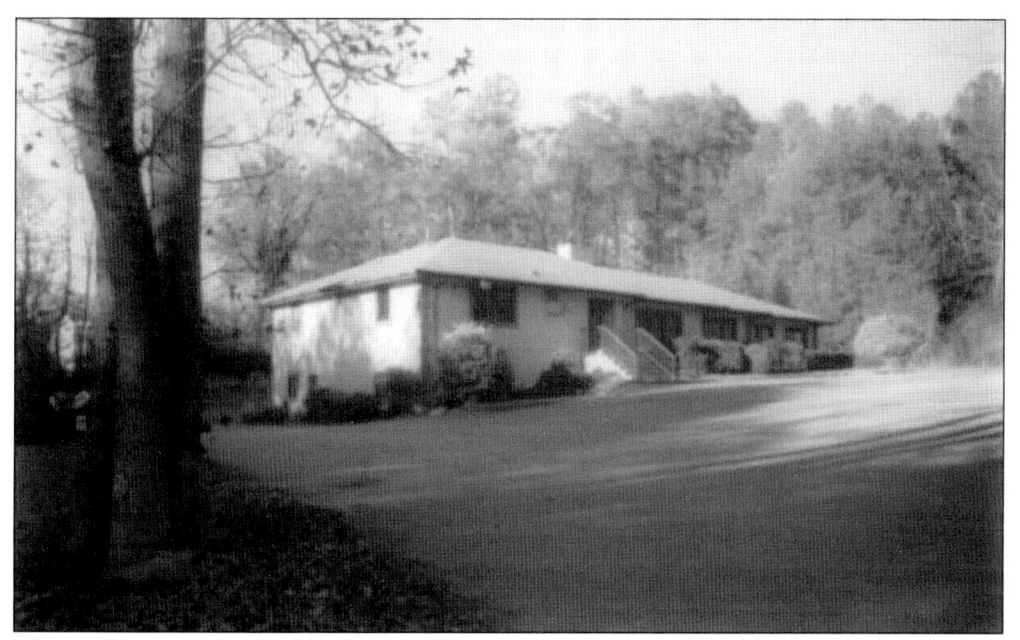

The actress Julia Roberts lived in this home on Maner Road as a teenager. She attended Smyrna's Campbell High. A movie poster of her first film, *Mystic Pizza*, is on display at the Smyrna History Museum. The poster was donated by Bob Lezinski, who was the lounge piano player in the hotel occupied by the movie's cast. Roberts has been known to occasionally sneak into town to meet with former classmates.

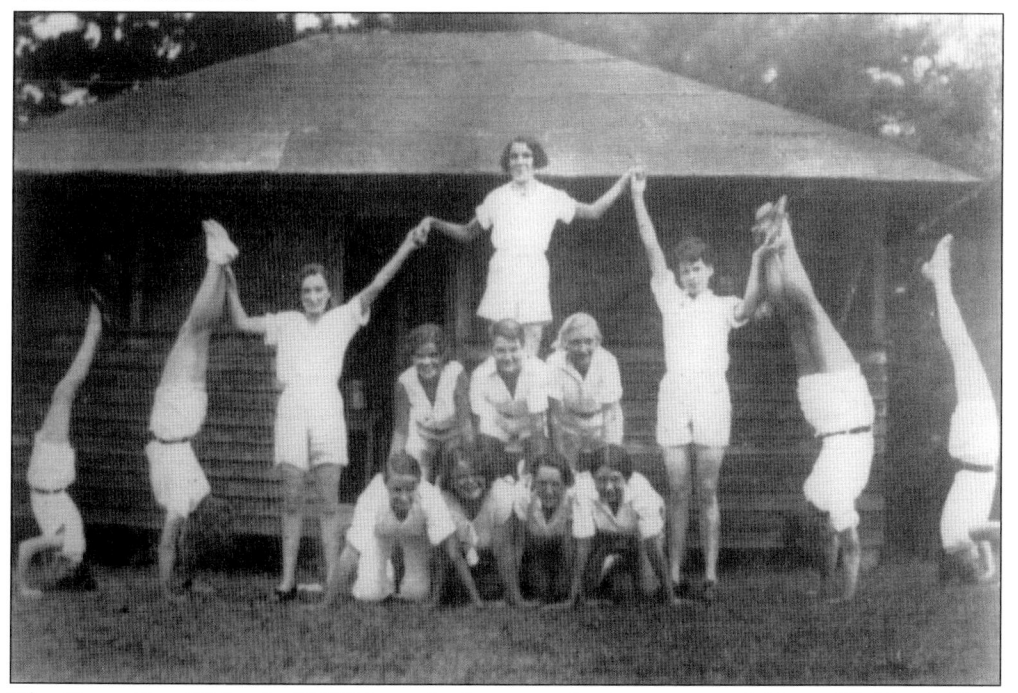

The Camp Fire Girls, the YWCA, and other organizations operated Camp Highland. This photograph from the 1920s was provided by local resident James Stephens, whose aunt Elsie Stephens, at the top of the pyramid, was a frequent camper there. (Courtesy James Stephens.)

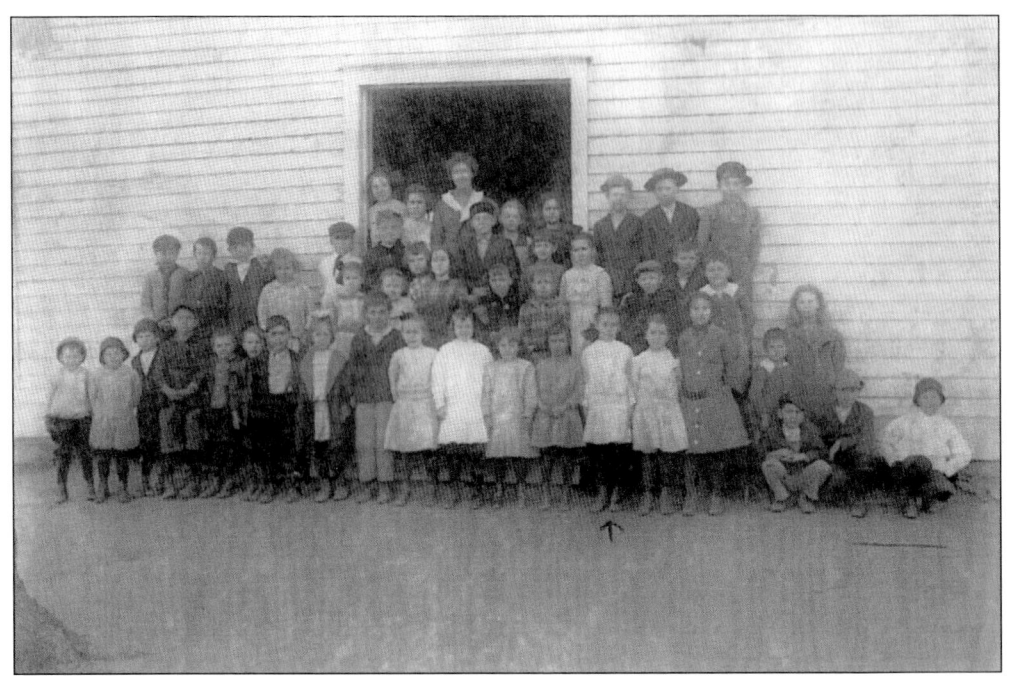

Locust Grove School began as a one-room log cabin in 1896. In 1915, the wooden building shown here replaced the one-room log cabin. This is the 1914–1915 second- and third-grade class of Lillie Wicks of the Locust Grove School. (Courtesy Clyde Dempsey.)

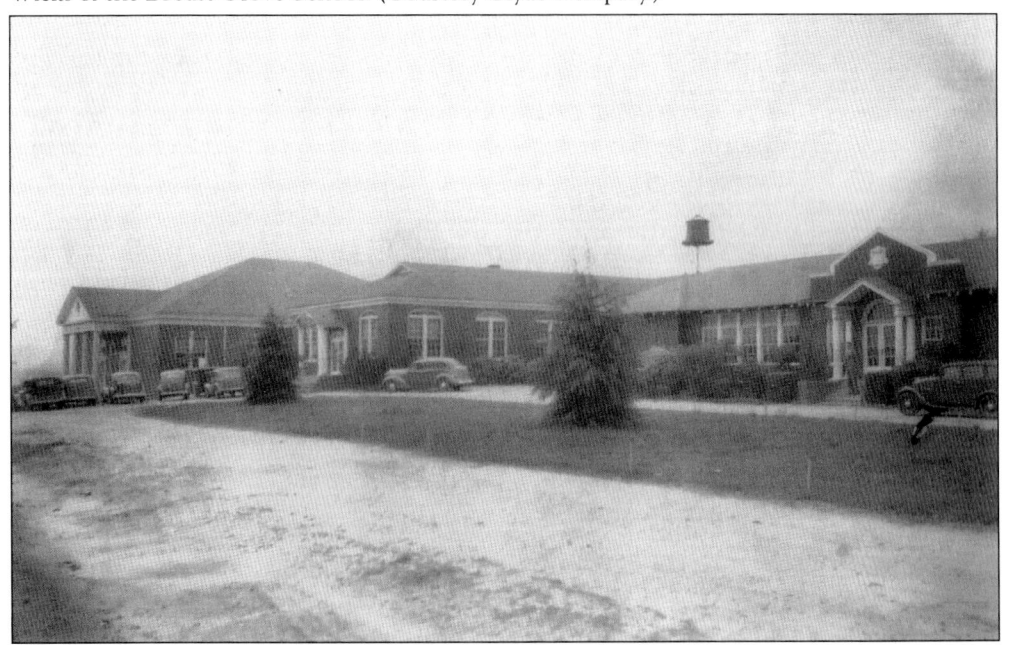

Fitzhugh Lee School was organized in 1896 as Locust Grove School. In 1936, it was renamed after a prominent soldier-citizen of Marietta and a great nephew of Gen. Robert E. Lee. Fitzhugh Lee was also a descendent of "Light Horse Harry" Lee of Revolutionary War fame. The present-day auditorium/gymnasium was built in 1938 with a Work Progress Administration grant of $25,000 and through local bond issues of $27,000.

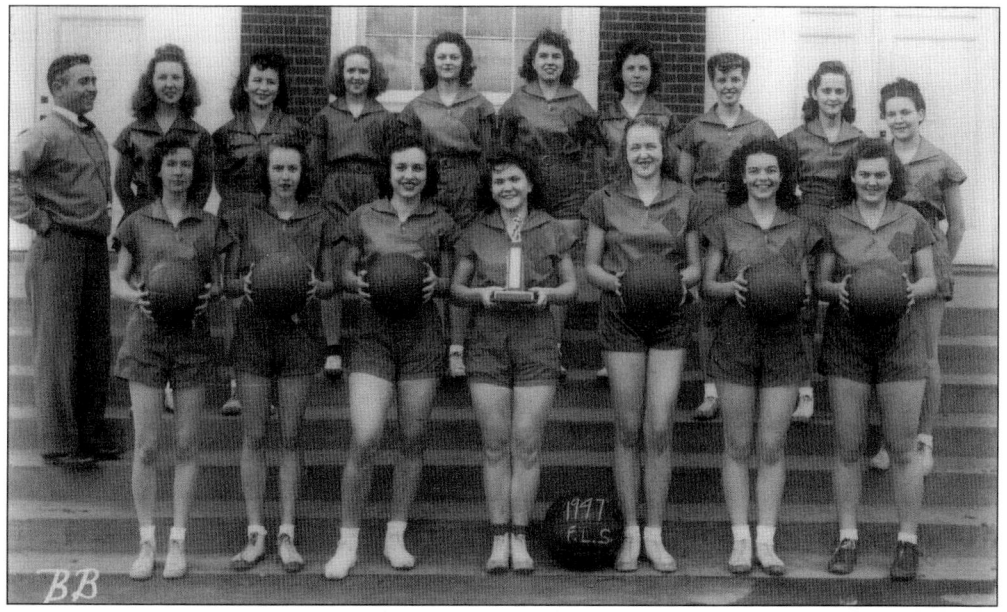

The 1947 Cobb County champion Fitzhugh Lee High School girls' basketball team was coached by William O. "Bill" Smitha. Shown here are, from left to right, (first row) Jeane Pruitt, Mary Ellen Cantrell, Barbara Morris, Mary Seagraves, Virginia Switzer, Mary Annie McDaniel, and Dorothy Rogers; (second row) Coach Smitha, Jean Johnson, Jean Watkins, Carolyn Bourne, Sheila Connaly, Martha Laird, Syble Browning, Dorris, Brown, and Saydie Fowler. (Courtesy Fitzhugh Lee School.)

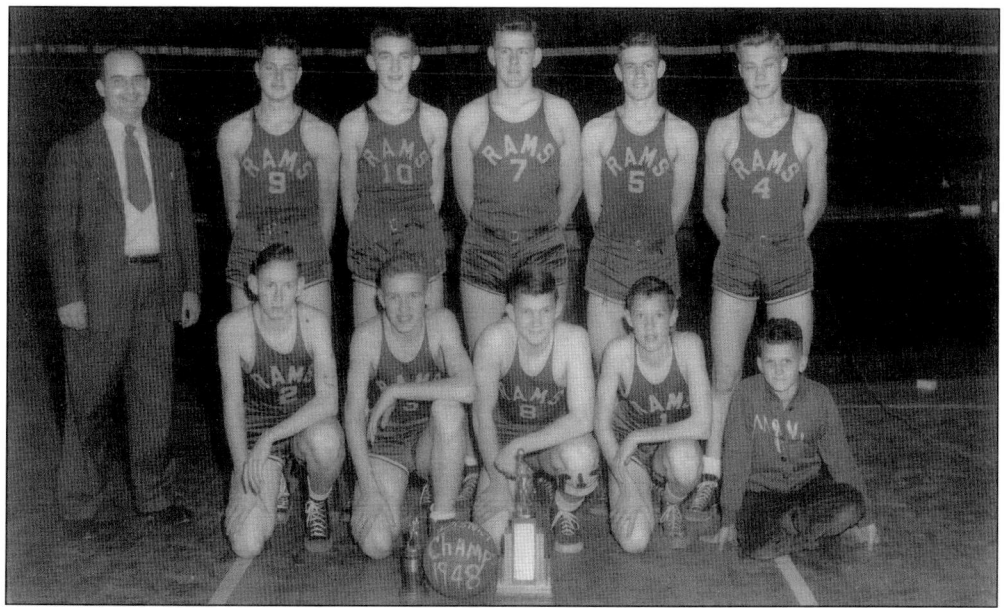

The 1948 Fitzhugh Lee School boys' basketball team were the Cobb County champions and the Seventh District champions. The team was coached by Robert L. "Bob" Ash. Shown here are, from left to right, (first row) Jack Coletrane, Dayle Smith, Kenneth Myers, Charles Beasley, and Walter Broom (manager); (second row) Coach Ash, Ed Poss, Raymond Dempsey, Raymond Smith, Ted Brown, and Buck Poss. (Courtesy Fitzhugh Lee School.)

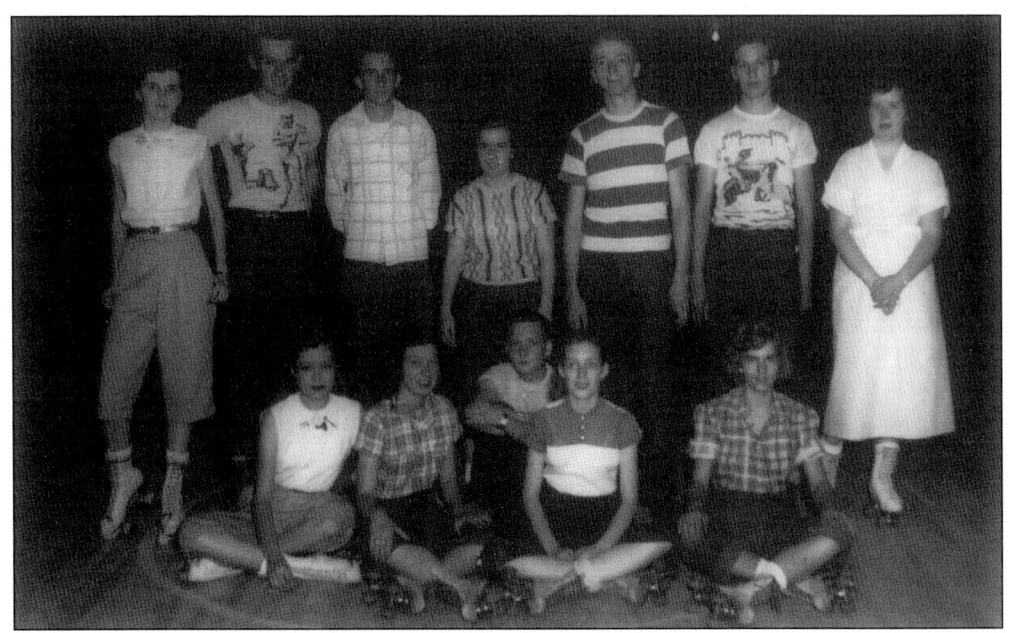

The 1951 Senior Day for Fitzhugh Lee School was held at the B&H Recreation Center in Oakdale. Posing here are, from left to right, (first row) Peggy Jo Addison Walker, Wilma Chandler Hale, George Stevens, Kay Boyles, and Billie Jane Billingsley; (second row) Dorothy McDaniel Jeffares, Grady Moore, Roger Cook, Mildred Street Patterson, Charles Switzer, Pete Fowler, and Vivian Meek. (Courtesy B&H Recreation Center.)

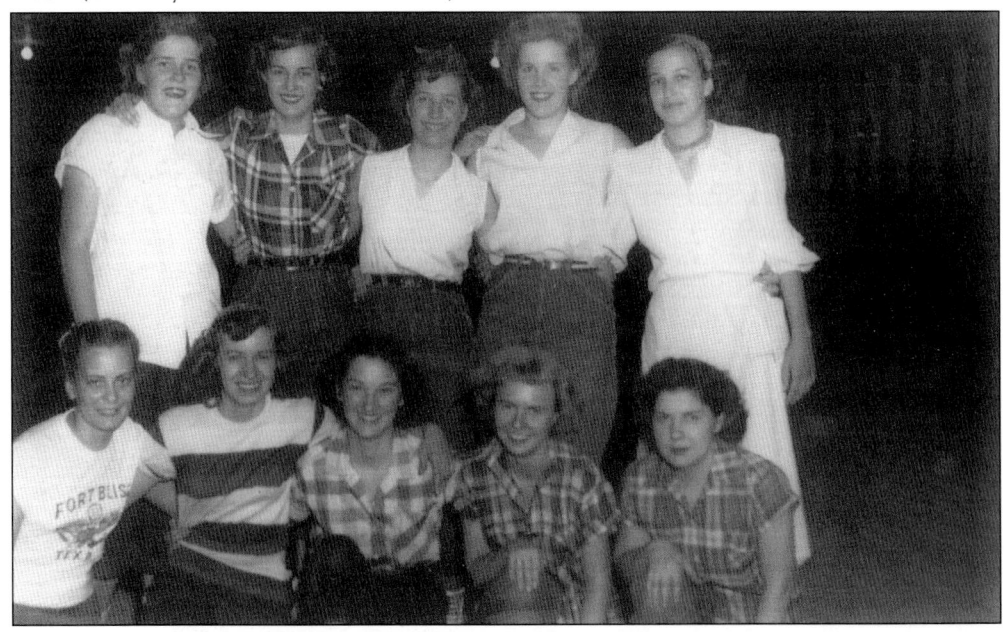

The girls of rival schools Fitzhugh Lee and Smyrna High did occasionally socialize, at places like B&H. Some "invaders" from Smyrna High are shown here. They are, from left to right, (first row) Mildred "Millie" Clayton Broyles, Charlene Clark Gunter, Jean Faucett Barden, and Jean Black Reese; (second row) Jean Bennett, Jean Scoggins Zimmerman, Doris Bailey Fowler, Joan Bennett, and Louise Akins. Both schools closed at the end of the 1950–1951 school year.

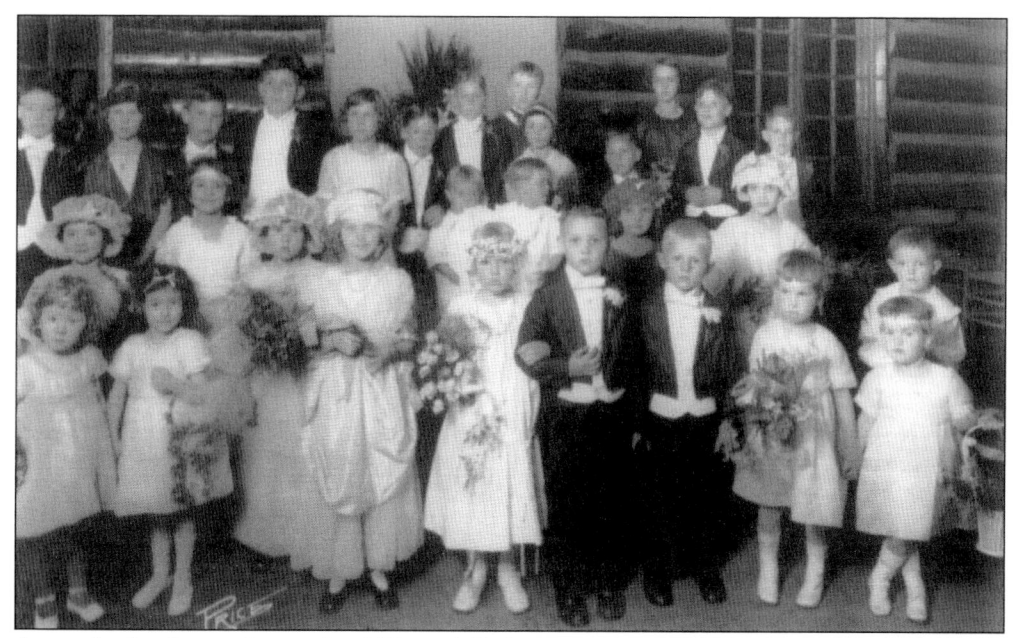

A popular fundraiser during the 1930s and 1940s was to stage elaborate Tom Thumb weddings featuring children. This one, presented by Brownie Troop 77 at the Log Cabin Community Church, took place on October 23, 1942. The bride and groom were Gennie Vee Valentine and Charles Switzer. The bride's father and mother were played by Raymond Dempsey and Patsy Ann McManus. (Courtesy Ann Johnson and Cecil and Gennie Haralson.)

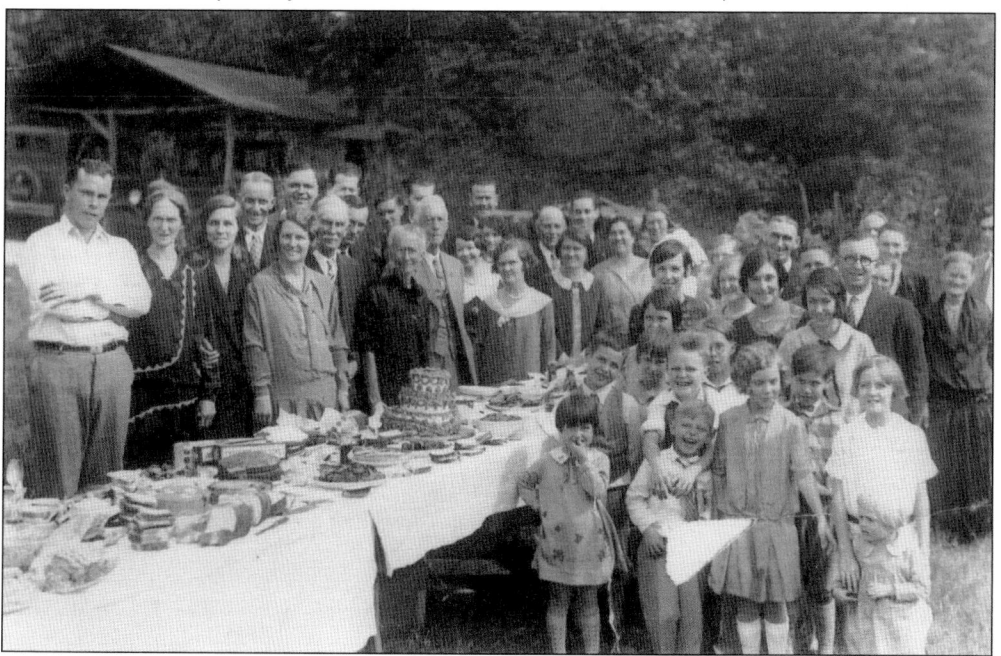

This was the 50th wedding anniversary of John and Roxie Herren (standing near the cake), in 1929. They are surrounded by family (Dempseys, Hogues, Spratlins, Bolings, and Argos) and friends, some of whom are current residents of the Oakdale, South Cobb, and Smyrna areas. (Courtesy Suzanne Spratlin Walker.)

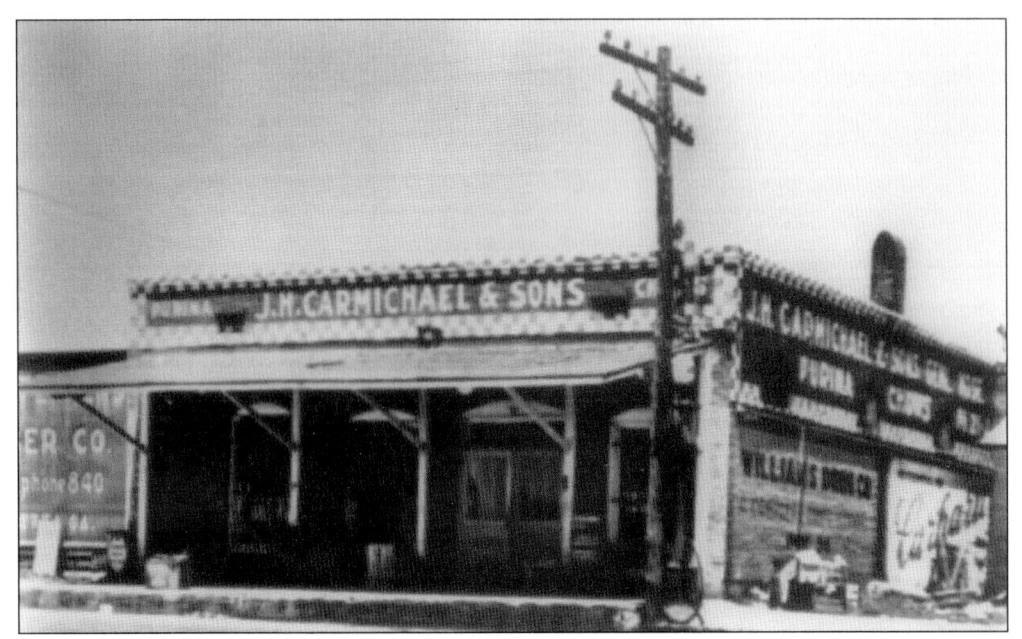

This building was located on the east side of Log Cabin Drive, just south of present-day I-285 and Atlanta Road. It was operated by the Carmichael family. They also had a residence and a blacksmith shop on the property. The buildings were demolished in the early 2000s to make way for mixed-use, single-family residences, townhouses, and multifamily housing. (Courtesy Virginia Carmichael.)

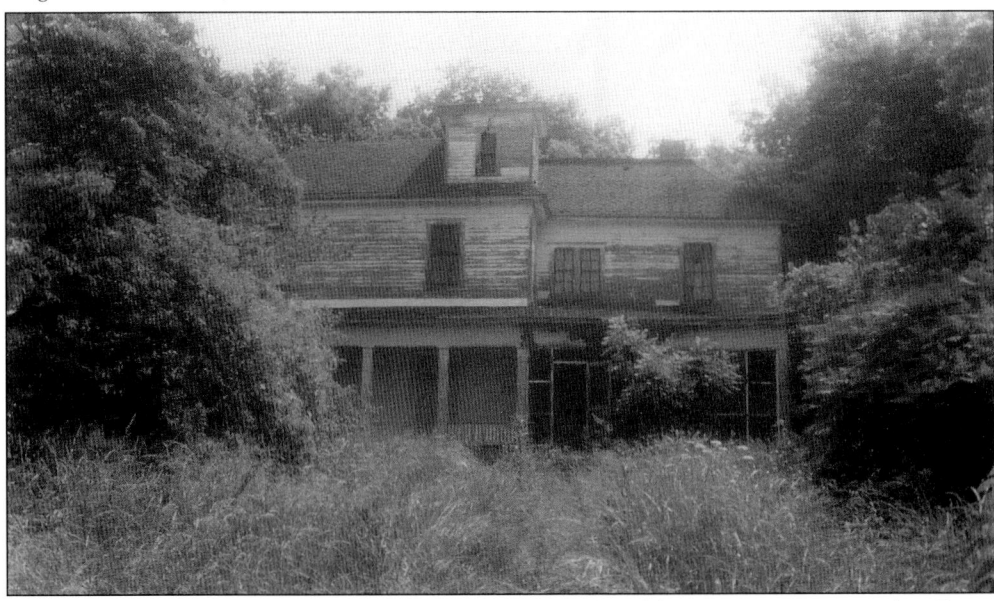

The former home of James "Jimmy" Vinson Carmichael and his parents on Log Cabin Drive is pictured on March 26, 1989. Carmichael was an influential lawyer who helped to secure the location of the 1942–1946 Bell Bomber Plant. The plant, which built B-29 bombers for the Army Air Corps, was a big business for Smyrna and Cobb County during the early 1940s. Carmichael, who later ran for governor of Georgia, was general manager of the plant. Many Smyrna residents worked there. (Courtesy Larry Blair)

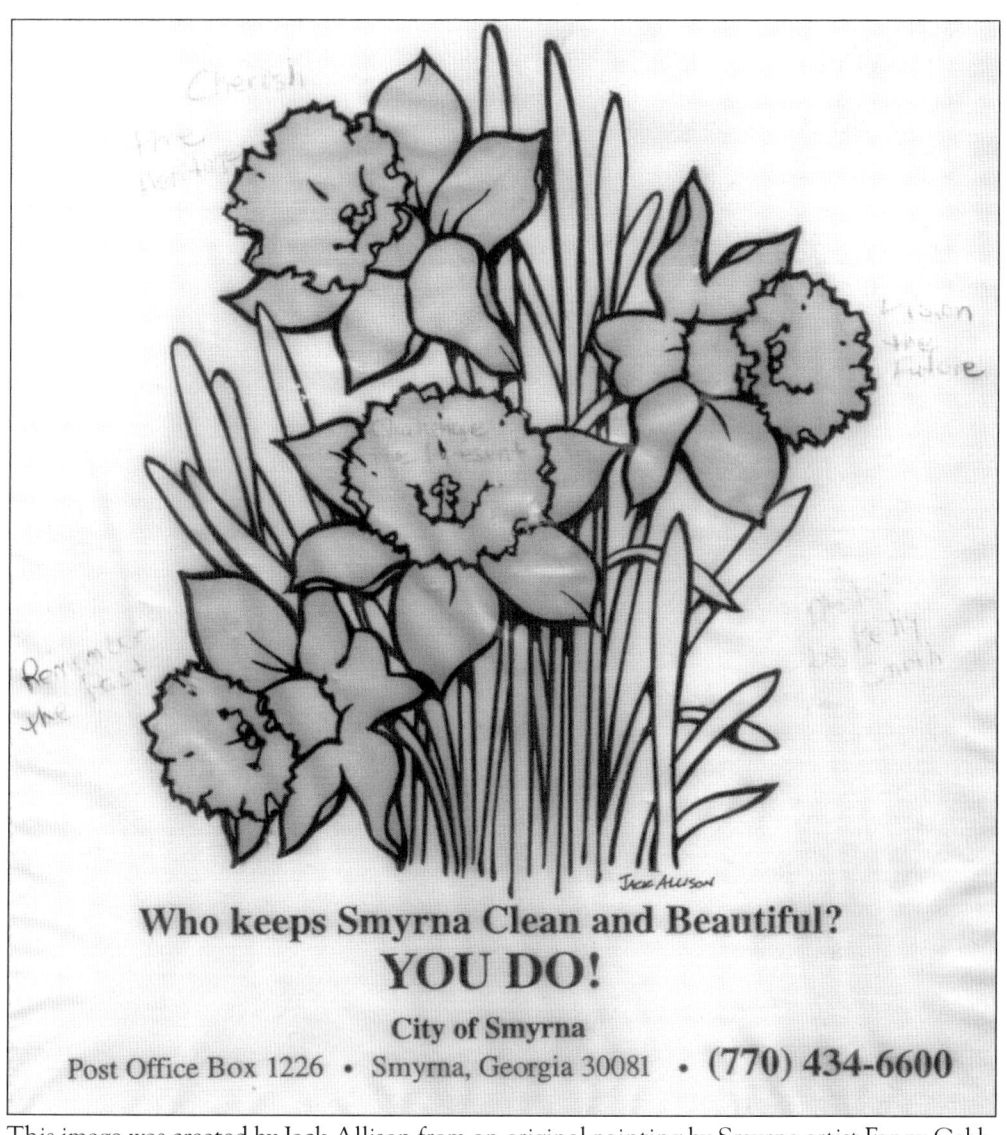

This image was created by Jack Allison from an original painting by Smyrna artist Fanny Cobb. Only three blooms of Smyrna's adopted flower, the jonquil, were printed on a plastic bag that was designed for distribution for Smyrna's first recycling organization, Keep Smyrna Clean and Beautiful. Light hand printing can be seen near the blooms that were used to display the creation of an early motto developed by Betty Smith and Kathy Barton: "Challenge the Present, Vision the Future, Remember the Past, Cherish the Heritage."

About the Smyrna Historical and Genealogical Society

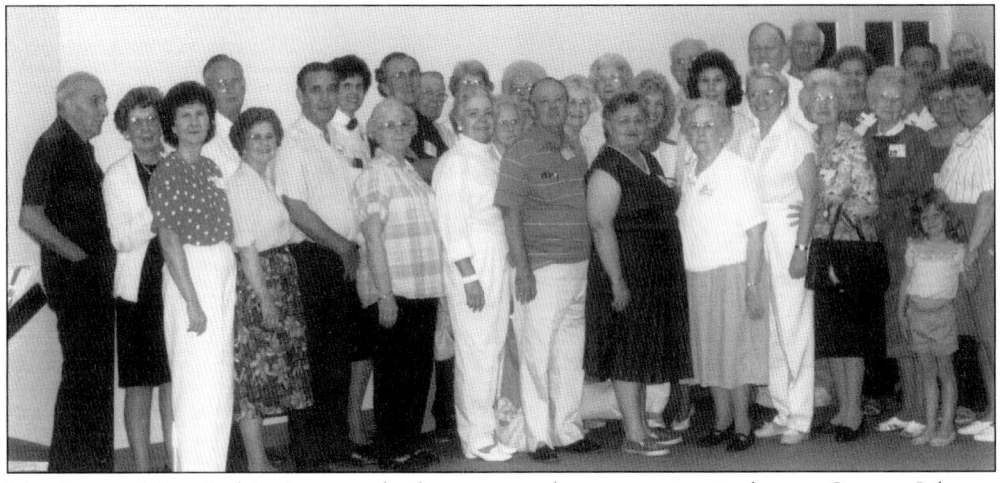

The Smyrna Historical Society was the first group to have a meeting in the new Smyrna Library. It took place on July 1991. The official opening was on August 3, 1991.

The Smyrna Historical and Genealogical Society was chartered as a nonprofit organization under Georgia law on May 17, 1985. The incorporators were Harold Smith and his wife, Betty; Emmett Yancey; and attorney George Carraker, who volunteered his service. The purposes were to establish a membership-organization museum for preserving structures and collecting photographs, documents, videos, and memorabilia related to the City of Smyrna and Cobb County. Since then, the organization has grown from a handful of members to almost 300. It is one of the largest civic and service organizations in Smyrna. The society's bimonthly publication, *Lives & Times*, was first published in March 1986. The Smyrna Museum opened for the first time on Saturday, April 25, 1992, after the city gave the historical society permission to establish the museum in the former Smyrna Health Clinic in 1991. The building had been constructed by the Smyrna Jaycees in 1965. Ribbon-cutting and dedication ceremonies for the current Smyrna Museum were held on April 25, 1999. The museum, a replica of the railroad depot demolished in 1959, houses thousands of artifacts, photographs, documents, videos, oral histories, and a genealogical research room. It is operated by volunteers; there are no paid employees. The officers and board of directors are required to chair the standing committees. Current officers are: Harold Smith, president; Kara Hunter-Oden, vice president and curator; Norma McHann, treasurer; and Roberta Cook, secretary. The directors are Forster Puffe, Nancy McGee, Pat Burns Roche, Jennifer Dixon, Andrea Searles, Don Taylor, and Cheryl Emmett Bennett. The hours of operation are Tuesday through Saturday, 10:00 a.m. to 4:00 p.m. Admission is free, and donations are welcomed.

BIBLIOGRAPHY

Argyle House Guest Register, 1885–1970. Donated by Gretna Poole.
But Thou Art Rich: A History of Methodists in Smyrna, Georgia. Columbus, GA: Quill Publications, 1990.
Cobb County Census, 1834 and 1840.
Cubbison, Douglas R. *Fireworks Were Plenty: Operations of the Fifteenth and Sixteenth Army Corps Near Ruff's Mill, Georgia.* Mableton, GA: Protect Endangered Areas of Cobb's History, 1993.
Duncan, Frank and Carolyn. *Smyrna: 125 Years.* Creative Publishing, 1997.
Facts and Figures About Cobb County, Georgia. Cobb Chamber of Commerce, 1970.
Facts and Figures About Smyrna, Georgia. Cobb Chamber of Commerce, 1969.
Linton, Calvin D. *American Headlines: Year by Year, 1776–1984.* Nashville, TN: Thomas Nelson Publishers, 1985.
Miles, Bill. *The People of Smyrna.* Smyrna, GA: Smyrna Herald, 1972.
Rice, P.M. Personal and business journals. Donated by Parker M. Lowry.
Roth, Darlene R. *Architecture, Archaeology, and Landscapes.* Cobb County Historic Preservation Commission, 1988.
Scott, Thomas Allan. *Cobb County, Georgia, and the Origins of the Suburban South.* Cobb Landmarks and Historical Society, 2003.
Smith, Harold. *Historic Smyrna: An Illustrated History.* San Antonio, TX: Historical Publishing Network, 2010.
———. *A Beacon for Christ: Centennial History of Smyrna First Baptist Church.* Roswell, GA: W.H. Wolfe Associates, 1984.
Smyrna Herald. Bill Miles, Bill Kenney, eds. Smyrna, GA.
Smyrna-Vinings Bright Side. Cathy and Allan Lipsett, eds./pubs.
Survey of the City of Smyrna, Georgia. Georgia Tech Planning Study, 1953.
Temple, Sarah Gober. *The First Hundred Years: A Short History of Cobb County, in Georgia.* Atlanta: Walter W. Brown, 1932.
Terry, Mike. *A Simpler Time, Story of the Taylor-Brawner House and the Brawner Hospital.* Madison, GA: Southern Lion Books, 2012.
Vanlandingham, A. 1832 Field Survey Journals, 17 & 18 Districts, Cherokee County, GA.
Whitfield Nelson, Mazie. *Past, Present, Future: Memoirs of Smyrna, Georgia.* Smyrna, GA: Vintage Press, 1967.
Wood, Charles "Pete." *The Paper Boy: A Collection of Memories from the Middle of the Twentieth Century in Smyrna, Georgia.* Smyrna, GA: 2006.

Newspapers: *Cobb County Times, Cobb Chronicle, Atlanta Journal-Constitution, Vinings Gazette.*

Oral histories conducted by Harold Smith in 1980–1982: Mayor J.B. Ables, Lewis Anderson, Rev. E.B. Awtry, Mayor Arthur Bacon, E.I. Bacon, Robert Baldwin, Robert Brooks, Annie Groover Brown, Lois Brown, Mary Carson, Robert Deborde, Agnes Feeley Faucett, Jay Foster, Marjorie Hiatt, Mayor Frank Johnson, police chief Hoyt Langston, Judith Lowry, Joe Brown McDowell, Sarah Miles, Louise "Bill" Morton, Evelyn Mulkey, Parker Norton, postmaster L.C. Parks, Maude Vaughan, postmaster Zelan Wills and his wife, Mary, and G.B. Williams.

Discover Thousands of Local History Books Featuring Millions of Vintage Images

Arcadia Publishing, the leading local history publisher in the United States, is committed to making history accessible and meaningful through publishing books that celebrate and preserve the heritage of America's people and places.

Find more books like this at
www.arcadiapublishing.com

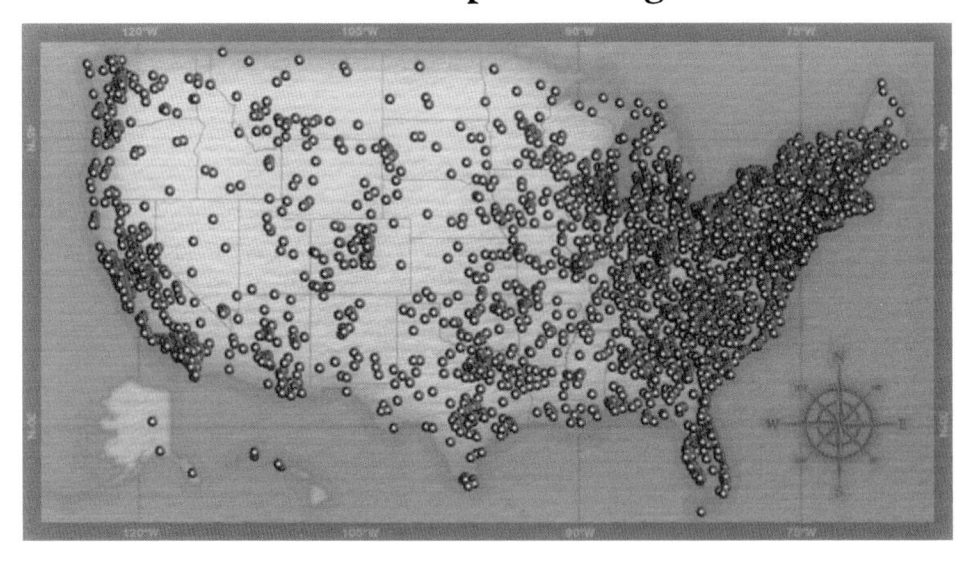

Search for your hometown history, your old stomping grounds, and even your favorite sports team.

Consistent with our mission to preserve history on a local level, this book was printed in South Carolina on American-made paper and manufactured entirely in the United States. Products carrying the accredited Forest Stewardship Council (FSC) label are printed on 100 percent FSC-certified paper.

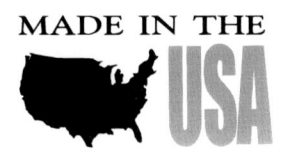

MADE IN THE USA